POTTERY OF THE GREAT BASIN AND ADJACENT AREAS

Number 111 1986

POTTERY OF THE GREAT BASIN AND ADJACENT AREAS

Edited by

Suzanne Griset

Contributions by

ROBERT L. BETTINGER, B. ROBERT BUTLER, SUZANNE GRISET,
STEVEN R. JAMES, JOANNE M. MACK, LONNIE C. PIPPIN,
EUGENE R. PRINCE, FRANCIS A. RIDDELL, HARRY S. RIDDELL, JR.,
MARY B. STRAWN, DONALD R. TUOHY,
WILLIAM J. WALLACE, AND RICHARD A. WEAVER

UNIVERSITY OF UTAH
ANTHROPOLOGICAL PAPERS

C. Melvin Aikens, Editor
Sharon S. Arnold, Associate Editor

University of Utah Press
Salt Lake City, Utah

We would like to dedicate this volume to Robert Crabtree and Rollin Enfield, participants in the pottery workshop who have since passed away. Bob Crabtree had a long-standing interest in pottery, stemming from some of the first extensive surveys of the northern Great Basin in the 1950s. He was always willing to share his expertise with others and was working on a summary of the many varieties of pottery from the southern Basin at the time of his passing.

Rollin Enfield was admitted to the intensive care unit of the Bishop Hospital shortly before the pottery workshop in April 1983. He insisted that Grace, his wife and lifelong partner in the study of Owens Valley archaeology, go ahead and attend the workshop. Midway through the afternoon session, Rollin arrived with an oxygen tank and his doctor in tow and stayed long enough to share his enthusiasm for pottery with the other participants.

CONTENTS

Contents

ILLUSTRATIONS

PREFACE

This volume of individual papers results from the Great Basin/California Pottery Workshop held at the White Mountain Research Station, Bishop, California, April 1983. Participants of the workshop responded to an invitation to "get together to talk ceramics," specifically brown wares of western North America.

In contrast to the vast volume of literature devoted to the analysis of decorated wares, plain or "utility" wares are understudied, often neglected, and largely misunderstood. Plain sherds outnumber decorated sherds in most ceramic assemblages and are the only pottery found in large portions of the Great Basin and surrounding areas.

Our purpose in meeting was to stimulate discussion, assess the current status of ceramic analysis in these areas, and gain a general idea of what topics should be addressed in future research. Participants were asked to bring examples of the sherds they were studying, to supply annotated bibliographic references for their areas, and to share their thoughts with the other members of the workshop in the form of informal data reports. The second half of the proposed agenda was to be devoted to several specific topics such as typology, chronology, and questions concerning pottery making and the cultures which employed this technology. Not surprisingly, the data-sharing portion of the agenda took up the entire day and we were left with as many, if not more, questions than when we started. There seemed to be a consensus, however, that the workshop had been worthwhile if only as a means of bringing together and stimulating discussion among the people involved in ceramic analysis and enabling researchers from across this wide research area to compare their study sherds with those of other areas.

PAPERS IN THIS VOLUME

To sum up the issues raised during the workshop and preparatory to convening a second meeting with specific topics, the participants were asked to submit papers on the topic of their choice. As will be seen in the pages that follow, the interests and theoretical viewpoints of the workshop participants were diverse and sometimes in direct opposition. Like the workshop, this volume is a status report, as of 1983. The papers include data reports, literature reviews, statements of theoretical position, and analytical methodology. The disparate topics are accurate reflections of the many opinions expressed at the workshop and are characteristic of the complications inherent in the analysis of plain ceramics. Despite this diversity, there is a general unifying theme: all papers address ceramic assemblages composed primarily of undecorated brown wares, of similar construction and form, from a cultural and geographic area known as the Great Basin and from areas contiguous to it (Figure 1).

At the end of each paper we have listed all references which do not relate specifically to ceramic analysis. Complete citations for ceramic references are provided at the end of the volume in an annotated and indexed ceramic bibliography. Although this involves an additional search for the reader, the intent is to maintain the annotated bibliography specifically as a reference tool for ceramic analysis of plain wares of the Great Basin and adjacent areas.

We have included photographs or drawings of complete vessels whenever possible and have provided basic descriptive data for each.

CERAMIC BIBLIOGRAPHY

The Annotated and Indexed Bibliography of the Ceramics of the Great Basin and Adjacent Areas is a compilation of references submitted by the following workshop participants: R. Bettinger, B. R. Butler, C. Drover, R. Enfield, S. Griset, M. L. Heuett, S. James, D. Jenkins, C. Lockett, J. Mack, S. McFarlin, L. Pippin, J. Swarthout, D. R. Tuohy, and W. J. Wallace. We have also consulted C. Fowler's Great Basin bibliography (Fowler 1970).

As with the papers in this volume, the bibliography covers a wide range of topics and geography. It does not pretend to be comprehensive, rather we have included the citations deemed most important or helpful in researching the pottery in these areas. Annotations vary in degree and depth. The index attempts to cross-reference all citations in a minimum of three categories: geographic location by state; ethnographic/archaeological group; and kind of pottery (types, wares, figurines, pipes). In addition, we have noted references of pottery-making techniques, ceramic analysis methods, and typology.

Because of the nature of compilations of papers such as this one, we appreciate the reader's patience with any oversights, errors, or unevenness in coverage.

ACKNOWLEDGMENTS

Simply put, credit for the success of the workshop held in Bishop goes to the following people:

Participants

Eleanor Bethel	Mary Lou Heuett	Ruth D. Simpson
Robert L. Bettinger	Dennis Jenkins	Charles Slaymaker
S. J. Bouscaren	George Kritzman	Jeanne Swarthout
B. Robert Butler	Eric Levy	Donald R. Tuohy
Robert H. Crabtree	Carl Lockett	Edith Wallace
Christopher Drover	Sheila McFarlin	William Wallace
Robert Elston	Lonnie C. Pippin	N. Peterson-Walter
Pamela Endzweig	Ron Reno	Claude Warren
Grace and Rollin Enfield	Francis A. Riddell	Richard A. Weaver
Joyce Faber	Harry S. Riddell, Jr.	Normal Weller
Matthew C. Hall	Edwin Rockwell	Robert West
John Hedrick	Charles Rozaire	Philip Wilke

Contributors not present at workshop

Steve James   Joanne M. Mack   Eugene R. Prince

Special thanks are extended to Richard A. Weaver of the Inyo National Forest for his help in arranging the logistics of the conference and spreading the word; to the staff of the White Mountain Research Center for being such gracious and helpful hosts; to Nancy McLaughlin and Gayle Bacon of the University of California, Davis, Anthropology staff; and to Charlie Slaymaker and Bob Bettinger for their encouragement, support, and occasional well-timed harassment.

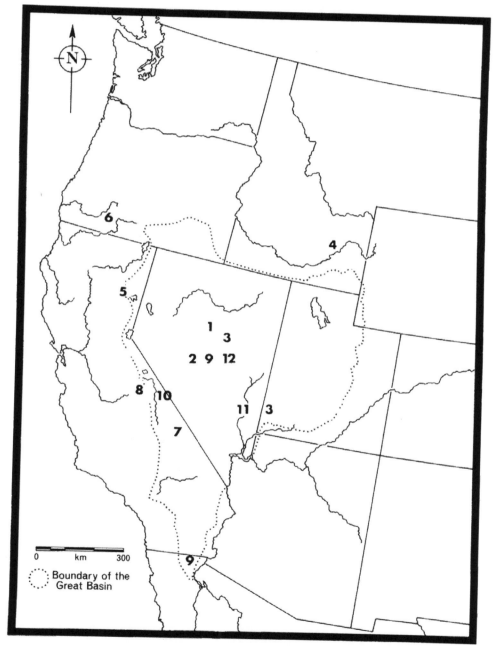

Figure 1. The Great Basin and adjacent areas showing the location of the areas addressed by the papers in this volume. Numbers refer to individual papers as listed in the contents.

CONTRIBUTORS

Robert L. Bettinger is an Associate Professor in the Department of Anthropology at the University of California, Davis. He has worked in the Great Basin since 1971, principally in Owens Valley and adjoining areas of eastern California. His interests include the ecology of hunter-gatherers, adaptive change, and the economic basis of ethnic spreads among nonagricultural peoples. The author of numerous scholarly articles on the prehistory of eastern California, he is perhaps best known for his research on adaptive change in Owens Valley and on the late prehistoric movement of Numic-speaking peoples into the Great Basin.

B. Robert Butler is the Curator of Archaeology and Associate Professor of Anthropology at the Idaho Museum of Natural History and Idaho State University since 1960. He was educated at the University of Washington, 1945-1960, with breaks for fieldwork at the Dalles of the Columbia River and at Mesa Verde National Park during the 1950s. He is a Fellow of the American Association for the Advancement of Science. He is self-described as a "primitive ceramist" planning to retire between 1988 and 1990 to devote full time to potting.

Suzanne Griset received an M.A. from the University of California, Davis (1978), and is curator of the Department of Anthropology's collections. She is completing a Ph.D. dissertation on the brown ware pottery of southern California, specifically the paddle and anvil wares of San Diego County. She has published several articles on Owens Valley Brown Wares of eastern California, and worked with Southwestern pottery from the Mesa Verde region. She organized the Great Basin/California Pottery Workshop held in Bishop in April 1983.

Steven R. James is an archaeologist with ten years' experience in the Great Basin, Colorado Plateau, and California, as well as field excursions in Texas, Wyoming, Hawaii, and Belize. He received his M.A. in anthropology at the University of Utah in 1982 and is currently studying for his Ph.D. at the University of New Mexico. The majority of his research is concerned with various aspects of faunal analysis including paleoenvironmental reconstructions and prehistoric subsistence strategies, but he has maintained a long-term interest in prehistoric ceramics, particularly in the Great Basin.

Joanne M. Mack is a Research Associate at the Department of Anthropology and Sociology, Pomona College. Her archaeological training was received from California State University, Chico, University of Wyoming (M.A. 1971), and the University of Oregon (Ph.D. 1978). Her archaeological interests are the hunting and gathering cultures of the Cascade Mountain area in southern Oregon and northern California, in the Northern Great Basin, and in the Klamath Basin. An additional research focus concerns the ethnohistory of the coiled basketry of the southern Californian Cahuilla.

Lonnie C. Pippin received the Ph.D. from the University of New Mexico in 1979 for archaeological research in the Southwest. He has spent more than eight years conducting cultural resources management projects in Nevada and California and research projects for the U.S. Forest Service in California and the Bureau of Reclamation in Idaho. He is the Principal Investigator for the cultural resources programs at the Nevada Test Site and Tonopah Test Range for the Department of Energy. He is an expert on the palynology of the Intermountain West having been trained at Washington State University by Peter J. Mehringer.

Eugene Prince received a B.A. in Anthropology from the University of California, Berkeley, in 1955 with an emphasis on the archaeology of California and the Great Basin. For the past 25 years he has been the head of the photographic department, R. H. Lowie Museum of Anthropology at Berkeley. Current fieldwork and research interests include the historic archaeology of California, Nevada, and Virginia, and the development of data-gathering methods for historic archaeology.

Francis A. Riddell received an M.A. in Anthropology from the University of California, Berkeley, in 1954. He has conducted extensive field research throughout the western United States, Alaska, and Peru. He recently retired from the position of supervisor of the Cultural Heritage Section of the California State Park System, and was the State Archaeologist for 28 years. As president of the nonprofit California Institute for Peruvian Studies, he has returned to earlier interests in Peruvian archaeology.

Harry S. Riddell, Jr. has maintained a lifelong interest in California archaeology in Lassen, Inyo, Kern, and Sacramento counties since 1934, and particularly in eastern California. After receiving a B.A. from the University of California at Berkeley in 1949, he went to work for the Los Angeles Department of Power and Water in the Owens Valley and continued to pursue his archaeological interests there. He contributed some of the early seminal articles on eastern California archaeology and brought important sites, such as Rose Spring, to the attention of other archaeologists. He is currently living in retirement in Carson City, Nevada.

Mary Strawn is an Emeritus Professor of Geology at Idaho State University. She earned a B.A. in Geology at Idaho State College and an M.S. in Geography at the University of Utah. Her research has focused on Quaternary geology, particularly the soils of southeastern Idaho. Since her retirement she has been doing petrographic analysis of pottery thin sections from throughout the Great Basin.

Donald R. Tuohy holds a B.A. in Social Science from San Francisco State University and an M.A. in Anthropology from the University of Nevada, Las Vegas. He also pursued graduate study in Anthropology at the University of Washington and the University of Arizona. He has been associated with the Nevada State Museum in Carson City since 1960, and presently is curator and head of the Museum's Department of Anthropology. He holds adjunct faculty appointments in the departments of anthropology at the University of Nevada at Reno and Las Vegas. He has authored and edited more than a hundred reports, articles, booklets, and monographs on American archaeology, and has had a special interest in Great Basin ceramics. Most recently he has expanded this research to include comparisons with the ceramics of

Baja California. In 1978 he was recipient of the First Annual Clark J. Guild Award for Outstanding Service to the Nevada State Museum and to the people of the State of Nevada.

William J. Wallace is Emeritus Professor of Anthropology, California State University, Long Beach. He received a Ph.D. in Anthropology from the University of California, Berkeley, in 1946, and has conducted extensive fieldwork and published approximately one hundred articles and monographs on the prehistoric and historic Indian cultures of California. He conducted many of the initial archaeological investigations in Death Valley, Anza Borrego Desert, southern San Joaquin Valley and many other areas of southern California. He is a recipient of the Society for California Archaeology Lifetime Achievement Award for Contributions to California Archaeology (1983).

Richard A. Weaver received his B.S. in Anthropology from the University of California, Riverside, in 1976 and subsequently began graduate studies in both Anthropology and Environmental Administration. He has, for fifteen years, been involved in both research and management activities in interior and coastal southern California and the western Great Basin. This has included serving as a private consultant and staff archaeologist with both the Bureau of Land Management and the Forest Service. He is presently an archaeologist with the U.S. Army Corps of Engineers, Sacramento District. He has maintained an active involvement in research and the integration of academic-management efforts and has authored or co-authored a number of papers and publications on the history, ethnohistory, and prehistory of these regions.

OVERVIEWS OF GREAT BASIN CERAMIC ANALYSIS: 1959 and 1983

Two views of Great Basin brown ware analysis are presented here: Prince's paper from the 1959 Great Basin Anthropological Conference, and Pippin's review derived from the Pottery Workshop in 1983.

We have included Prince's paper in this volume because it is often cited but difficult to obtain in its unpublished form. It should be read within the context of the times. In 1959 there were fewer than ten published reports on archaeological ceramics from the Basin. Most of these were summary reports dealing with the following:

Schellback 1930	Shoshoni ceramics from Idaho
Mulloy 1942	Shoshonean ceramics from Montana
Malouf 1944	Shoshonean ceramics from Utah
Baldwin 1942 and 1950a	Southern Paiute Utility Ware from south-eastern Nevada, western Utah and eastern California
Riddell 1951	Owens Valley Brown Ware from eastern California
Rudy 1953	Shoshonean Brown Ware from western Utah and eastern Nevada
Tuohy 1956	Shoshoni pottery from southern Idaho
Mulloy 1958	Intermontane Tradition wares from Wyoming

Prince presented thin-section data from sherds that were surface collected from the eastern half of Nevada and compared them to sherds thin-sectioned by Rudy (1953) and Riddell (1951), and to the published descriptions for Southern Paiute Utility Ware and Owens Valley Brown Ware. In addition to the data presented, Prince proposed that "Great Basin Plain Ware" be used as a general term for Great Basin ceramics, and that regional variations be described as "types" within the overall "ware."

As Pippin's title suggests, he follows Mulloy's "Intermontane Tradition" nomenclature in his discussion of Basin ceramic analyses of the previous twenty years. He presents a review of ethnographic data on pottery making by Great Basin groups and a critical discussion of the interpretations made of archaeological data. Of particular interest is his review of "dates" attributed to Basin ceramics. He surveys the research topics that have preoccupied analysts to date, notes the lack of satisfactory answers for many of these, and suggests new directions that should be investigated.

SHOSHONEAN POTTERY OF THE WESTERN GREAT BASIN

EUGENE R. PRINCE

The pottery that is to be discussed is the utility ware of the Shoshoni, Northern Paiute of Owens Valley, and the Southern Paiute. The area under general consideration comprises the western, central, and southern Great Basin in what is today the state of Nevada and the eastern desert section of California.

The earliest mention of pottery in the central Nevada area would seem to have been made by Zenas Leonard in 1834. He reported in his journal that "They cook in a pot made of stiff mud, which they lay upon the fire and burn; but from the sandy nature of the mud, after cooking a few times, it falls to pieces, when they make a new one" (Leonard 1934: 166-68). John C. Fremont, eleven years later in 1845, saw pottery in use in the Elko, Nevada, area. His party "found a single Indian standing before a little sage-brush fire over which was hanging a small earthen pot filled with sage-brush squirrels" (Fremont 1886:435). There is a dearth of information on pottery by these early travelers, and it would seem quite likely, as others have pointed out (Baldwin 1950a:50), that such crude pottery was given up as soon as the White Man's goods became available. It probably also indicates the lack of emphasis placed upon pottery by these peoples.

Although archaeologists interested in western North America have long worked on the pottery of the Southwest and adjacent areas, it has been only in recent years that serious attempts have been made to describe and classify the pottery of the Shoshonean peoples of the Great Basin.

Pottery is described ethnographically from the western Great Basin and adjacent areas by Steward (1941b), Gayton (1929), and Kroeber (1925). Archaeologically the pottery of the Shoshoni is described by Wedel from the central and upper Yellowstone drainage in Montana and Wyoming (Wedel 1954). Schellbach (1930) and

Tuohy (1956) offer the most comprehensive description of Shoshoni pottery from southern Idaho. Sherds were found by Cressman in eastern Oregon though it is unclear just how they relate to the pottery to the east (Cressman 1942:91). Rudy has noted Shoshoni pottery from western and southern Utah (Rudy 1953).

The following pottery-bearing sites are largely confined to the area set forth by Steward (1938: Fig. 1) as being inhabited by the Shoshoni. In all too many cases the records lack vital information. Pottery is simply noted at some sites; little or no sherd description is present. This lack of information gives rise to many gaps in the pottery description.

The work of H.S. Riddell (1951) and G. Baldwin (1950a) describe and define pottery of Owens Valley and Southern Paiute pottery of Southern Nevada, respectively. A brief discussion of these pottery types and their possible relationships to each other and to the Shoshoni pottery will follow the pottery descriptions.

The identification of the Puebloan sherds was made by Richard Shutler of the University of Arizona. Nevada State Museum numbers are given where possible. UCMA refers to the University of California Museum of Anthropology specimens.

Elko County

26-El-2 is a small campsite located at Hog Tommy Spring about fifteen miles (24 km) southeast of Elko, Nevada. Twenty-five small body sherds and one rim sherd were collected. None are larger than 1 1/2 in. (3.8 cm) diameter. UCMA 1-45589--'90.

Construction:	Coiled and scraped
Firing:	Uncontrolled but mainly oxidizing atmosphere
Core color:	Ranges from brown to black
Temper:	Large angular quartz grains with traces of mica
Texture of core:	Coarse
Fracture:	Friable
Surface finish:	Rough and uneven
Surface color:	Brown to gray
Rim:	Outcurved
Thickness:	6 mm average
Decoration:	Absent

26-El-11 is a rockshelter near the confluence of the South Fork Humboldt River and the Humboldt River proper. One small body sherd of the same kind of pottery as that at El-2 is noted.

NSM-288-L-1 is located generally in the Ruby Mountains, Elko County. The jar is 31 cm high, 30 cm in diameter at the mouth, and the base is 9 cm in diameter. The base shows a twined basketry impression. Two small holes have been drilled just below the rim on either side of a crack.

Construction:	Coiled and scraped
Firing:	Uncontrolled, but mainly oxidizing atmosphere
Temper:	Coarse granite sand
Surface finish:	Rough and uneven
Surface color:	Brown to black
Form:	Conical, flanged base
Rim:	Straight
Decoration:	Absent

This jar and the following piece are like those described from southern Idaho (Schellbach 1930; Tuohy 1956) and western Wyoming (Wedel 1954).

Elko County - No location. The Nevada State Museum has in its possession a complete basal sherd.

Construction:	Coiled and scraped
Temper:	Coarse sand
Form:	Conical, flanged base
Thickness, wall:	7 mm
Base:	7.5 cm in diameter

Lander County

26-La-3 is located in the vicinity of Battle Mountain. One body sherd was collected. UCMA 1-45586.

| Construction: | Scraped. Cannot determine if piece was coiled. |

Firing:	Oxidizing atmosphere
Core color:	Brown to gray
Temper:	Large angular quartz grains. Mica is abundant.
Core texture:	Coarse
Fracture:	Medium strong
Surface finish:	Rough and uneven
Surface color:	Brown
Thickness:	9 mm

26-La-4 is a small campsite in the vicinity of Battle Mountain. Two small body sherds were collected. UCMA 1-45587-8.

Construction:	Coiled and scraped
Firing:	Oxidizing atmosphere
Core color:	Brown to very dark brown
Temper:	Angular quartz grains and small amounts of mica
Core texture:	Medium
Fracture:	Friable
Surface finish:	Rough and uneven
Surface color:	Brown
Thickness:	7-8 mm

26-La-8 is located in the vicinity of Battle Mountain. UCMA 1-68028. Two rim sherds were collected.

Construction:	Coiled and scraped
Firing:	Oxidizing atmosphere
Core color:	Brown to dark gray
Temper:	Angular quartz grains with little mica
Core texture:	Medium coarse
Fracture:	Friable to medium strong
Surface finish:	Rough to smooth
Surface color:	Reddish brown
Thickness:	6-7.5 mm

Lander County - No location. UCMA 2-15767.

Construction:	Scraped. One sherd shows coiling.
Firing:	Predominantly oxidizing though reducing atmosphere is found in some sherds.
Core color:	Dark brown to dark gray
Temper:	Medium quartz sand
Core texture:	Medium
Fracture:	Friable sherds predominate though there are a few strong sherds.
Surface finish:	Rough and uneven
Surface color:	Gray to reddish brown
Rim:	Outcurved
Thickness:	8 mm average

Lincoln County

NSM 9-14. Black-on-white and corrugated sherds are reported but no locations are given.

Mineral County

26-Mi-5 is a campsite at the southern edge of Whiskey Flat. Only several small crude, gray sherds were found.

26-Mi-18. Pottery is reported from Truman Meadows by local collectors.

Nye County

26-Ny-7 is located at Ash Meadows near the Nevada-California boundary. One sherd of what appears to be a lid was collected. UCMA 1-40032-33.

Construction:	Coiled and scraped
Firing:	Oxidizing atmosphere
Core color:	Black
Temper:	Small quartz grains with a small amount of mica.
Core texture:	Fine to medium
Fracture:	Medium strong
Surface finish:	Rough and uneven
Surface color:	Reddish brown
Thickness:	4 mm

26-Ny-19 is located in the Timber Mountain, Forty-mile Canyon Skull Mountain area. Four small rim sherds are recorded as coming from here. UCMA 2-12597 is one sherd of Middleton Black-on-red, three sherds of North Creek Black-on-gray. UCMA 2-12598 is one sherd of Tsegi Orange Ware.

Construction:	Coiled and scraped
Firing:	Oxidizing and unoxidizing
Core color:	Brown to black
Temper:	Large angular quartz grains
Core texture:	Coarse to medium
Fracture:	Strong to friable
Surface finish:	Rough and uneven
Surface color:	Reddish brown to black
Thickness:	Averages 7.5 mm

26-Ny-25 is an open site near Big George Cave. NSM 12-8.

Construction:	Coiled and scraped
Core color:	Brown
Surface finish:	Rough and uneven
Surface color:	Brown and gray
Form:	"Flower pot"

26-Ny-26 is located in Forty-mile Canyon. Fifteen sherds are noted but no further information is available.

26-Ny-27 is located at Tippipah Spring. Black-on-white and plain corrugated types are noted. Further description of this pottery is unavailable. One rim sherd of crude utility ware is noted, NSM 12-10.

Temper:	Large angular quartz grains
Core color:	Gray
Surface color:	Brown

A small (1.5 mm) hole was made by a twig or piece of straw while the clay was still wet. It is placed 1 cm below the rim. It may have been used to suspend the vessel for cooking (Fremont 1886: 435) or carrying (Heizer 1954: 6-7).

26-Ny-29 is a campsite at Ammonia Tanks. A Black-on-white sherd is also noted at this site. NSM 12-13 is a concave base and is reminiscent of some Owens Valley forms (Riddell 1951: 21).

Construction:	Coiled and scraped
Surface color:	Brown to black
Form:	"Flower pot"
Thickness:	5 mm average
Base:	Concave
Height:	17 cm
Diameter, mouth:	19.5 cm

26-Ny-30 is located in the Foyle area. One corrugated sherd, NSM 12-14, is noted from this site.

Construction:	Scraped
Core color:	Black
Temper:	Large, angular quartz grains
Surface finish:	Rough
Surface color:	Gray

26-Ny-31 is the designation given Johnny Water Cave. Two small body sherds and one rim sherd are in the Nevada State Museum. NSM 12-17.

Construction:	Scraped
Core color:	Black
Temper:	Large quartz grains. Mica is noted.
Surface finish:	Crude, rough
Surface color:	Gray to brown
Decoration:	Vertical fingernail incising in a single band below the rim.

26-Ny-32 is located at Whiterock Spring. A Black-on-white pottery is also noted from this site. NSM 12-18.

Core color: Brown
Surface color: Gray
Rim: Straight

26-Ny-33 is located at Indian Retreat, Paiute Mesa, in southern Nye County. NSM 12-19.

Construction: Coiled and scraped
Surface finish: Rough
Surface color: Brownish gray
Rim: Incurved
Decoration: Vertical fingernail
                      incising

26-Ny-36 (NSM 12-11) is noted only as Cave (Cane ?) Spring and the pottery is described as a gray-black utility ware.

26-Ny-38, 39, 40 are sites where pottery is noted. No locations or sherd descriptions are given.

26-Ny-41 (MAI-HF) is located in the vicinity of Carrara. No sherd descriptions are given.

26-Ny-42 is located near Beatty. Two sherds are described as a Black-on-white pottery. One corrugated sherd is also noted.

26-Ny-43 is located in the Beatty area. No sherd descriptions are given.

26-Ny-45, 46 are located in the vicinity of Fairbanks Spring. No sherd descriptions are given.

26-Ny-48 is an open site noted in the Nevada State Museum records as being located 1/4 mile south of McKinney Tanks, Monitor Range.

Construction: Coiled and scraped
Core color: Black
Fracture: Sharp
Surface finish: Rough and uneven
Surface color: Dark gray
Thickness: 6 mm
Base diameter: 8.5 cm
Height: 7.5 cm

"The base is irregularly punctate with small holes 1 to 2 mm in diameter and also has a few marks made by grass or other vegetal material."

Nye County - no location. A complete jar was found on or near the Riordan Ranch. NSM 12-1.

Construction: Coiled and scraped
Firing: Unoxidized
Surface color: Gray
Form: Conical, pointed base
Rim: Straight
Thickness: 6 mm
Diameter, mouth: 31.5 cm
Height: 30 cm
Decoration: Absent

Two small holes have been bored just below the rim, apparently to repair a break.

Nye County - no location, at or near the the Whipple Ranch. One small Black-on-white rim sherd was collected. NSM 12-1.

White Pine County

26-Wh-8 (Wheeler 1936; 1937:196). Three sherds are identified as Snake Valley Corrugated, Snake Valley Gray, and one that is probably Snake Valley Black-on-gray. One small sherd is tentatively designated North Creek Black-on-gray.

26-Wh-12. One sherd was found in the Baker Creek Caves by Alan LeBaron. NSM 18-1-114.

Puebloan Pottery in UCMA Nevada Collection.
R. Shutler

Wh-8	7-20-77	Snake Valley Corrugated (Rudy 1953: 88) – Pueblo I-II
"	"	Snake Valley Gray (Meighan et al. 1956)
Ny-19 (?)	2-12597	Middleton Black-on-red (Colton 1952)
"	"	North Creek Black-on-gray (Colton 1952)
"	2-12598	Tsegi orange ware (Colton 1952)
"	"	North Creek Black-on-gray (Colton 1952)
Wh-8	no number	Probably Snake Valley Black-on-gray. Decoration and surface finish match my type specimens but temper is a little different.

All the aforementioned nonpuebloan pottery, with the exception of one conical pointed base form, differs little, if at all, from the crude Shoshoni pottery from southern Idaho, western Wyoming, Montana, and western Utah. This would extend the type of pottery attributed to the Shoshoni at least as far south as central Nye County in south-central Nevada, using form as the most distinctive characteristic. One of the interesting things about the Shoshoni pottery of central and southern Nevada is its relative scarceness as compared to Southern Paiute pottery and the pottery of the Owens Valley Paiute. The sherds number not in the thousands (Baldwin 1950a: 52), but the hundreds. Part of this is probably due to the small amount of work done in the area but it is, I think, indicative of the relative importance of pottery in the life of the Shoshonis. A great deal more survey work must be carried out in order to define with any exactness the distribution and full range of form of this pottery.

The table comparing the crude utility pottery of this Nevada area was taken from the following sources: Southern Paiute Utility Ware from Baldwin (1950a), Owens Valley Brown Ware from Riddell (1951), and Shoshoni Ware from Schellbach (1930), Rudy (1953), and Tuohy (1956).

Almost all of those who have worked with Shoshoni Ware, Owens Valley Brown Ware and Southern Paiute Utility Ware have noted the close similarity of these "wares" (Bennyhoff 1958:99; Malouf 1946:121; Riddell 1951:22; Rudy 1953:96; Steward 1937:43). There seems to be a tendency for each type to emphasize certain characteristics which occur to a lesser extent in the others. Certain forms, paddle-and-anvil technique, and possibly some types of decoration and handles appear to be restricted to fairly limited areas. This tendency of emphasis of characteristics also present in the other wares appears in the so-called reducing atmosphere, for example; although predominant in Southern Paiute Utility Ware, it is also found to some extent in Owens Valley Brown Ware and Shoshoni Ware, undoubtedly because of the relatively uncontrolled nature of the firing. The term reducing atmosphere is not used in this paper following Shepard's suggestion (1956:221) as no criteria other than color is used. The descriptions available at the present time give the impression that mutually exclusive traits are relatively uncommon.

A series of pottery thin sections ranging from Lander County in central Nevada through the western, Southern Paiute area to the Mono-Yokut territory in the southern San Joaquin Valley of California were analyzed by H. Williams of the University of California Department of Geology.

Differences in the materials used in the manufacture of these three types of pottery appear to reflect the local geology. For example, the Shoshoni pottery from Lander County and southern Nye County contains a preponderance of materials of volcanic origin. The samples analyzed come from within an area of volcanic formations in central Nevada where granite formations are relatively scarce (Williams, personal communication). The pottery sampled from southern Nye County and well within Shoshoni territory was from a site fairly close to an area where granitic rocks occur with some abundance. It would seem that pottery was not carried any great distance from the place of manufacture.

The Southern Paiute Utility Ware, containing mostly granitic substances, lies within a southern Nevada, Colorado River area characterized by granite rocks.

Yokut pottery or Owens Valley Brown Ware (Riddell 1951) from the southern San Joaquin Valley in California is derived from the gran-

ites of the Sierra Nevada. Thin sections from Inyo-2, the Owens Valley Brown Ware type site, show the parent rock to be volcanic. The northernmost extension of this pottery type is somewhat south of Mono Lake in eastern California and shows a plutonic or granitic rock derivation. Both volcanic and granitic formations occur in profusion in this area just east of the Sierra Nevada Mountains.

Additional thin-section analysis should be made of the pottery from the adjacent areas in the Great Basin to determine with greater precision the closeness of the relationship to the local geology. It may, at some future date, be possible to set up subtypes of Great Basin pottery by identification with the local geology.

The use of decorative technique for typing these sherds is also limited. It would appear from the available information that decoration is relatively rare. Not only are decorated sherds fairly uncommon but rim sherds, where most of the decoration is found, are scarce. The only difference, apparently, is the lack of overall decoration by Owens Valley Brown Ware (Riddell 1951:21).

Although the table shows the presence of handles to be restricted to Owens Valley Brown Ware, handles are mentioned ethnographically from the Shoshoni by Steward (1941b:340) so that this criterion may not be as important as it would seem at first glance.

The criteria just mentioned simply exclude only one of the three wares as possibilities when typing sherds. For example, the presence of overall decoration eliminates Owens Valley Brown Ware but leaves the worker with two alternatives. This appears to be the case with the firing atmosphere, core and surface color also. If mutually exclusive traits other than those already mentioned exist in this crude utility pottery they must await future definition. This is especially true of Shoshoni Ware and Owens Valley Brown Ware.

Form seems thus far to be the most useful criterion for typing. Form is, however, subject to some of the same limitations as the others. Sizeable body or rim sherds and basal sherds are required. These, however, are not abundant due to the weak nature of the pottery and paucity of ceramics in general. The conical pointed base type so characteristic of Southern Paiute pottery has not been found, in any great numbers (Rudy 1953:94), outside Southern Paiute territory and the "flower-pot" form does not occur outside the central and southern Shoshoni territory. The flanged base is not found in the Southern Paiute area.

It may be then, at least, that some subtypes may be postulated on the basis of form. As Tuohy points out in a comparison of the Shoshoni pottery of southern Idaho (Tuohy 1956:68), and that described by Rudy (1953:98) from western Utah and eastern Nevada, the conical

flat base pots seem to be restricted to the
northern Shoshoni territory. On the basis of
the examples cited in the site descriptions
this type or subtype can be extended, at the
present time, as far south as the Elko-Ruby
Mountains area in northeast Nevada. The
"flower-pot" form Rudy reported from western
Utah (Rudy 1953:96) is apparently not found to
the west and south in central Nye County,
Nevada. At present, differences in form seem
to have some reality as a criterion for typing
pottery. It must be kept in mind, however,
that a great deal more work must be done
starting with thorough surveys of the area to
obtain a greater sample than is now available.

Although the writer is unacquainted with
the pottery of the Southwest and the Great
Plains, the pottery types of the Shoshonean
peoples of the Great Basin seem to resemble
each other much more than they do the wares of
these adjacent areas. This is, of course, not
a new idea (Mulloy 1952:290-296). The crude
utility pottery of the central and western
Great Basin would appear to constitute a
distinct ware. It appears that archaeologically, we are dealing with local variations
within a single pottery-making tradition.
Southern Paiute Utility Ware, Owens Valley
Brown Ware, and Shoshoni Ware are so similar
that it becomes difficult to assign small sherd
lots to one or another of these "wares" with
any degree of surety. Euler has discussed the
similar problem of the pottery of southern
California (Euler 1959).

Using the term "ware" somewhat in Colton's
sense (Colton and Hargrave 1937:2) it might be
more useful to place these three so-called
"wares" into one inclusive ware category. The
designation Great Basin Plain Ware is
suggested.

This ware can be said to possess the
following characteristics. It is coiled and
shaped by either scraping or using a paddle and
anvil. The latter is the predominant shaping
technique in the southern part of the Basin.
The firing atmosphere is uncontrolled and as a
result color ranges from a reddish brown to
black, the unoxidizing atmosphere being the
rule to the south. The temper is quartz and is
usually coarse. The fracture is usually
crumbling and irregular. The surface is rough
and uneven with a dull luster. Forms consist
of conical jars with flat, pointed, and flanged
bases and small round- and flat-bottomed bowls.
Decoration, when present, consists only of
fingernail impressions around the rim or, infrequently, over the entire surface of two of
the types.

It is suggested that the pottery of the
Southern Paiute, Owens Valley Paiute, Yokut-
Western Mono, and Shoshoni can be seen as types
or regional variations of a single "ware."
This ware corresponds roughly as to greater
geographical area; the peoples manufacturing
this pottery are closely related and have a
similar material culture. Whether these types
constitute a series with historical meaning is
yet to be determined.

A large amount of additional work must be
done in the Great Basin to determine the full
range of variation and the historical relationships of this Great Basin Plain Ware. At the
present time we are hampered by a general lack
of stratigraphical association, except in a few
cases (Riddell 1951; Steward 1937), and by the
quantity and quality of material available for
study. The extent and areas of borrowing and
the role which trade may play in the development of this ware is, as yet, undetermined.
Those differences between types that are due to
the passage of time and those which are due to
the process of borrowing must remain unknown
until more work is done in the Great Basin.

ACKNOWLEDGMENTS

An earlier version of this paper was read
at the 24th annual meeting of the Society for
American Archaeology, Salt Lake City, Utah,
April 1959. Support for this research was pro-
vided through the National Science Foundation,
Project No. G3917.

REFERENCES CITED

(Citations not listed here will be found
in the Annotated and Indexed Bibliography of
Ceramics at the back of this volume.)

Bennyhoff, J. A.
    1958 *The Desert West: A Trial Corre-
         lation of Culture and Chronology.*
         University of California Archaeo-
         logical Survey Reports No. 42,
         pp. 98-111.

Mulloy, W.
    1952 *A Preliminary Historical Outline
         for the Northwestern Plains.* Ph.D.
         dissertation. Department of Anthro-
         pology, University of Chicago.

INTERMOUNTAIN BROWN WARES: AN ASSESSMENT

LONNIE C. PIPPIN

INTRODUCTION

Although the making of pottery by Great Basin hunters and gatherers has been recognized for over a century, it has not been generally considered an important attribute in either their cultural adaptation or characterization. Hence, while the aboriginal peoples in the Great Basin are often used to exemplify a hunting and gathering life-style, they are seldom used as an example of pottery making by nonagriculturalists (Driver 1961:67). But, what do we know about the brown ware pottery made by these nomadic inhabitants of the Intermountain West or about its role in their adaptation to this arid environment? As voiced by Shepard (1956: 102) over two decades ago, what we learn about pottery is directly related to the questions we ask of it. Most previous research concerning the brown ware pottery in the Great Basin has revolved around questions regarding its classification, age, and origins. But is it sufficient to continue to classify this brown ware pottery into traditional "styles," "types," or "wares" and monitor their distribution through time and space? If not, what should be our purpose(s) behind studying Intermountain Brown Wares?

As in any line of scientific inquiry, it is not only worthwhile, but often essential, that researchers pause and critically assess the directions of their scholarly activity. How well have we answered previously posed questions and what other questions should we be asking of our data base? This paper will address these issues by first reviewing the nature of our current understanding of Intermountain Brown Wares and then by examining several avenues of research, new and old, which I feel may provide valuable information about this pottery and its role in understanding Great Basin prehistory. The term Intermountain Brown Ware, as used in this paper, refers to

the pottery made by the aboriginal peoples in the Great Basin during both historic and prehistoric times. As will be pointed out below, several other terms have been applied to this pottery, but these terms have not been used consistently and often imply an assumed affiliation that has not been adequately demonstrated. Rather than perpetuate those implications, I have selected a new term to refer to this pottery in a general sense.

THE ETHNOGRAPHIC RECORD

The existence of pottery making among certain aboriginal hunting and gathering groups of the Great Basin was known as early as the middle of the 19th century (Euler 1966:62, 115; Fremont 1845:263; Minto 1901; Palmer 1878: 601-603). But, as Baldwin (1950a:50-51) and Coale (1963:2-3) outlined, little attention was given this crude pottery by these early explorers or the ethnographers who followed them. As a result, we have only a vague notion of what this pottery was like, how it was made, and the role it played in aboriginal Great Basin cultures.

Although Lowie (1909:177) noted that the Shoshoni of southern Idaho had pottery, he failed to provide a description of these vessels. In fact, except for Driver's (1937: 122) description of two truncated, cone-shaped pottery vessels belonging to the Panamint Shoshoni, the only other available ethnographic information about pottery among the Shoshoni comes from the cultural element distribution surveys of Steward (1941b:242, 295; 1943:375). According to these surveys, coiling was the most commonly employed method of construction. However, Steward (1943:375) noted that the Lemhi Shoshoni formed the base and lower sides of their large conical pots in holes in the ground and then modeled the upper walls out of "pats" of clay. The Bear River and Promontory Shoshoni also purportedly hand modeled their pottery from "pats" of clay. Surfaces were smoothed (scraped) with fingers, deer horns, sticks, and cobbles. Vessel shapes included shallow bowls, jars with both outflaring rims and constricted necks, and large conical pots with round, pointed, or flat bases. Decoration, when present, was usually by incising or fingernail indentations; however, the Spring, Antelope, and Snake Valley Shoshoni were said to have painted their pottery with both red and black pigments after firing (Steward 1941b:242).

Steward (1933a:266-268) also described the large, flat-bottomed pottery of the Owens Valley Paiute. He felt that pottery making among this well-known group was a specialized art form limited to only a few women. As with most Shoshoni groups above, the Owens Valley Paiute pottery was manufactured by first laying a pancake-shaped base, then building the walls with coils of clay. Walls were smoothed with the fingers dipped in a syrup made by boiling desert globe mallow (*Sphaeralcea fremontii*). The vessel was then sun-dried, the exterior painted with globe mallow syrup, and then baked in a sagebrush fire (Steward 1933a:267). Kaolinitic clays were obtained from special localities which contained decomposed granitic inclusions to serve as temper. Apparently, these clays required grinding before use. Steward (1933a:345, Plate 5) illustrated two vessel forms for the Owens Valley Paiute: one globular with recurving rims and one conical with direct rim. Finally, Steward (1933a:267) noted that the specimens recovered from archaeological sites in the region reflected a larger, "better made," thinner-walled, round-bottomed style. Noting that the flat-bottomed vessels of Owens Valley Paiute resembled the pottery of the Yokuts and Western Mono (Gayton 1929:246-250), Steward (1933a:267-268) hypothesized a western origin for this pottery.

Lowie (1924:225-226), referring to the Shivwits Paiute of southern Utah, indicated that although this group previously made pottery, it formed only a minor element in their material culture. This pottery was manufactured by coiling, surfaces were scraped with a turtle shell, and rims were left undecorated. Lowie (1924:226) reports that the vessels had pointed bottoms so that they could be stuck in the ground and fires built around them during cooking. Kelly (1964:77-78) also described the pottery of the Southern Paiute of Utah. According to one of her informants, the Kaibab Paiute learned how to make pottery from the Hopi. Natural clays were apparently first pounded, then mixed with "dirt" (temper ?) and water. The undecorated, flat-bottomed vessels were then constructed by molding the base and using coils of clay to form the vessel walls. Another informant of Kelly's (1964:77), however, claimed that aplastics were not added to the natural clays used in the manufacture of this pottery and that the pottery was used for boiling meat.

There are several references to the pottery made by the Utes of eastern Utah and western Colorado, but all of these are based on the memory of older informants who, themselves, had never made pottery (Lowie 1924:226; Opler 1939; Stewart 1942:273, 341). According to Stewart (1942:273, 341) this brown ware pottery was constructed by coiling and finished by scraping, but he cites an amateur anthropologist who stated that she observed some vessels made by smearing clay on the outside of willow baskets which were then filled with dung and burned. He also notes that the Ute occasionally added pounded cactus, as well as sand, as an inclusion in the clay (Stewart 1942:273). Opler (1939:162) mentions that the Ute of southwestern Colorado used a micaceous clay, "found in the bluffs of New Mexico," for their pottery. Interestingly, one of Stewart's (1942:341) informants thought that the Mowatci Ute of the San Luis Valley, Colorado, learned pottery making from the Taos Indians who are well known for their micaceous brown ware.

In summary, although the above ethnographic data are incomplete and sometimes confusing, they do reveal several interesting aspects of aboriginal pottery in the Great Basin. First, it is apparent that some degree of variability in manufacturing techniques and vessel shapes occurred within the same ethnographic group. Hence, both flat-bottom and rounded- or pointed-bottom vessels were apparently made by the Shoshoni of Utah, the Shivwits Southern Paiute, and the Paiute of Owens Valley. Likewise, some groups apparently relied on natural inclusions in their clay sources to provide the essential aplastics, whereas others added "dirt." It is possible, of course, that at least some of this perceived variability might be due to differing perspectives of the ethnographers and/or to post-contact cultural change. But, it is not unreasonable to expect that such variability also existed during aboriginal times. In fact, one might wonder why there was not more variability noted in the pottery made by these nomadic hunters and gatherers whose life-style precluded any large degree of craft specialization.

The ethnographic record also provides an indication of the geographical distribution of pottery-making in the Great Basin. There is little doubt that both the Bannock and Shoshoni of Idaho possessed, if not made, pottery at the time of contact (Lowie 1909:177; Steward 1943:319, 375). Likewise, the Shoshoni in eastern Nevada and western Utah also apparently made pottery (Steward 1941b:242, 295; 1943:375). But, excluding Owens Valley, Stewart (1941:389) reported an absence of pottery among the Northern Paiute further west. And, although the Shivwits and Kaibab Southern Paiute were credited with pottery (Lowie 1924:226), Steward (1943:273) felt that pottery making was restricted to the Southern Paiute groups west of the Kaibab Plateau.

THE ARCHAEOLOGICAL RECORD

The above review of the ethnographic record also indicates that, notwithstanding detailed studies of ethnographic specimens in museums (Fowler and Matley 1978:32-33), most information concerning brown ware pottery in the Great Basin must be gleaned from the archaeological record. In fact, as Baldwin (1950a:51) notes, it was archaeological specimens that were first used in defining Southern Paiute pottery (Harrington 1926:71; 1927:271; 1930:24). Similarly, most scholars have used Coale's (1963:1-2), Rudy's (1953:94-98), and Tuohy's (1956) descriptions of archaeological specimens to reference the pottery made by Shoshoni speakers. But, the information obtained from the archaeological record is, of course, subject to interpretation and dependent on the questions we ask of that record. In this section, I will review that questions that have been previously asked of the prehistoric brown ware pottery in the Great Basin and assess how well we have been able to answer those questions.

Typology and Description

Most archaeological references concerning brown ware pottery in the Great Basin have focused their attention on presenting brief descriptive statements about a particular pottery assemblage and assigning that assemblage to a previously defined pottery "type," "style," or "ware" (Bettinger 1975:163-165; Elsasser 1960:30-31; Fowler, Madsen, and Hattori 1973:15-17; Heizer, Baumhoff, and Clewlow 1968; Layton 1970:105-108; Magee 1964; Meighan 1955; Thomas and Bettinger 1976:345-346; Wallace and Wallace 1978 and others). During this exercise, some researchers present relatively detailed descriptions of their pottery assemblages, but others simply cite an existing "type description" as being representative of what was found. Occasionally, there may be statements on how the particular assemblage differs from or conforms to a certain "type description." More often than not, however, the typological assignment concludes the discussion of pottery and one gains the impression that this assignment is viewed as an end in itself.

As Fowler (1968a:10) noted, the terms "ware," "type," and "variety" have been used loosely in the discussion of Intermountain Brown Wares. This usage, seldom following the concepts advanced by Colton (1953:51-58), has caused considerable confusion in typological assignments and in the interpretation of those assignments. This problem has been compounded by the fact that few scholars have presented formal typological descriptions of Intermountain Brown Wares. Nevertheless, most scholars (Beck 1981:1; Fowler 1968a:10; Madsen 1975:82) have recognized three major "wares" within this brown ware pottery: Southern Paiute Utility Ware, Shoshoni Brown Ware and Owens Valley Brown Ware. Some researchers (Fowler 1968a:10) have lumped all three "wares" under the Shoshonean tradition and use the term Shoshonean Brown Ware to refer to the pottery made by all Numic speakers. However, this distinction between Shoshonean and Shoshoni brown wares has not been followed consistently and it is often difficult to discern whether authors are referring to only Shoshoni speakers or all Numic speakers when applying the term Shoshonean Brown Ware.

Baldwin (1942:187; 1950a:53-54) is credited with defining Southern Paiute Utility Ware. According to that description, based on more than 7,000 sherds recovered from over 130 different archaeological sites near Overton, Nevada, Southern Paiute Utility Ware has the following characteristics:

Construction: Normally coiling and thinning with paddle and anvil, although many vessels evidently were also thinned by scraping.

Firing atmosphere: Uncontrolled, but probably mainly reducing.

Core color: Dark gray to black, occasionally dark brown.

Temper: Very coarse, quartz and mica.

Texture core: Coarse.

Fracture: Usually crumbling, occasionally rather sharp.

Surface finish: Normally rather rough, particularly on interior surface; exterior partially smoothed, occasionally finger indented; mica and quartz grains show through interiors, less often on exteriors; interior surface has tendency to flake.

Luster: Dull.

Surface color: Very dark gray to grayish brown to black; and occasional specimen may be varying shades of reddish gray or reddish brown.

Firing clouds: Yes.

Forms: More common are small to large deep bowls and tall narrow jars, both with pointed or semipointed base and more or less conical in form; also rather large jars with very wide mouth.

Vessel size: Bowls range from 20 to 38 cm in diameter and from 18 to 22 cm in depth; jars range from 18 to 35 cm in diameter and from 15 to 40 cm in height.

Base: Extremely thick and either pointed or slightly rounded.
Thickness of vessel walls: Bowls, 3.5 mm to 7 mm, averaging 5 mm; jars, 4 mm to 13 mm at the base, averaging 6 mm.
Rims: Bowls, straight to slightly out-curving, rounded or flattened, often uneven, jars slightly outcurving, uneven.
Handles or lugs: None.
Decoration: Often none. A number of jars have small fingernail indentations over entire surface, but usually this occurs as a narrow single band just below rim.
Slip: None.
Paint: None.

Baldwin (1950a:54) felt that the distinctive features of this pottery type were "the thick pointed or semi-pointed base; conical form; absence of true neck; dark, roughened surface; straight, uneven rim; and fingernail indentations below rim, when present." Euler (1964:279) has concurred with Baldwin's description of Southern Paiute pottery "except for his contention that it was usually fired in a reducing atmosphere." On that point, Euler noted that most sherds are brown or reddish brown in color and thereby reflect an oxidizing atmosphere during firing.

Alice Hunt (1960:202-207) distinguished three varieties of Southern Paiute Utility Ware from Death Valley. The first variety, including bowls and jars with wide mouths, out-flaring rims, and rounded, rather than flat or pointed bases, was marked by a paddle-and-anvil finish; granitic temper; round or flat, but not bulbous rims; and rough surfaces and vessel walls ranging between 4 to 9 mm. The second Southern Paiute ware from Death Valley, finished by scraping, was "easily recognizable by its outflaring or straight rim, fingernail decorations, and round or pointed base" (A. Hunt 1960:205). Finally, the third variety, "believed to be Southern Paiute ware, resembles the above Southern Paiute ware in its associations but resembles Shoshoni ware in form" (A. Hunt 1960:205). According to Hunt, the Shoshoni ware from Death Valley was distinguished by straight or incurving rims and round or small flat bases.

Shoshoni Brown Ware, as a pottery "type" or "ware" has been defined by Rudy (1953:94-98) and Coale (1963:1-2), although Tuohy's (1956:56-67) descriptions of four pottery vessels and several groups of pot sherds from Idaho have also been taken as a "type description" of this ware. Rudy's (1953:94) "preliminary description," based on approximately 900 sherds from western Utah and an assemblage of undisclosed size from northeastern Nevada, follows:

Construction: Coiled and molded.
Firing: Uncontrolled atmosphere (?).
Core color: Generally reddish brown, ranging from dark gray through reddish brown to almost black.
Temper: Variable; when viewed with a hand lens it appears as quartz sand ranging from fine to coarse . . . thin section analysis shows the temper to be "crushed granitic rock or subangular sand that has been derived from granitic rock."
Texture of core: Coarse, occasionally medium.
Surface finish: Poorly smoothed; scraped by a stick; striations common. Surface usually undulating. Occasional sherds well smoothed but not polished.
Surface color: Reddish brown or buff, occasionally gray grading into dark brown; some almost black.
Vessel walls: Strong to friable - principally friable.
Shapes: Sherds indicate "flower pots" and jars with pointed bases.
Rims: Straight and outcurved.
Wall thickness: Average, 7 mm; range, from 4 to 8.5 mm.
Decorative techniques: Occasionally fingernail impressions vertically placed in horizontal bands just below the rims; most sherds plain.

Rudy (1953:96-97) noted that "the sherds studied are very similar to the Southern Paiute pottery described by Baldwin (1950a)," as well as to sherds from the Wyoming Basin (Mulloy 1958).

Coale's (1963:1-2) less detailed, but more often cited, description of Shoshonean pottery is similar to that Rudy presented. He found the most diagnostic trait of this ceramic ware to be its flat-bottomed, straight-walled shape with, or without, slightly inverted rims and with, or without, "an annular flange" around the base. Surface treatment was said to vary from "roughly scraped to well smoothed and floated." Decoration, seldom present, was "limited to incised or indented geometric designs in a narrow zone around the [rim], either inside or out" (Coale 1963:2). The "grit, sand or crushed rock" temper was said to be "ordinarily quite coarse" (2.5 to 3.0 mm), but Coale (1963:2) noted a finer tempered (0.3 to 2.0 mm) variety represented by sherds from the Snake River area and cited Osborne's unpublished thesis that this "Snake River Shoshone Fine" pottery could reflect a distinct "ware" (Coale 1963:2).

As I will discuss below, a central focus of Coale's (1963) paper was to discount a Southwestern origin for Shoshonean pottery and to propose a cultural connection between this pottery and Eskimo wares. Hence, when discussing construction methods, he (Coale 1963:2) stated "both coiling and modeling techniques appear to have been used to fashion the vessels," but suggested that "coiling *per se* is

. . . the result of Southwest influence, and that the noncoiled technique of construction can be isolated as the method originally concomitant with the [Shoshonean] ware being described." Like Baldwin (1950a), Coale used the gray or grayish cast of most sherds to represent a reducing atmosphere during firing, but noted that "brown to buff splotches . . . are frequently present" (Coale 1963:2). Unfortunately, Coale did not specify the particular assemblage(s) used for his characterization of Shoshonean pottery.

Tuohy's (1956:56-57) descriptions of Shoshoni Brown Ware may be more representative of the brown ware pottery from Idaho. Tuohy (1956) consistently identified this pottery as constructed by coiling and scraping. Similarly, vessel forms, including those of four complete specimens, usually had flat bottoms, with or without flanges, and recurvate or straight walls with slightly incurving rims. The one exception (Tuohy 1956:66-67), marked by very fine sand temper similar to Coale's "Snake River Fine Shoshoni" variety, was a sherd from a "necked" vessel having an outward curving, lipped rim. Excluding this above sherd, which also has a very smooth, slightly lustrous surface, surface finish was characteristically rough with striations. Tuohy (1956:67) noted that the "predominance of the flat-bottomed vessel form and the absence of decoration set the Idaho specimens apart from some of the Shoshoni ceramics of western Utah and eastern and southeastern Nevada."

The final, major brown ware pottery type identified in the Great Basin has been termed "Owens Valley Brown Ware." Riddell's (1951: 20-21) description of this pottery type was based on over 900 sherds from a historic/protohistoric Northern Paiute village (4-Iny-2) in Owens Valley and specimens illustrated by Steward (1933a, Fig. 1a-i, Plate 5a, b, d) and Lathrap and Meighan (1951, Plate 3a).

> Construction: Coiling with thinning by
> scraping.
> Fired: In oxidizing atmosphere, although
> often uncontrolled as exhibited by
> numerous sherds that range in color from
> gray to black.
> Core color: Variable; exterior often
> ranges from light red to browns while
> the interior will often range from light
> grey to black.
> Temper: Very fine rounded quartz sand to
> large rounded quartz sand; mica present
> in amounts ranging from small to very
> noticeable. Iron pyrites are occasionally present.
> Carbon streak: Occasional.
> Texture core: Ranges from fine to coarse.
> Walls: Weak to medium strong.
> Fracture: Variable, from crumbling to
> sharp; fractures very often occur at

> coil lines.
> Surface finish: Variable, though normally
> rather rough. Exterior often exhibits
> finger indentations and vertical and/or
> diagonal striations, interior exhibits
> horizontal striations . . . Smoothing
> may be occasionally done with wet hands
> rather than with scraping tool.
> Exterior surfaces sometimes lumpy;
> quartz grains and mica often show on
> surface. Flaking of pottery rare.
> Luster: Dull.
> Surface color: Variable, ranges from
> reddish brown to brown or from light
> grey to black.
> Forms: Vessels from Iny-2 are fragmentary
> but appear to be wide mouth bowls and
> jars having either a flat bottom or a
> rounded bottom.
> Vessel size: Reconstructed diameters of
> two jars (?) are 34 cm and 28 cm;
> reconstructed diameters of two bowls (?)
> are 22 cm and 19 cm.
> Base: Moulded out of a lump of clay, are
> either flat or rounded.
> Thickness of vessel walls: Range from
> 3 mm to 8 mm.
> Rims: Often variable and uneven on the
> same vessel. The curvature of the
> vessel walls generally tends to make the
> rim incurving.
> Handles or lugs: None recovered from
> Iny-2.
> Decoration: Occasional; fingernail indentation in a single band on rim top or
> just below rim on interior or exterior.
> Slip: None.
> Paint: None.

Riddell (1951:22) proposed that the basic differences between Owens Valley Brown Ware and Southern Paiute Utility Ware "include the use of the paddle and anvil and a reducing atmosphere for the Southern Paiute ware in opposition to the use of the coiling (and thinning by scraping) technique and an oxidizing atmosphere in the manufacture of Owens Valley Brown Ware." Further distinguishing attributes were said to be the flat bottoms and slightly incurving rims on Owens Valley Brown Ware vessels and other than flat bottoms and straight or outcurving rims on Southern Paiute Utility Ware.

These criteria are similar to those used by Alice Hunt (1960:205-207) to separate Shoshoni Brown Ware and Southern Paiute Utility Ware from Death Valley. Shoshoni Brown Ware, of course, had not been defined as a separate type when Riddell named Owens Valley Brown Ware and, therefore, he did not provide criteria to distinguish Owens Valley Brown Ware from Shoshoni Brown Ware. When faced with this problem, Alice Hunt (1960:205) restricted the category of Owens Valley Brown Ware to "pottery tempered with Sierran (Cretaceous) granite" and assigned other (Precambrian) granitic tempered brown ware pottery to either "Shoshoni Ware" or "Southern Paiute Ware." However, Charles Hunt (1960:198) noted that "the two kinds of (granitic) rocks are not easy to distinguish."

Several other "types" of brown ware pottery have been recognized in the Great Basin. Hunt (1960:207-209) used the presence of schist temper to define a "Death Valley Brown" "variety" of Shoshoni Brown Ware from Death Valley; Tuohy (1963:62-63; Tuohy and Palombi 1972) defined a Riddle Textile-Impressed "variety" of Shoshoni Ware from southwestern Idaho; Plew (1979:330-331) refers to the finer tempered pottery from the Snake River drainage (Osborne's "Snake River Shoshone Fine") as "Southern Idaho Plain Ware"; Fenenga (1952:345) has used the term "Tulare Plain Ware" to refer to brown ware pottery from Slick Rock Village in the Sierra Nevada; and Mack (1983:81-90) has described Siskiyou Utility Ware from the Klamath River region in Oregon as a "variety" of Shoshonean Brown Ware. Fowler, Madsen, and Hattori (1973:16, 62) reported two "varieties" of Shinarump Brown, apparently an Anasazi Brown Ware (Colton 1952:57-58), from O'Malley and Conaway shelters in southeastern Nevada. In addition, Tizon Brown Ware (Colton 1958; Euler 1959; Euler and Dobyns 1958; May 1978) and possibly other Lower Colorado River ceramic types are known to occur in the southern Great Basin and further confuse typological studies (A. Hunt 1960:202-204). Finally, brown ware pottery similar, if not identical, to that described by Rudy (1953:97-98) and Tuohy (1956:69) occurs in southwestern Montana and western Wyoming (Kehoe 1959; Mulloy 1958; Wedel 1954), and Mulloy (1958:196-199) has proposed that these ceramics, as well as the three major "wares" of the brown wares described above, formed an "Intermountain Tradition."

It is clear, however, even without considering these other pottery types, that there is a great deal of confusion in the classification of brown ware pottery from the Great Basin. Hence, Southern Paiute Utility Ware is said to be characterized by pointed or rounded bases, straight or outflaring rims, and fingernail decorations (Baldwin 1950a:54; A. Hunt 1960:202-207), but Rudy (1953:94-98) classified jars with pointed bases and outcurved rims, apparently sometimes displaying fingernail decoration, as Shoshoni Ware. Similar rounded base vessel forms occur in the pottery assemblages described as Owens Valley Brown Ware (Riddell 1951:20-21) and have been noted in Grass Valley of central Nevada (Beck 1981:26) as well as in southern Idaho (Butler 1979a:4; 1983c, Fig. 13). Conversely, pottery marked by straight or incurving rims and flat bases, characteristics usually ascribed to Shoshoni Brown Ware, occasionally have been classified as Southern Paiute Utility Ware (A. Hunt 1960:205; Worman 1969:43).

Shape is not the only attribute that has been used in distinguishing the above three wares. Riddell (1951:22) argued that Owens Valley Brown Ware must be distinct from Southern Paiute Utility Ware because coiling and scraping were used to construct the former, whereas Southern Paiute Utility Ware was made by the paddle-and-anvil technique. We begin to get an indication that something may be amiss, however, when Riddell (1951:22) compares Owens Valley Brown Ware to Mono-Yokuts pottery, and Coale (1963:2) uses the Mono-Yokuts pottery as exemplary of his paddle-and-anvil constructed Shoshonean Brown Ware. Not to single out Riddell or Coale, this contrast between "paddle and anvil" and "coil and scrape" construction techniques is widely echoed in Great Basin literature and oral tradition. Shepard (1956:59) and Baldwin (1950a:54) are clear in their distinction between processes of building and thinning. Coiling is a form of building that may be contrasted with molding or modeling; whereas scraping, paddle and anvil, hand (finger) smoothing, etc., are methods of thinning and shaping the vessel wall after it has been built. None of these manufacturing techniques are mutually exclusive. Rogers (1936:8-11, Plate 2) provides a good description of the use of paddle-and-anvil technique to thin pottery built by coiling.

As Tuohy (1956:68) pointed out, some of the inconsistency between the three major Intermountain Brown Wares might be due to mistakes in classificaiton. Hence, Tuohy (1956:68) accused Rudy (1953) of lumping flat-bottomed Shoshoni vessels with conical Southern Paiute vessels in his description of pottery from western Utah. Likewise, Lathrap and Shutler (1955) have questioned Fenenga's (1952) separation of Tulare Plain Ware as distinct from Owens Valley Brown Ware. And, Butler (1981b:1-3) has proposed that the fine-tempered, "Shoshonean" pottery from Wilson Butte Cave (Gruhn (1961:98-100) might actually belong to the Desert Gray Wares of the Fremont (Madsen 1977). But, I feel that the problems in the typology of brown ware pottery from the Great Basin run much deeper than the misclassification of a few pottery assemblages or even from the misinterpretation of defining characteristics.

Dunnell (1971:139-140) has argued that the "type descriptions" commonly employed in ceramic analyses, such as those for the Intermountain Brown Wares, "are in reality unstructured description of groups of artifacts which have already been identified with classes in a classification which has not been presented." In other words, these descriptions present a list of characteristics of a particular pottery assemblage already determined to represent a distinct and "historically significant" type. When Baldwin (1950a:53-54) and Harrington (1926:71) presented their descriptions of "Southern Paiute Utility Ware," they were describing a pottery assemblage presumed to belong to the Southern Paiute (Southern Numic speakers). This assumption appears to have been well founded at the time as the Southern Paiute were known to have occupied this region of the Great Basin and to have made brown ware pottery. But, there is no way to tell how well those archaeological assemblages actually represented the pottery made by the Southern Paiute, how much variability was exhibited by those collections or, most importantly, how those archaeological assemblages differed from the pottery made by other Numic speakers.

The classificatory intent behind the pottery type of Shoshoni Brown Ware is more complex. Rudy's (1953:94) "type description" was apparently intended to represent the pottery made by all Numic speakers who occupied western Utah and eastern Nevada. On the other hand, Tuohy's (1956) descriptions are clearly intended to characterize only that pottery assumed to be made by the Northern Shoshoni, even though Tuohy (1956:68) was careful to point out that this "cultural affiliation" was only suggested and not proven. Coale's (1963: 1-3) characterization of Shoshonean pottery was apparently even broader than Rudy's as he draws parallels between that "syndrome of traits" and the ceramic "traditions" of the Yokuts and Western Mono, Panamint Shoshoni, Owens Valley Paiute, Nevada Shoshoni, Gosiute, Northern Shoshoni, and Bannock. Unfortunately, Coale (1963) did not mention the Southern Paiute nor Baldwin's description of their pottery and, thus, researchers can only surmise that he would consider Southern Paiute Utility Ware a distinct type. Whatever the case, it is apparent that each of the three above authors had different perspectives of what was represented by the pottery "ware" they were describing.

Dating

In addition to its use as an indicator of linguistic and cultural affiliations, brown ware pottery from the Great Basin has also commonly been used as a "time diagnostic artifact." In this section I will not attempt to review all the data pertinent to the dating of Intermountain Brown Wares, a task of considerable magnitude. Rather, I will use selected evidence to argue that, although commonly asserted to date from about A.D. 1300 (650 B.P.) to historic times (Bettinger and Baumhoff 1982:493; Thomas and Bettinger 1976:346), the brown ware pottery from the Great Basin is not well, or even satisfactorily, dated. Its precise dating, of course, is not only essential to its use as a temporal indicator, but also has a direct bearing on

hypotheses of Fremont-Shoshoni and Anasazi-Shoshoni relationships as well as the nature of the purported Numic expansion (Aikens 1966a; Euler 1964; Fowler, Madsen, and Hattori 1973: 81-85; Madsen 1975).

When evaluating the use of artifacts as chronological indicators, Hester (1973:51-53) relied on Fowler's (1968a:33) "guess date" of post-A.D. 1300 to date Shoshoni Brown Ware, Shutler's (1961:69) hypothesis that the Southern Paiute entered southern Nevada during the Lost City Phase (A.D. 700 to A.D. 1100) to date Southern Paiute Utility Ware and Fowler's 1968a:10) passing reference of post-A.D. 1650 to date Owens Valley Brown Ware. Fowler (1968a:33) used the occurrence of brown ware pottery from Newark Cave in a stratum radiocarbon dated at 840 $\pm$ 340 B.P. (WSU 463) to substantiate his chronological estimate for Shoshoni Brown Ware, but brown ware pottery was mixed through several levels at Newark Cave and its direct association with this radiocarbon date is equivocal (Fowler 1968b:28, Table 6). Shutler (1961:69) used the occurrence of "Southern Paiute Brown Ware" at "almost all of the pueblo sites" in the Muddy and Virgin River areas and the co-occurrence of a "Paiute jar" and Washington Black-on-gray bowl in Burial No. 3 at Lost City to postulate the contemporaneity of Virgin Branch Anasazi and Southern Paiute. Nevertheless, Shutler (1961:29) states: "although . . . the excavation notes never state whether sherds come from the fill or the floor of a room, it seems reasonable to <u>assume</u> that at least some of the many Paiute sherds found . . . must have been deposited while the ruins were in use." It is plausible, as noted by Gunnerson (1969:189), that Lost City and other pueblo ruins in southeastern Nevada were reoccupied by Numic speakers after the departure of the Anasazi. Finally, Fowler's (1968a: 10) reference to a post-A.D. 1650 date for Owens Valley Brown Ware was derived from Riddell's (1951:23) estimate of a 200-year occupational span for the Cottonwood Creek site (4-Iny-2), but that site may not represent the earliest occurrence of Owens Valley Brown Ware.

Madsen (1975, Table 1) has also reviewed the evidence for dating "Paiute-Shoshone" pottery in Great Basin sites and lists Lost City, Stuart Rockshelter, O'Malley Shelter, Conaway Shelter, Scott site, Pine Park Shelter, Hogup Cave, and Swallow Shelter as providing well-controlled, stratigraphically associated dates. The evidence for the age of "Paiute-Shoshone" pottery at Stuart Rockshelter (Shutler, Shutler, and Griffith 1960:14, Fig. 5) and at the Scott site (Fowler, Madsen, and Hattori 1973:68, Table 26) consisted only of its apparent association with Virgin Branch Anasazi pottery. Madsen (1975, Table 1) interpreted this evidence as indicating this brown ware pottery dates "prior to A.D. 1150," but I suspect that, at both sites, the mixing of "Southern Paiute" and Anasazi pottery could be due to turbation. At O'Malley Shelter, "Shoshonean Ware" was recovered along with both Fremont and Anasazi ceramics from Cultural Units V and VI (Fowler, Madsen, and Hattori 1973:16-19, Table 2). Two radiocarbon dates, 890 ± 100 (RL-42) and 870 ± 100 (RL-43), were taken from Cultural Unit V, but this unit contained only 9 percent (10 sherds) of all Shoshonean ware recovered from O'Malley Shelter; the remaining 91 percent occurred in the above, undated, Cultural Unit VI (Fowler, Madsen, and Hattori 1973: Tables 1, 2). The existence of several, large (80 cm diameter) pits extending from Cultural Unit VI into Cultural Unit V indicates to me that, here again, the apparent association between Fremont, Anasazi, and Shoshonean pottery types might have been due to the aboriginal turbation of these geological deposits (Fowler, Madsen, and Hattori 1973:13, Fig. 4). Hence, Madsen's (1975, Table 1) reference to the "Paiute-Shoshone" pottery from O'Malley Shelter as being well dated between A.D. 1050 and A.D. 1250 is misleading.

Madsen (1975, Table 1) also referred to the Paiute-Shoshoni pottery from Conaway Shelter as dating prior to A.D. 1250. However, at Conaway Shelter, most (67 percent) Shoshonean ware occurred as the only pottery type in Stratum 1, radiocarbon dated (RL-36) at 230 ± 100 B.P. (Fowler, Madsen, and Hattori 1973:58-59, Tables 19, 20). The remaining Shoshonean ware, mixed with Fremont pottery types, occurred in underlying cultural strata II, III, and IV. Stratum II appeared to be a small depression "dug and then filled . . . by the occupants of the site," and Stratum III was a small, crescent-shaped lens restricted to the rear of the shelter (Fowler, Madsen, and Hattori 1973:60, Map 4). Stratum IV, apparently continuous throughout the site, produced a radiocarbon date of 1050 ± 100 B.P. (RL-37), but contained only 7 percent of all the Shoshonean pottery recovered from the site. Conversely, Strata II and III produced only 8 percent of the Fremont and none of the Anasazi pottery recovered from Conaway Shelter. Although Conaway Shelter is well known for containing sterile alluvial strata between cultural levels, these sterile levels do not occur continuously between Cultural Units I through IV and the post depositional turbation of these cultural units could easily account for the above percentage mixes of Fremont and Shoshoni pottery.

Pine Park Shelter (Rudy 1954:94-98) is one of numerous archaeological sites in western Utah which contained both Fremont and Shoshonean pottery (Rudy 1953:23-55). With few exceptions, however, these sites, including Pine Park Shelter, have not been radiocarbon dated, and Rudy (1953:71-72) summarized the situation as: "Shoshone ware to date has

always been found in the topmost levels of sites where other pottery types occur." At Swallow Shelter, six sherds of "possible Shoshoni Ware" occurred with abundant Fremont ceramics in Stratum 9 (Dalley 1976:56, Table 9). A radiocarbon date of 1120 ± 110 B.P. (RL-108) was recovered from the bottom of Unit 9 (Dalley 1976, Table 3). But where Dalley (1976:71) used the occurrence of Shoshonean pottery to indicate a terminal date of A.D. 1300 for Unit 9, Madsen (1975: Table 1) used the radiocarbon date to indicate an age of A.D. 850 for the Shoshonean pottery.

A similar situation occurred at Hogup Cave where abundant Shoshonean pottery was found with abundant Fremont ceramics in Strata 12 through 16 (Aikens 1970:32, Table 3). Radiocarbon dates from these strata ranged from 2920 ± 80 B.P. to 480 ± 80 B.P. (Aikens 1970, Table 2). Aikens explained this inconsistency between early and late radiocarbon dates by the "contamination of portions of these strata by older, underlying materials excavated from their depth by aboriginals during the course of past occupation." The apparent association of Fremont and Shoshoni pottery at Hogup Cave, therefore, might also be due to this process. Hence, where 57 percent of all Shoshoni ware was retrieved from Stratum 16, acceptably radiocarbon dated at 480 ± 80 B.P., 81 percent of all Fremont ceramics was retrieved from Strata 12 to 14, acceptably radiocarbon dated between 1530 ± 80 B.P. and 620 ± 70 B.P. (Aikens 1970, Tables 2, 3). More precise evidence for the age of Paiute-Shoshoni pottery in this region might have been obtained from Remnant Cave where "Paiute-Shoshoni" pottery was in direct, indisputable, association with a hearth dated (SI-2334) at 405 ± 60 B.P. (Berry 1976:117, 119, Tables 24, 26).

Wright (1978:121-122, Table 2) and Butler (1981b:14-15) have reviewed the scant evidence for the age of Intermountain Brown Wares in Idaho and Wyoming. Wright (1978, Table 2) listed a radiocarbon date of 450 ± 80 B.P. (WSU-1441) from a pottery-bearing site near the northern end of the Blackfoot Reservoir in Idaho, but Fowler (1975:489) reported that an additional date of 720 ± 70 B.P. (WSU-1478) from that site which was also "tentatively associated with Northern Shoshone pottery." Other dated occurrences of Intermountain Brown Ware listed by Wright (1978: Table 2) include a 425 ± 150 B.P. (M-1088) radiocarbon assay from Wilson Butte Cave, Idaho, radiocarbon dates of 340 ± 100 B.P. (M-1747) and 370 ± 100 B.P. (M-1746) from Piney Creek, Wyoming, and a 370 ± 110 B.P. radiocarbon assay from Mummy Cave, Wyoming. As noted above, Butler (1981b:2-3) has argued that the pottery associated with the radiocarbon date from Wilson Butte Cave is actually of Fremont derivation.

Butler (1981b:14-15) concluded that "the Shoshoni filtered into the eastern Idaho region only very recently, onto the Snake River Plain no earlier than the middle of the 16th Century and into the mountains north of there perhaps no earlier than the beginning of the 18th Century." His evidence for this statement, however, is circumstantial and not well documented. Nevertheless, the earliest, indisputable dates for Intermountain Brown Ware throughout the Great Basin fall only within the 15th to 18th centuries (Stratum I at Conaway Shelter, Stratum 16 at Hogup Cave, and the hearth at Remnant Cave), and it is possible that this pottery dates later than commonly assumed. On the other hand, the frequent co-occurrence of Intermountain Brown Wares with Fremont and Anasazi pottery in western Utah and southern Nevada is seductive. One can only sympathize with Gunnerson (1969:189) when he states "perhaps the largest single problem in explaining the various 'Shoshonean' wares is the lack of good dating information."

Origins

The next major question anthropologists have asked about Intermountain Brown Wares concerns their origin. The underlying assumption, made by most scholars who have addressed this question, has been that this pottery was not a product of independent development, but rather, was borrowed from a donor with little or no modification (Willey et al. 1955:19-20). However, researchers have not only differed, but also vacillated in their ideas about the presumed donor(s). Based on similarities in vessel form, Steward (1933a:267) postulated that the Paiute of Owens Valley learned to make their pottery from the Yokuts and Western Mono. When considering the Ute and Southern Paiute, however, he speculated that these Numic speakers acquired their "paddle and anvil made pottery" from the Yumans (Steward 1940:479; also see Donnan 1964). Hence, in one case Steward viewed vessel shape as indicating the supposed donor, whereas, in the other he viewed "construction" (surface finishing) techniques as the common link between pottery traditions.

When defining Southern Paiute Utility Ware, Baldwin (1950a:54, 55) considered that its ties laid more with the "general Woodland type" rather than with the Pueblo or Hohokam. Tuohy (1956:70; 1963:63) also initially pointed to Eastern Woodland affinities for Shoshonean Brown Ware and suggested that the Northern Shoshoni might have learned pottery-making on the Northern Plains. Wedel (1954:406, 408) had previously pointed to the similarities in vessel form between Shoshoni pottery and certain steatite vessels from the upper Yellowstone drainage and between that pottery and the Paint Creek ceramics of central Kansas and the Baumer and Crab Orchard wares of Illinois. But, Wedel (1954:406), himself, saw "no good

reason for postulating a direct connection" between these ceramics and Intermountain Brown Wares. Later, Tuohy (1973:55, 58) apparently also changed his mind as he assumed the Numic speakers of Nevada "ultimately derived the idea of pottery making from their kin in the Southwest culture area." Butler (1983c:16), however, has recently revived the idea of a Northern Plains influence on Intermountain Brown Wares when he postulated: "much of the so-called 'Shoshonean' pottery of eastern Idaho may represent a fusion or blending of late Plains and Basin pottery-making techniques and may not be typical of Basin Shoshonean pottery as a whole." He based this interpretation on the purported use of "molding and patching" techniques of pottery construction in both areas.

As mentioned above, the main thrust of Coale's (1963) study of Shoshonean pottery was to address the problems of origins. He (Coale 1963:1) began his study by observing: "Even casual inspection . . . reveals that the ceramic traditions of the southwestern United States can in no way be the direct progenitor of the plain Shoshonean ware." Coale (1963:4) then turned further afield to "find analogous flat-bottomed wares" in the Middle Woodland and Early Mississippian periods in Louisiana, Texas, Arkansas, and Ohio, but concluded that "the spatial separation and probable time gap are too great to admit any immediate inference in that direction." Rather, he (Coale 1963:4) pointed to the typological and temporal similarities between Shoshonean pottery and the Eskimo wares described by Giddings (1952:93-94) and others, and argued for a direct link between the two pottery traditions. It is revealing that Coale, as well as those who have turned to the Eastern Woodlands for examples of pottery styles analogous to those of the Great Basin, deemed that Intermountain Brown Wares could have developed only from a ceramic tradition exhibiting similar vessel shapes and surface finishes. But, it is not unreasonable to expect that changes in vessel shape and finishing techniques might accompany the adoption of a pottery tradition by the hunters and gatherers of the Great Basin (Willey et al. 1955:20-23).

Gunnerson (1969:181-193) has postulated that the Numa were Fremont peoples who, due to climatic change, reverted to a hunting and gathering life-style. Rudy (1953:168-169) and Jennings and Norbeck (1955) have presented similar hypotheses. Gunnerson (1969:189-190), pointing to Malouf's (1946:119) difficulty in distinguishing "Shoshoni pottery" from "Great Salt Lake Buff," argued that "the change in shape from round-bottomed vessels to pointed-bottomed or conical vessels probably reflects to some extent changes in cooking methods." Hence, he (Gunnerson 1969:191) suggested that Intermountain Brown Wares are "basically decadent Pueblo (Virgin, Fremont, Sevier) pottery that received influence from other pottery traditions and from an outside stone-vessel tradition and that underwent some further changes in response to changing cooking techniques." Rudy (1953:16, 75), on the other hand, suggested that the Promontory Brown Ware pottery might be "proto-modern" Shoshoni, but did not attempt to explain the differences in these pottery styles. Although few prehistorians currently favor either Gunnerson's (1969) or Rudy's (1953) hypotheses concerning the fate of the Fremont culture (Berry 1980), the suggested relationship between Fremont pottery and Intermountain Brown Wares should not be discarded lightly.

Distribution

Fowler (1968a: Table 11, Fig. 2) and Tuohy (1973:55-56, Fig. 3) have examined the geographical distribution of Intermountain Brown Wares. According to their cited data, this pottery occurs throughout southern and eastern Nevada, western Utah, southern Idaho, western Wyoming, and into the upper Yellowstone region of Montana. For the most part, this distribution corresponds with the known distribution of Numic speakers at the time of Euroamerican contact. However, Tuohy (1973) has defined an area in western Nevada that is largely devoid of brown-ware ceramics and notes that this "non-ceramic cultural sphere" appears to conform with the geographic distribution of Northern Paiute (Western Numic) speakers. Important exceptions to this correspondence, of course, occur in northwestern Nevada (Layton 1970:105-108, 1973) and southern Oregon (Cressman 1942:91; Mack 1983), as well as in Owens Valley. Tuohy (1973:58) explained this lack of pottery making in western Nevada by postulating that "the Northern Paiute left their ancestral homeland in southeastern California prior to the arrival of ceramic containers in that area." The occurrence of pottery in the High Rock area of northwestern Nevada was attributed "to the passage through the area of mobile, mounted, pottery-using Idaho Shoshoni" (Layton 1973:25).

Madsen (1975:84, Fig. 1) and Wright (1978: 120-123) have used the distribution of Intermountain Brown Wares to corroborate a northeastward spread of Numic-speaking peoples from the southwestern Great Basin. I have already reviewed the evidence for dating this hypothesized Numic expansion and must conclude that the data are simply not yet sensitive enough to establish a migration direction or rate. More germane to evaluating this migration hypothesis, however, is the assumption of a direct correlation between Intermountain Brown Wares and Numic-speaking peoples. Tuohy's (1973) definition of a non-pottery-making sphere among

the Northern Paiute would indicate that not all Numic-speaking peoples made pottery. Likewise, the fact that flat-bottomed pottery was noted among the Gros Ventres (Flannery 1953:65), Blackfoot (Ewers 1945), and several other tribal groups in the northwestern Plains (Mulloy 1958) indicates that its manufacture was probably not restricted to only Numic speakers. The use of material culture, such as pottery styles, as indicators of linguistic groups is extremely dangerous. The Hupa, Yurok, and Karok of northwestern California are a classic example of cultural homogeneity combined with extreme linguistic heterogeneity (Sapir 1921: 213-214). Closer to the case under consideration, Steward (1970:225) cites an example of Southern Paiute absorption into Navajo culture while retaining their Numic language. Pottery, of course, can be borrowed, traded, copied, and/or modified regardless of language.

Recognizing this possibility, Wright (1978:121) posited that if the spread of Intermountain Brown Wares was due to diffusion rather than migration, then its distribution should exhibit no major gaps and portray a wavelike pattern. Conversely, if migration was responsible for the spread of this pottery, then its distribution should follow a definite migration route with diffusion to adjacent areas only during considerably later time. Wright (1978:122, Table 1) then used the absence of pottery at several late-dated archaeological sites in Idaho and Wyoming to support the migration hypothesis. But, Butler (1979a:8) has suggested that "the geographic disparity in the distribution of pottery in southern Idaho may not be so much a function of time as Wright would have us believe, but of differential food gathering and hunting activities." To support this hypothesis, Butler (1979a:8) noted that pottery finds in the upper Snake River region are more abundant near camas meadows than in areas he interpreted to be hunting grounds.

Butler is not the only researcher to note a correlation between the distribution of brown ware pottery and environmental zones. Thomas (1970:696) has proposed a positive association between Shoshoni Brown Ware pottery and the pinyon-juniper woodlands in the central Great Basin. Purporting to test this hypothesis against Fowler's (1968a: Table 7) list of recorded sites in eastern Nevada, Thomas (1970: 696) speculated that "this correlation may be due to (1) more intensive exploitation of the pinyon-juniper zone in later times, or (2) a seasonal round that emphasized use of containers only in the pinyon-juniper zone." In Grass Valley, situated immediately adjacent to the Reese River Valley, however, Beck (1981: 9-13, Tables 1, 2) noted that most pottery-bearing sites were located in the lower foothills or on the sagebrush-covered valley floor. She (Beck 1981:13) raised the possibility that the settlement patterns in Grass Valley may be quite different than those Thomas noted in the Reese River Valley to hypothesize the association between pottery and the pinyon-juniper woodland. The presence or absence of pottery might have more to do with the nature of social activities conducted at these sites than with the particular environmental zone in which they occur.

WHERE DO WE GO FROM HERE?

The above literature review has revealed what I consider to be several weaknesses in our knowledge about the brown ware pottery traditionally included under the rubrics of "Shoshonean Ware," "Southern Paiute Utility Ware," and/or "Owens Valley Brown Ware." I have argued that the problems in the typology of this pottery stem not only from the attributes archaeologists have used to distinguish these "wares," but more important, from the classificatory intent behind their definition. Although it may be theoretically convenient to assume that variability in this pottery directly reflects sociolinguistic divisions, neither ethnographic nor archaeological records verify this correlation. Hence, I have followed Mulloy's (1958:196-199) suggestion and referred to these three pottery "wares" and their various subdivisions as Intermountain Brown Wares. This should not be construed to mean that significant differences do not occur in this brown ware pottery tradition, but only that the significance or meaning of these differences have yet to be demonstrated. If prehistorians remain content simply to classify their pottery assemblages according to the existing "type descriptions" and then use these types or "wares" as indicators of cultural affiliations, then our knowledge about Intermountain Brown Wares is likely to remain about the same.

Second, I have tried to dispel the notion that this brown ware pottery tradition is well dated. Although it could be argued that the existing chronological control of Intermountain Brown Wares can be used to identify archaeological sites dating within the last seven to nine centuries or so, this degree of accuracy is not very useful for assessing temporal variability in typological attributes, or addressing questions of pottery origins and modifications or rates and directions of its dispersal. The frequent coexistence of Anasazi and/or Fremont pottery styles with Intermountain Brown Wares at archaeological sites might reflect their coterminous production or use, but this apparent association also can be explained by natural and cultural turbation. My point here is not to discredit previous attempts to date this pottery, but rather to emphasize the need for additional chronometric

control. As Wilke aptly pointed out during the Great Basin/California Pottery Workshop, the sooted and gummed surfaces of brown-ware vessels provide a unique and, to my knowledge, heretofore unexploited means of dating this pottery.

I have also attempted to show that in the search for the origins of these brown-ware ceramics, most scholars have constrained themselves by assuming that pottery-making was adopted from a donor with little or no modification. This assumption has led researchers to propose sources which lie at great distances from the Great Basin and which have few, if any, other demonstrated connections with the cultural development of this area. A more appropriate assumption might be that these brown wares reflect a pottery tradition the occupants of the Intermountain West have modified to conform more closely to their lifestyle. The ways in which this pottery tradition was modified, of course, may not only reveal significant aspects about aboriginal Great Basin-Plateau societies, but also about the general processes involved in the adoption of a pottery tradition by hunters and gatherers. Why would the highly mobile hunters and gatherers of the Intermountain West want to adopt pottery in the first place?

An examination of the geographical distribution of Intermountain Brown Wares reveals that not all aboriginal occupants of the Intermountain West adopted pottery. Tuohy (1973:58) has postulated that this "nonceramic cultural sphere" might be due to the timing of population movements, but these movements and their timing have not been adequately demonstrated. Even if such migrations occurred prior to the advent of pottery manufacture, what precluded the subsequent adoption of pottery by these Northern Paiute and Washoe groups? In this regard it is interesting to note that the Northern Paiute and Washoe of western Nevada are traditionally considered to have been more sedentary in their adaptation than their pottery-making and highly nomadic Western Shoshoni neighbors. Considering the bulky and fragile nature of pottery, one might suspect that it would have fit better in a less mobile life-style. Hence, in order to address questions concerning the geographic distribution of pottery, we need to understand not only the chronological sequence of events, but also something about the role that pottery might have filled in these aboriginal hunting and gathering societies.

The identification of the above problem areas in the existing literature concerning Intermountain Brown Wares, of course, is the first step in evaluating appropriate directions for future research. But, endeavors should not be restricted to gathering data and devising hypotheses to address previously posed questions. Many of the above questions were posed during a phase in American archaeology dominated by a concern over reconstructing cultural histories. However, today we have incorporated a desire to explain the processes of cultural dynamics as well as to understand variability in past lifeways. Hence, I believe that the starting point in formulating future directions for research should rest in assessing how pottery articulates with behavior in a hunting and gathering adaptation and devising theoretical constructs allowing us to model how pottery might reflect aspects of aboriginal life-styles and cultural adaptations.

Rather than perpetuating a classificatory scheme based on the assumed, but improbable direct correspondence between pottery "wares" and linguistic groups, I suggest that researchers focus their attention on identifying and understanding the factors and processes influencing variability in Intermountain Brown Wares. As Binford (1965:205) aptly stated two decades ago, "we should partition our observational fields so that we may emphasize the nature of variability in artifact populations and facilitate the isolation of causally relevant factors." For example, previous researchers have pointed to variability in vessel shape and size as indicating differences in the linguistic affiliations of aboriginal potters. But changes in vessel shape and size might reflect differences in vessel function, period of manufacture (age), aesthetic viewpoints, as well as alterations in the size, composition, and organization of domestic groups. Likewise, differences in the design motifs, surface finishes, rim styles, and other stylistic features of Intermountain Brown Wares might be due to such factors as the nature and extent of aboriginal information systems, social group composition, idiosyncratic behavior of individual potters (motor habits), and symbolic intent. Variability in the paste and nonplastic inclusions of pottery assemblages might provide information not only regarding where and how aboriginal potters obtained the raw materials used in their craft, but also information about their seasonal movements and exchange relationships.

There is no reason to assume that variability in any one of these attribute classes reflect the same factors or processes that influence differences in any other attribute class. I suggest that future pottery analyses should focus on delineating the ways in which various attribute classes are represented within specific, provenienced assemblages. Hence, the pottery assemblage, rather than the pottery type, should be taken as the unit for comparison. This approach would maximize the usefulness of previous descriptions of Intermountain Brown Wares, while avoiding many of the pitfalls characterizing current typology. More important, it would help to emphasize

variability in Intermountain Brown Wares rather than hide it under type descriptions emphasizing the norm.

Finally, our efforts at modeling aboriginal behavior as reflected by pottery should not be restricted to typological or attribute analyses. Archaeological sites produced by hunters and gatherers consist of a wide variety of potential functional types (residential bases, temporary field camps, caches, resource procurement localities, information gathering stations, etc.), and the prehistorians' ability to decipher the past depend, at least in part, on their ability to identify these various site types and the activities conducted at each. The occurrence of pottery in the archaeological record might provide valuable clues as to the nature of activities conducted at any particular archaeological site. For example, in addition to indicating food preparation, the variety, quantity, and spatial distribution of pottery at an archaeological site might be used to estimate the structure and size of the group occupying the site, the duration of this occupation, and/or the frequency of site reoccupation.

During the above review, I have attempted to critically assess our current knowledge concerning Intermountain Brown Wares and offer suggestions for future research. Although other researchers may not agree with my specific viewpoints concerning the adequacy of traditional approaches, I hope that this exercise has helped clarify the foundations on which our current understanding of Intermountain Brown Wares is based. Similarly, I hope that my recommendations for future avenues of study outline the need for new directions in Great Basin pottery analysis.

ACKNOWLEDGMENTS

The idea for this paper was initiated by comments from Suzanne Griset and its contents and quality have been greatly enhanced through discussions with and editorial comments by Catherine S. Fowler, Suzanne Griset, Brantley Jackson, Cari Lockett, Ronald L. Reno, and Donald R. Tuohy.

REFERENCES CITED

(Citations not listed here will be found in the Annotated and Indexed Bibliography of Ceramics at the back of this volume.)

Berry, Michael S.
    1980 Fremont Origins: A Critique. In
          Fremont Perspectives, edited by
          D.B. Madsen, pp. 17-24. Utah State
          Historical Society Antiquities
          Section Selected Papers No. 16.

Binford, Lewis R.
   1965   Archaeological Systematics and the
          Study of Culture Process. *American
          Antiquity* 31(2):203-503.

Driver, Harold E.
   1941   *Indians of North America*.
          University of Chicago Press,
          Chicago.

Dunnell, Robert C.
   1971   *Systematics in Prehistory*. The
          Free Press, New York.

Jennings, Jesse D., and Edward Norbeck
   1955   Great Basin Prehistory: A Review.
          American Antiquity 21(1):1-11.

Rudy, Jack R.
   1954   *Pine Park Shelter, Washington
          County, Utah*. University of Utah
          Anthropological Papers No. 18.

Sapir, Edward
   1921   *Language: An Introduction to the
          Study of Speech*. Harcourt, Brace,
          and World, New York.

Steward, Julian H.
   1940   Native Cultures of the Intermontane
          (Great Basin) Area. In *Essays in
          Historical Anthropology of North
          America, Published in Honor of John
          R. Swanton*, pp. 445-502. Smith-
          sonian Miscellaneous Collections
          No. 100.

   1970   The Foundations of Basin-Plateau
          Shoshonean Society. In *Languages
          and Cultures of Western North
          America*, edited by E.H. Swanson,
          Jr., pp. 113-151. Idaho State
          University Press, Pocatello.

Thomas, David H., and Robert L. Bettinger
   1976   *Prehistoric Piñon Ecotone Settle-
          ments of the Upper Reese River
          Valley, Central Nevada*. American
          Museum of Natural History
          Anthropological Papers 53(3).

Willey, Gordon R., C. C. DiPeso, W. A. Ritchie,
I. Rouse, J. H. Rowe, and D. W. Lathrap
   1955   An Archaeological Classification
          of Culture Contact Situations.
          In *Seminars in Archaeology: 1955*,
          edited by R. Wauchope, pp. 1-30.
          Society for American Archaeology,
          Memoir No. 11.

AREAL REPORTS

The papers in this section have been grouped according to geographical areas of interest: Eastern and Central Basin, Northwestern Basin and Plateau, and Southwestern Basin. Like the overviews presented in the previous section, they present data from earlier research as well as recent work.

EASTERN AND CENTRAL BASIN

The first of the two papers dealing with this area of the Basin is a short report by Don Tuohy intended to publish photographs of whole ethnographic pots and relevant descriptive data. During the Pottery Workshop, the point was made that it was often difficult for ceramic analysts dealing with sherd collections to compare them to the relatively few complete specimens of known provenience. Published reports often failed to illustrate or describe these specimens completely. Tuohy's paper is an attempt to begin rectifying this problem.

Butler's paper discusses the ceramic assemblages of a particular area--eastern Idaho--and also presents illustrations and descriptions of complete specimens. He describes the available data, previous analyses, and his own conclusions as to the explanation of ceramic diversity observed in the area.

NORTHWESTERN BASIN AND PLATEAU

The papers by the Riddells and Joanne Mack have been grouped together despite their seeming difference in cultural area, because both deal with the northwestern boundary of Basin and Plateau and report ceramics in areas that were previously thought to be devoid of them.

Riddell and Riddell present a short report concerning three sherds found in the late 1930s near Honey Lake in northeastern California. The significance of these sherds is that to this day, many reports on this area fail to acknowledge that pottery is occasionally found here. Although some researchers may be aware of the finds reported here, without published notification, this information was restricted to a narrow network. Once it is recognized that a baked-clay tradition existed in these regions, other researchers may review old collections or direct new research toward uncovering additional specimens. Mack's paper derives from her dissertation research in southern Oregon (Mack 1979). In summarizing data from previously unpublished excavations she noted the presence of crude vessels associated with house floors. Her continuing research is uncovering additional sherds, vessels, and clay pipes from throughout southern Oregon/northern California. She provides a description of "Siskiyou Utility Ware" and includes photographs of the southern Oregon vessel fragments.

SOUTHWESTERN BASIN

The final region to be treated here is the Owens Valley/southern California desert on the western border of the Great Basin. The first paper is a summary by William Wallace of surveys he conducted in Death Valley in the 1950s and 1960s. He describes the overall ceramic assemblage for one particular area of Death Valley—Mesquite Flat.

Weaver incorporates Wallace's survey data along with other information contained in the site records for the counties that comprise the Inyo National Forest. This includes the areas around Mono Lake, Owens Valley, and Death Valley. Although Weaver is cognizant of the limitations of these data, he provides a good example of the kinds of questions that can be addressed and uses ethnographic analogy to elicit plausible explanations for the patterns observed in the ceramic distributions within these counties.

A third paper dealing with this area, Bettinger's analysis of sherds from three sites in Owens Valley, has been included in the next section since it focuses on an analytical technique he feels has potential application for distinguishing brown wares elsewhere in the Basin.

ETHNOGRAPHIC SPECIMENS OF BASIN BROWN WARE
Donald R. Tuohy

The purpose of this report is to put on record several photographs and a brief description of complete specimens collected in the course of ethnographic research and now at the Peabody Museum of Harvard University, Boston, at the Heye Foundation of the Museum of the American Indian, New York, and at the Nevada State Museum, Carson City. These specimens include: four vessels from the Edward Palmer collection --three from Southern Paiutes on the Santa Clara River in southern Utah (1875-1877) and one from central Nevada (1908); two Snake River Shoshoni vessels collected in Idaho by R.P. Erwin (1929); one "Shoshoni" pot from Austin, Nevada (1970); and another from Lund, Nevada, in an area utilized by both Southern Paiute and Shoshoni (1931). We have attempted to provide as much descriptive data as is available for each pot.

Edward Palmer Collection

The notes on the three Southern Paiute pottery vessels and one Nevada Shoshoni vessel in collections at the Peabody Museum were written by Wilbert K. Carter. Carter was responding to a letter of inquiry about these vessels made to J.O. Brew by H. Douglas Osborne, then at the University of Washington, Seattle. Osborne was trying to obtain information on three Southern Paiute pottery vessels collected by Edward Palmer in 1875-1877, as mentioned in R.L. Lowie's "Notes on Shoshonean Ethnography" (Lowie 1924).

Carter was assigned the task of responding to Osborne's inquiry, and he described four "Paiute" vessels in a letter dated June 5, 1950. Osborne sent this letter and other documents in his file to the Nevada State Museum in the early 1960s when Richard Shutler, Jr., and I had begun further studies of Nevada "Shoshoni" ceramics. Carter's photographs (Figures

2-4) and descriptions comprise an excellent record of three vessels made by Southern Paiutes on the Santa Clara River in southern Utah in 1875-1877, and one vessel recovered from central Nevada in 1908, all in the Palmer collection at the Peabody Museum. As Carter explains:

Dr. Edward Palmer was a botanist, who while doing field work in the Southwest in 1875 and 1877, was commissioned to collect for Peabody. He purchased materials and also did a little digging. In 1875 he worked the Santa Clara River country and he is reported to have made excavations in a great mound called the St. George Mound in 1875 and 1877. He also worked Kane County around Salt Lake and Paragonah. A brief statement of his work may be found in the *11th Annual Report of the Peabody Museum*, published in 1878, pp. 198-200. Also in this same report, pp. 269-272, is an article by Palmer entitled "Cave Dwelling in Utah." Other publications by Palmer include "Exploration of a Mound in Utah," *American Naturalist* Vol. X, pp. 410-414 (1876) and "Manufacture of Pottery by Mohave Indian Women," *Proceedings of the Davenport Academy of Natural Science*, Vol. 11, part 1, pp. 32-34 (1877).

He goes on to say that a great deal of confusion exists regarding the term "Paiute." This term had been used to identify makers of all four of the pottery vessels in question despite the fact that Tybo, Nevada, where one vessel (Pot 4) was found, is located in Nevada Shoshoni territory. Carter notes that:

. . . The term "Paiute" has been used in such a broad and confused manner that "Paiute" pottery could refer to that made by people in five or six states, but these

Tuohy

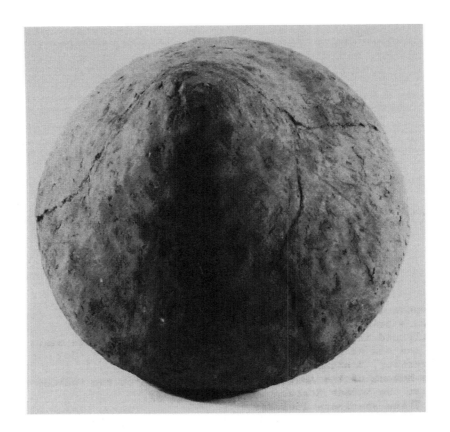

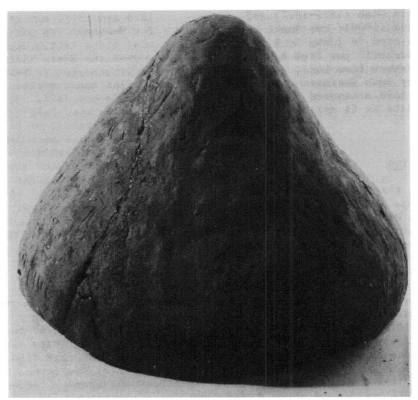

Figure 2. Southern Paiute pot collected in 1875 by E. S. Palmer, now in Peabody Museum collections, No. 9448. The vessel is 14.7 cm high. Note the "fingernail" designs on the neck of the vessel. Courtesy Peabody Museum, Harvard University. Photographs by F. P. Orchard, 1936 (N14191, N14192).

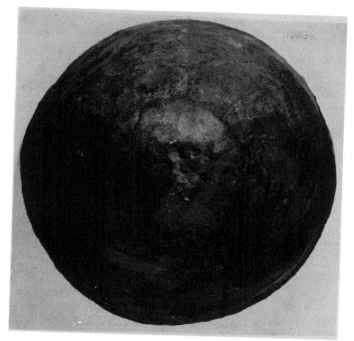

Figure 3. Southern Paiute pot collected in 1877 by E. S. Palmer, now in Peabody Museum collections, No. 12131(a). The vessel is 40 cm high. Courtesy Peabody Museum, Harvard University. Photographs by F. P. Orchard, 1936 (N14190, N14188).

Figure 4. Southern Paiute pot collected in 1877 by E. S. Palmer, now in Peabody Museum collections, No. 12131(b). The vessel is approximately 40 cm high. Courtesy Peabody Museum, Harvard University. Photographs by F. P. Orchard, 1936 (N14187, N14189).

three items were collected on the Santa Clara River in Southern Utah; one in 1875 and two in 1877. The fourth Paiute pot measured was collected near Tybo, Nevada, in 1908. The two pots collected in 1877 bear the same catalog number (12131), so I have designated them 12131(a) and 12131(b). For some strange reason two or more similar items were sometimes assigned one number in the early records at Peabody.

In general appearance all are crude cooking pots with more or less pointed bottoms. These appear dark grey; the third (9448) is grey on the outside except for an inch or two near the rim, which is a buff-red as is all the inside surface. None are slipped. All are uneven in thickness, irregular in contours and all have uneven rims. There are marks inside and outside made by crude scraping tools, perhaps corn cobs, pieces of wood or sherds. No evidence of tempering material is evident. The paste appears to be buff and it is fired very hard. Three are smudged inside (perhaps to aid in holding water) and appear grey outside due to smudge also. The paste color was observed in conical, crack-lacing holes which are mentioned below.

Carter's descriptions of the pots follows, with Tuohy's comments and additions in brackets. Some of the information has been reorganized for clarity.

Pot 1. Catalog No. 9448 (Figure 2).
  Collected by Dr. Edward Palmer in 1875.
Catalog notations: "Cooking pot (to sit in sand) Pah Ute Indians So. Utah"
Remarks: "(Made in Imitation of old pots)"
Dimensions and description:
  Shape: Conical with slightly rounded bottom.
  Height outside: 5/3/4" [14.7 cm] [Inside depth 12.9 cm]
  Top diameter: 7-3/8" [18.8 cm] Bottom pointed; slightly rounded off in area having diameter of 2 to 3 inches [5-8 cm].
  Thickness: The rim thickness is an uneven 1/4" [0.7 cm]. Thickness increases toward the bottom of the pot to about 3/4" [2 cm]. [This estimation is confirmed by comparison of inside depth with outside height].
  Color: buff-red inside and extending down from rim for about 1-3/4" [4.5 cm] on the outside. Remainder of outside is light grey. The portion near the lip, which is buff-red inside and out, is the thinnest section of the pot. Apparently the pot was fired in

an inverted position; thus the inside retained heat for a longer period and was fired sufficiently to turn red to a depth of perhaps 1/4 to 3/8" [0.7-1 cm]. Near the rim the pot was thin enough so that the red section reached through and appears in an uneven (lower on one side than the other) band of red.
  Surface: There is no indication of a slip. The inside shows scraping marks of a crude tool. Note the thumb nail marks about 1/4" below the rim [Shown in the profile photo, Figure 2].

Pot 2. Catalog No. 12131(a) [Figure 3].
  Collected by Dr. Edward Palmer in 1877.
Catalog notations: [apply to both 12131(a) and (b)] "Earthen cooking pot, broken. Pah Ute Indians, South Utah."
Dimensions and description:
  Shape: high cone
  Height outside: 15-3/4" [40 cm] [Inside depth 37.5 cm]
  Top diameter: 12/3/4" [32.5 cm]
  Thickness: 1/4" [0.7 cm] [uneven]. Pot walls thicken below the rim to about 1" [2.6 cm] in places. This thickness is known since many sections [shown in Figure 3] are restored. The wall thickness varies greatly from point to point. Thickness at bottom is 1". Bottom pointed with slightly rounded-off area of diameter about 1-1/2" [3.9 cm].
  Color: dark grey. Heavily smudged (black) inside, perhaps to aid in holding water.
  Surface: There is no slip and no decoration. Some marks [see Figure 3, obverse photo] appear to have been impressed by materials pot laid on during prefiring drying. Note the 12 holes [shown in the profile photo, Figure 3], apparently drilled for lacing to repair cracks. These are conical holes drilled from the outside, such as a stone drill would make.
  Core: In the lacing holes the paste is a buff or buff-grey color. It appears to be of good clay and is fired very hard.

Pot 3. Catalog No. 12131(b) [Figure 4]
  Collected by Dr. E. Palmer in 1877.
Catalog notations: [apply to 12131(a) and (b)] "Earthen cooking pot, broken. Pah Ute Indians, South Utah."
Dimensions and description:
  [This pot is intact to a height of roughly 8-10". Above this it has been built up entirely by restoring material to a height equal to 12131(a). For this

reason it has not been measured].

Shape: Conical, similar to 12131(a),
but less elliptical, having a pointed
bottom, rounded off slightly in an
area of 2-3".

Surface: 12131(b) is smudged inside and
out similar to 12131(a). The paste is
also similar and fired to a like hardness. Three conical lacing holes have
been drilled along a crack (see photo
of bottom). 12131(b) has been scraped
a bit more carefully than 12131(a) but
it is still very crude.

Pot 4. Catalog No. 72975 [not
illustrated]

Catalog notations: "Cooking pot. Paiute.
Found near Tybo, Nevada. Gift of Lewis
H. Farlow. Collected by C. L. Hartman,
1908. Purchased from an Indian by Mr.
Hartman."

Dimensions and description:

Shape: Conical with a small but flat
bottom on which it stands nicely on
the display case floor. The profile
shape is thus: [Sketch shows typical
"Shoshoni" vessel with recurved or
"S"-shaped sidewalls.]

Height outside: 9 to 9-1/4" [22.9 -
23.4 cm] [Inside depth 8-1/2 to
8-3/4" or 21.6 - 22.3 cm].

Top diameter: 12 to 12-1/4" [30.7 -
31.3 cm]. Contour uneven.

Bottom diameter: 2-3/4" [7 cm]

Color: dark grey heavily smudged inside
and out. Rim thickness 3/16" [0.5
cm]. This pot is thin all the way
down except in the bottom which is
rounded inside and square out with a
thickness of about 1/2" [1.3 cm].
There is no slip or decoration. There
are two conical lacing holes, one on
each side of a crack near the rim.
The paste appears grey or buff. The
pottery is fired very hard. The pot
is roughly smoothed, having a very uneven rim. Except for the flattened
bottom and relative dimensions (rim
diameter greater than height), this
pot collected in 1908 is very similar
to those collected in 1877 (Carter
1950).

Thus, Carter's descriptions and photos are
extremely useful "type" descriptions of
Southern Paiute and Shoshoni vessels found in
Utah and Nevada between 1875 and 1908.

The second "type" illustrated here is
represented by two "Snake River Shoshoni Ware"
vessels from the collections of the Heye
Foundation, Museum of the American Indian, New
York. R.P. Erwin, an early day Idaho collector, gave five vessels to Louis Schellbach and
Godfrey J. Olsen who were employed to do

research in Idaho by the Heye Foundation at the
time (Schellbach 1930). Eventually, two of the
restored vessels returned west, one going to
the Idaho State Historical Museum in Boise
(Tuohy 1956:56) and the other to the Washington
State Museum in Seattle. Three restored
vessels, two of which are illustrated here
(Figure 5) were retained by the Heye Foundation
(Coale 1963:4). These photographs of two of
the New York specimens are published through
the courtesy of Osborne and the Heye Foundation's Museum of the American Indian. It
is important to note that even though the
restoration work distorted all maximum diameters of these two vessels, all of the "Snake
River Shoshoni Ware" vessels known at that time
were flanged base forms with flat bottoms and
wide, flaring mouths and outward sloping sides.
Complete descriptions of attributes and dimensions cannot be given, as the data are incomplete. Overall dimensions of the vessels
are given in the caption (Figure 5).

The final brown ware vessels to be
discussed are two cooking pots in Nevada State
Museum collections which show variations in
"standard" coil-and-scrape manufacturing techniques. The first of these two vessels is a
typical "Shoshoni" ware pottery vessel (Figure
6). This vessel was found in Nevada Shoshoni
territory near Austin, Nevada, and was previously described by Tuohy and Palombi (1972:
46-48). Metric data for this vessel are
repeated below:

Fig. No.: 6
Specimen No.: Mc-1-1
Provenience: vicinity of Austin, Nevada
Ceramic "Type": "Shoshoni" ware
Vessel Form: jar
Vessel Shape - rim: IIIA2 (Colton 1953:44)
Method of Construction: coiled and wiped
Surface (exterior)
       Texture: rough, with
        wiping marks
       Mohs hardness: 4
*Surface (interior) - if different from
exterior)* *Texture:* carbonized
Decoration (indicate kind and placement)
"Fingernail" impressions in a single
row, ca. 1.4 cm below lip of rim.
Dimensions -
Height (interior): 23.2 cm
Diameter @ mouth (interior): 27.3 cm
      @ base (exterior): 12.5 cm
Wall thickness @ rim: 0.7 cm
     @ body: 0.7 - 0.9 cm
Remarks: Basketry impression of open-work
twining present on the bottom side of
the base.

The importance of this Nevada Shoshoni
vessel lies in the fact that it illustrates the
manufacturing practice of placing the basal
lump of clay for the vessel on a fragment of a

Figure 5. Two "Snake River Shoshoni Ware" vessels from the R. P. Erwin collection in the Museum of the American Indian, Heye Foundation, N. Y. Upper, vessel 16/6888 which is 24.1 cm high, has a rim diameter of 27.3 cm, and a base diameter of 13.9 cm; Lower, vessel 17/5229, 23.5 cm high, with a rim diameter of 22.8 cm and a base diameter of 11.4 cm. Photographs courtesy of the Museum of the American Indian, Heye Foundation, N. Y.

Figure 6. Central Nevada Shoshoni pottery vessel with basketry impression on the bottom side of the base and "fingernail" decorations on the neck of the vessel. The vessel is 23.2 cm high (after Figure 1 in A Basketry Impressed Shoshoni Pottery Vessel from Central Nevada [Tebiwa 15(1): 48] by Donald R. Tuohy and Barbara Palombi, 1972).

finger-woven textile before building up the body of the vessel by coiling. Warp-face or twill-twined and possibly coiled basketry fragments have also been similarly utilized in the manufacture of other Nevada Shoshoni ceramic pots (Tuohy 1963). Also, the McCloud vessel aptly illustrates the practice of wiping the vessel with a coarse material and decorating the vessel with so-called "fingernail impressions." The latter actually are incisions gouged out of the vessel before the clay hardened, and before the vessel was fired.

The final vessel to be considered here is a small, conical brown ware vessel made by coiling. While the exterior has been scraped and otherwise smoothed, the individual coils showing on the vessel's interior have been only partially obliterated (Figure 7). Thus, the manufacturing technique results in a kind of interior corrugated design often found only on the exterior surfaces of southwestern textured ceramics.

This vessel was recovered near Lund, in southern White Pine County, Nevada. This White River area is right on the boundary between areas utilized by both the Southern Paiute and Shoshoni. The conical shape of the vessel and the partially obliterated coils on the interior suggest that the pot is of Southern Paiute manufacture and it was so identified by the finder, James C. Riordan. The metric data pertinent to this vessel are given in the following description.

Fig. No.: 7
Specimen No.: 11-G-1
Provenience: Riordan Ranch, near Lund, White Pine Co., Nevada.
Ceramic "Type": Southern Paiute?
Vessel Form: jar
Vessel Shape - rim: IA3 (Colton 1953:44)
   body: conical
   base: pointed
Method of Construction: coiling
Surface (exterior)
   Texture: scraped and smoothed
Surface (interior) - (if different from exterior) Texture: coils only partially obliterated
Dimensions -
 Height: 17.0 cm
 Diameter @ mouth (interior): 16.5 cm
Remarks - Other descriptive data not available at present.

This unusual vessel appears to be unique. Others may be represented in sherd collections, but not at the Nevada State Museum. This description concludes this brief discourse on rare and unusual or "type" specimens of brown ware in the pottery collections of several museums.

Figure 7. Conical pottery vessel probably of Southern Paiute manufacture; Specimen 11-G-1, Nevada State Museum Collections, Carson City. Photograph by J. Toms.

THE POTTERY OF EASTERN IDAHO

B. ROBERT BUTLER

The title serves to distinguish this article
from an earlier one (Butler 1979a) treating the
pottery of the same region--the Upper Snake and
Salmon River country of eastern Idaho. Identifications made in the earlier article need to
be revised in light of more recent studies, and
there are new findings to be reported as well.
Beyond that, something also needs to be said
about the problems inherent in attempting to
classify the pottery of this region.

GENERAL DISTRIBUTION OF POTTERY IN THE
UPPER SNAKE AND SALMON RIVER COUNTRY
OF EASTERN IDAHO

The northern limit of pottery in this
region is the Salmon River Canyon from the
North Fork to the Middle Fork (Figure 8); however, pottery occurs as far west on the Salmon
as Riggins, Idaho. The east-west course of the
Salmon also marks the approximate limit of the
northeastern Great Basin culture subarea in
Idaho (Butler 1978). Pottery does not occur
uniformly throughout this region. There are
marked differences in distribution, differences
of considerable significance in the later prehistory of the area. More than 90 percent of
all the known pottery from this region has been
found in a zone across the southern part of the
state corresponding with the limits of the
Snake River Plain from the confluence of the
Henry's Fork with the main Snake westward, including the Camas Prairie basin on the northern
edge of the Snake River Plain in south-central
Idaho (Figure 9).

Pottery is extremely rare up the Lost
River valleys, a fact I have attributed in part
to a sexual division of labor in which male
hunting parties continued up the valleys to
hunt for bison, mountain sheep, and other big
game, while those remaining behind (i.e.,
women, children, and the elderly) collected

roots, especially camas, and seeds in the
meadows along the southern foot of the Rocky
Mountains (Butler 1979a).

I have also suggested that hunters from
the High Plains intruded into the mountains
north of the Snake River Plain during the Late
Period (ca. A.D. 500-1805), prior to occupation
of the region by horse-mounted Shoshoni after
ca. A.D. 1780, and to the exclusion of other
peoples, collectively referred to as the
Fremont. The Fremont centers of occupation
were along the Snake River and farther south
along the Great Salt Lake (Butler 1981b), and
it is their pottery that is found at sites pre-
dating Shoshonean occupation in southern Idaho
south of the Rocky Mountains. Thus far, no
Fremont pottery has been found beyond the
northern limits of the Snake River Plain.

Conversely, the flat-bottomed, flower-pot-
shaped pottery commonly attributed to the
Shoshoni is found nearly everywhere in the
region; however, as indicated earlier, it
rarely occurs at sites in the Lost River
valleys north of the Snake River Plain and is
more common at sites along the Middle Fork, on
the main Salmon below the Middle Fork, and in
the headwaters of the Middle Fork and the main
Salmon in the Stanley Basin area of central
Idaho than father east in the Salmon River
drainage.

That this distribution of pottery in the
region might be an accident of collecting or
the result of research bias is counterindicated
by large-scale, highly structured inventories
made of the Mount Bennett Hills, Challis,
Little Lost River-Birch Creek, and Camas-Little
Grassy BLM planning units (Cinadr 1976;
Epperson 1977; Kingsbury 1977; Roberts 1976)
and numerous other random and nonrandom inventories made throughout the region beginning in
1958 including U.S. Forest Service as well as
BLM lands (e.g., Harrison 1972).

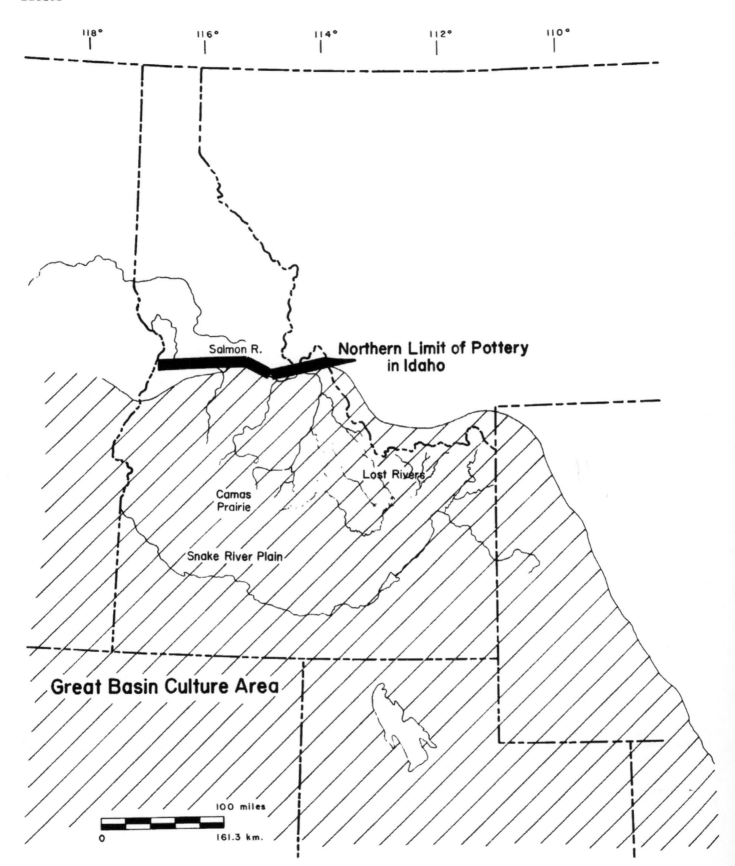

Figure 8. Northeastern portion of the Great Basin culture area showing northern limit of pottery in Idaho.

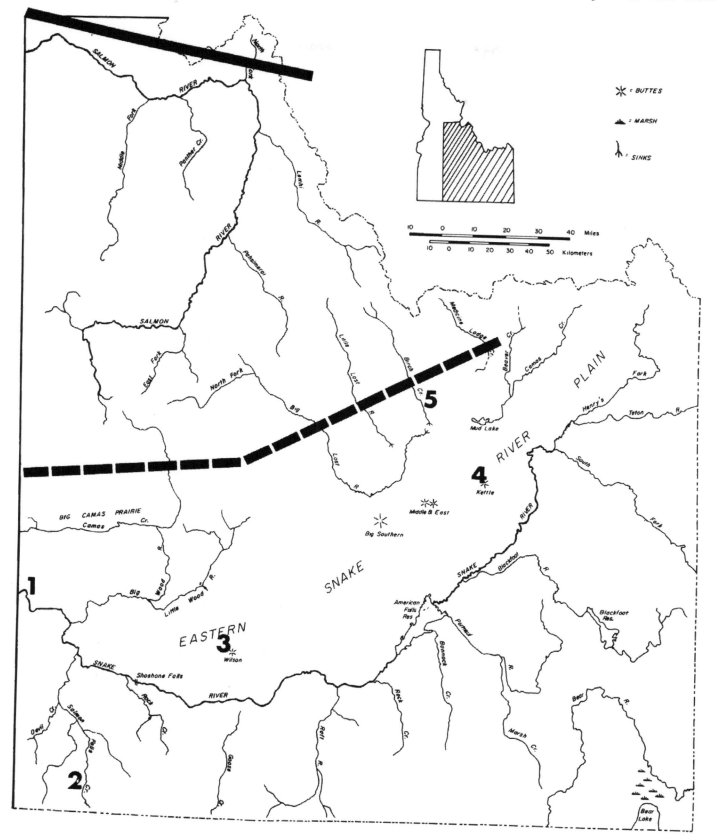

Figure 9. Eastern Idaho showing locations of the principal sites mentioned in text, northern limit of Fremont pottery (broken line) and northern limit of all pottery (solid line). (1) Clover Creek; (2) Dean site on Brown's Bench; (3) Wilson Butte Cave; (4) Wasden site; (5) 10-CL-100.

Painted as well as plain pottery occurs in the region. The painted pottery, all found either along the Snake River or its tributary streams draining the Owyhee Uplands in the southwestern corner of Idaho, consists mainly of isolated sherds of Moapa Black-on-gray (Butler 1982a), Sosi Black-on-white and Virgin Black-on-white, Anasazi wares dating from the 9th to the 12th centuries; and Snake Valley Black-on-gray, a southern Fremont ware dating from approximately the same time period (identifications made by R. Madsen, personal communication to B.R. Butler 1983). All of the aforementioned sherds were found west of Twin Falls, in south-central Idaho. Sherds of un-identified black-on-white or black-on-gray ware are said to have been found on a ranch just west of the Menan Buttes, upstream from Idaho Falls. I have not handled these sherds myself, as I have the others, but the information appears to be reliable. If confirmed, the sherds in question would represent the only known painted pottery found in southern Idaho east of Twin Falls. Far more common are finds of plain pottery. These finds are the focal point of this paper. However, they pose dif-ficult problems in identification and classi-fication.

PROBLEMS IN THE IDENTIFICATION AND CLASSIFICATION OF THE PLAIN POTTERY FOUND IN THE UPPER SNAKE AND SALMON RIVER COUNTRY

One of the problems in identification and classification is that of sample size. Approximately 4,200 potsherds have been collected from the entire region over the past 25 to 30 years, most by relic hunters who have donated their sherds to the Idaho Museum of Natural History's (IMNH) collections. This is about equal to the total number of sherds re-covered from a single Fremont site along the Bear River in Utah (Shields and Dalley 1978, Table 1). Most of the Idaho material consists of very small quantities of sherds, seldom more than 10 to 15 from any one site, with most of the sherds less than 5 cm across. A few sites, such as the Wasden site (Owl Cave) on the Snake River Plain near Idaho Falls (Butler 1968), have yielded as many as 450 to 500 sherds (un-published data), but even with a sample of this size, there is some disagreement as to exactly what ware(s) are represented.

Determination of vessel forms on the basis of the IMNH collections is often very dif-ficult, if not impossible. As indicated earlier, the most readily and commonly iden-tified form is the flat-bottomed, flower-pot-shaped vessel attributed to the Shoshoni, but other forms are also occasionally reconstruc-tible from available sherds (examples of each of these are shown in Figures 10-11).

Adding to the problems of sample size and reconstructibility of vessel forms are ambiguities encountered in using the term "ware" as applied to plain pottery found in the Basin generally. The term "ware" can refer to certain technological attributes of pottery, such as the size, shape, and composition of the temper or filler; it also can refer to a completely different set of parameters, such as the method of manufacture and surface finish of the pottery, or a combination of both of these. In any case, all of the pottery comprising a ware presumably share a common set of attri-butes. However, in the classification of flat-bottomed, flower-pot-shaped vessels from the Northeastern Great Basin, this conception of the term "ware" does not seem to apply. Although almost universally referred to as "Shoshonean ware," the pottery in question exhibits enormous variability in the size, shape, and mineral composition of the temper, in wall thickness, rim form and lip shape, in surface finishing, and in manufacturing tech-niques. About the only attribute these vessels have in common is the flat-bottomed, flower-pot-shaped form. As Mulloy (1958) pointed out, this was a *regional* style on the Northwestern Plains made by a number of different tribal groups, the Shoshoni among them, utilizing dif-ferent methods of manufacture (Simon 1979). Those Shoshoni who were Plains dwellers before being pressured westward over the Continental Divide by such rival Plains groups as the Blackfoot (Murphy and Murphy 1960) may have made their pottery in the fashion of the Plains rather than in the fashion of the Great Basin. Thus, not all of the pottery produced by Shoshonean speakers is necessarily "Shoshonean ware." Similar problems are encountered in classifying the Fremont (Desert) Gray wares, particularly Great Salt Lake Gray. The latter is a highly variable pottery, at times in-distinguishable from what is loosely called "Shoshonean" ware in Utah (Rudy 1953). In fact, type quality Great Salt Lake Gray sherds from Wilson Butte Cave on the Snake River Plain north of Twin Falls were originally identified as a Shoshonean ware (Gruhn 1961), an iden-tification later questioned but not corrected until 1981 (Butler 1981a). One cannot say there is an absolute difference between the wares, save that the Fremont did not make pottery with a flanged, annular base, although they did make jars with flattened bottoms. The Shoshoni, on the other hand, probably made vessels resembling some made by the Fremont, utilizing essentially the same residual clay bodies and techniques of manufacture (Rudy 1953).

In an attempt to determine whether there were systematic differences in the temper and paste utilized in manufacturing the pottery found in the Upper Snake and Salmon River country, I initiated a thin-section analysis of

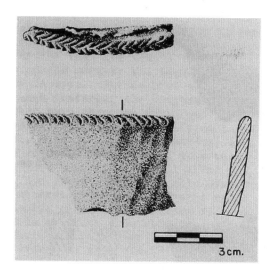

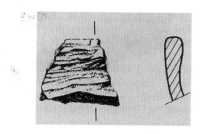

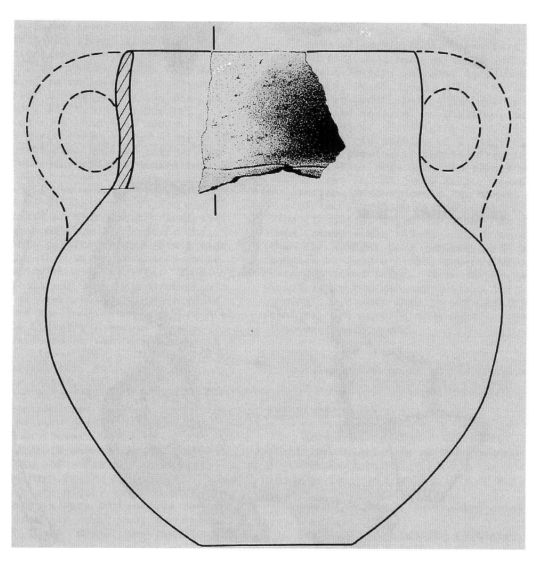

Figure 10. Examples of Great Salt Lake Gray (GSLG) and Promontory (P) wares (all rim sherds) from the Upper Snake and Salmon River country. <u>Upper left</u> (GSLG) from Wilson Butte Cave, Stratum A; <u>upper right</u> (P), from the Wasden site; <u>lower</u> (GSLG) from 10-EL-33 on Snake River above Clover Creek.

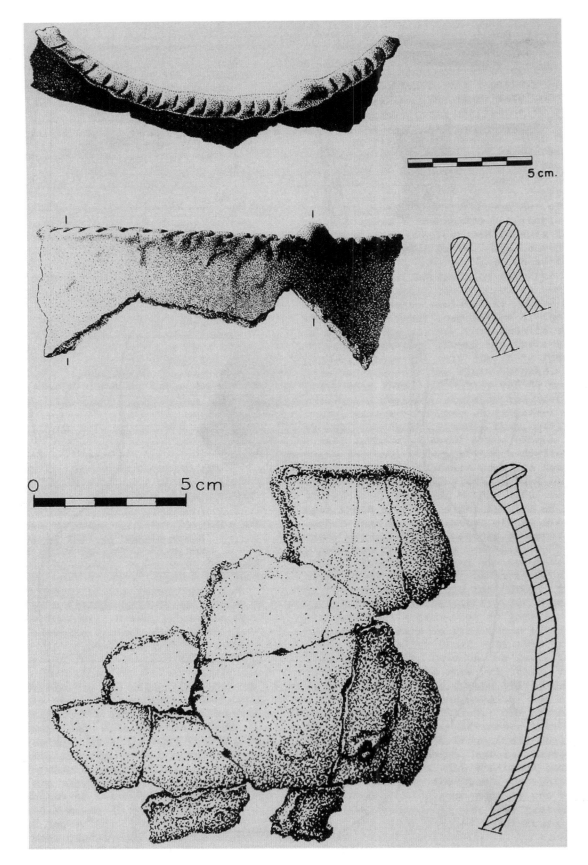

Figure 11. Examples of Promontory Ware from Upper Snake and Salmon River country. Upper, rim sherds (probably from a jar) from Little Lost River sinks; lower, partially assembled bowl from Wasden site.

a geographically dispersed sample of 50 different sherds from 40 different sites or site locations. At the time the sample was selected, none of the pottery had been formally identified as to type. Sherds were selected randomly in each instance, the only requirement being that when more than one sherd was selected from a site, each would be from a different vessel, such as at the Wasden site (Owl Cave), where at least 12 different pots were represented. The analysis is still under way. Thus far, it has revealed considerable diversity in the mineralogy, shape, and size range of the nonplastic elements (temper or filler) incorporated in the clay from which the pottery was made. There are only very broad geographical trends evident at this time: north of the Snake River Plain, the nonplastic elements in the clay reflect the mineralogy of the Idaho batholith, while to the south they reflect the mineralogy of the Snake River Plain. No two thin sections exhibited identical or closely similar nonplastic inclusions, except that nearly everywhere, the shapes of the nonplastic inclusions appeared to reflect an abundance of naturally occurring inclusions in the clay to which, on occasion, additional nonplastic materials (crushed rock) had been added. That is, for the most part, there are no clear indications that a particular body of clay or tempering material was selected for manufacturing a particular type of pottery. Thus, it seems unlikely that we will be able to distinguish consistently the local plain wares from one another on the basis of thin-section analyses. Such analyses may enable us to identify the locality in which a particular vessel was made, but by themselves, they will not enable us to identify the particular type of ware. This conclusion is consistent with D. Madsen's (1979) analysis of Great Salt Lake Gray wares from the Levee and Knoll sites in northern Utah and with Florence Lister's comments on the Desert Gray wares found at the Coombs site in southern Utah (R. Lister 1959). Yet, on the basis of other attributes, such as surface finish, hardness, vessel, and lip form and decoration, all of which can vary widely, we are reasonably certain that at least three different plain wares were manufactured in the region. These are: Desert Gray, of which Great Salt Lake Gray is one highly variable type; Generic Basin, of which the so-called "Shoshonean," Southern Paiute Utility, and Owens Valley Brown are highly variable types; and Promontory Gray, a very distinctive ware, quite different from the other two, but also highly variable. These "wares" are described below, in the order of their apparent antiquity in southern Idaho.

Before describing them, however, the often considerable assistance of various individuals in identifying some of the pottery involved should be acknowledged. Rex Madsen, who com-

piled the handbook of Fremont pottery (R. Madsen 1977), took time from his busy legal practice to examine sherds from a number of different sites, including Wilson Butte Cave, and provided substantial reports on the results, as did Joe Ben Wheat, University of Colorado Museum, Boulder, on the burnished pottery from the Wasden site, and Claude Warren and Margaret Weide, University of Nevada, Las Vegas, on the Moapa Black-on-gray ware from two sites in south-central Idaho (Butler 1982a). Also instrumental in the identification of the pottery in question were David Madsen, State Archaeologist, Division of State History, Salt Lake City, Utah, and Jesse Jennings, Richard Holmer, Frank Hull, and Patricia Wong in the Department of Anthropology at the University of Utah. In most instances, I asked for and received a publishable comment or report on the material in question, all of which proved extremely helpful.

Also of considerable value were comments some participants made at the Great Basin/California Pottery Workshop in Bishop, California, April 22-23, 1983. William Wallace, in particular, after several examinations of the material in question, pointed out that a group of sherds from south-central Idaho forming the rim section of a large globular pot that I had previously labeled Fremontlike (Butler 1979a: Fig. 1, upper right) could be easily lost in his Owens Valley Brown Ware collection. Subsequently, R. Madsen identified one of the sherds as typical Great Salt Lake Gray (letter of August 10, 1983, on file IMNH). This, among other things, led me to suggest that there might be a generic Basin ware comparable to Rudy's (1953) generic Desert Gray Ware described below. None of the individuals named is in any way responsible for the shortcomings or errors made in this article. Nevertheless, the article owes much to their generous assistance.

PLAIN WARES FOUND IN THE UPPER SNAKE AND SALMON RIVER COUNTRY

Desert Gray Ware

According to Rudy (1953:79-80), the principal characteristics of this generic Fremont utility ware are:

Construction: Coiled.
Firing: Poorly controlled reducing atmosphere.
Core color: Light to dark gray, although buffs and reddish grays appear; occasionally almost black.
Temper: Volcanic glass and quartz. In Great Salt Lake Gray and Sevier Gray volcanic glass predominates. It ranges from 0.1 to 3.0 mm in diameter and

averages 2.0 mm. The temper of the Snake Valley series is predominantly fine-grain quartz ranging from 0.2 to 0.5 mm in diameter. Varying amounts of mica are found in most sherds, but it is believed to be a natural constituent of the paste clay and not intentionally included as temper.

Texture of core: Fine to coarse.
Vessel walls: Medium strong to friable.
Surface finish: Both surfaces smoothed, exterior surface poorly polished. Striations occasionally visible on surfaces of heavily tempered sherds. Mica particles conspicuous on both surfaces.
Surface color: Predominantly light gray to dark gray but includes almost black to buff to reddish gray.
Fire clouds: Occasionally present.
Wall thickness: Average, 5.0 mm; range, from 2.6 to 7.0 mm.
Rims: Jars; the predominant form is the out-curved, rounded rim classified by Colton and Hargrave as IB3 type (Colton and Hargrave 1937:10). Variations of this rim form occur . . . Bowls; predomnant form is the straight lip with the rounded rim labelled IA3 by Colton and Hargrave.
Decorative techniques: The largest percentage of the sherds and specimens is undecorated. However, pinching, applique, punching, incising, and painting are found. Painting occurs on black-on-gray types only; the pigment used is carbon.
Designs: Various.

The northernmost variant of Desert Gray ware, characteristic of the Great Salt Lake Fremont, is Great Salt Lake Gray. The description of this variant, given below, is from Rudy (1953) as modified by D. Madsen (1979); another, more detailed, description can be found in R. Madsen (1977). Both of the latter (Madsen 1979 and Madsen 1977) incorporate original research on Great Salt Lake Gray Ware and differ from one another in certain details.

Great Salt Lake Gray

Construction: Coiled.
Core color: Predominantly dark gray with occasional buffs and reddish browns. Occasionally light gray.
Temper: Predominantly volcanic glass and small amounts of quartz. Ranges from fine to medium (0.1 to 3.0 mm). The paste is coarsely micaceous. Under a hand lens the temper appears as a medium-sized quartz.
Texture of core: Generally medium, ranging to medium coarse, occasionally fine. The sandy texture, due to large quantities of temper, results in a friable fracture. The temper makes up between 30 and 40 percent of the wall.
Surface finish: Smoothed to slightly polished. Mica conspicuous on both surfaces. The exterior surface is usually smoother than the interior surfaces. The exterior surface is lightly pitted but is not identical with Lino Gray. Striations are generally found on the interiors.
Surface color: Predominantly dark gray, ranging from light gray through dark gray to almost black. Some buffs.
Wall thickness: Average 4.9 mm; range, from 3.0 to 6.5 mm.
Rims: Out-curved.
Decorative techniques: Punching and applique [incising and fingernail impressions]. (Figures 10, 12.)

Although rarely recognized in the past, Great Salt Lake Gray is probably the most commonly found non-Shoshonean pottery in southern Idaho, particularly at excavated sites, as confirmed by independent analyses. The oldest examples are probably those recovered from Housepit 11 at the Clover Creek site on the Snake River near King Hill in south-central Idaho. Based on the associated projectile point configuration and the changes in this configuration between the upper and lower levels, the Clover Creek site was probably occupied repeatedly by Fremont groups between ca. A.D. 500 and 1350 (Butler 1982b; R. Holmer 1982, personal communciation). Great Salt Lake Gray sherds (75 in all) were found in every level of Housepit 11. Definitely younger than these sherds were the Great Salt Lake Gray sherds recovered from Stratum A at Wilson Butte Cave. The radiocarbon date for Stratum A at Wilson Butte Cave is A.D. 1525 $\pm$ 150 (M-1088, uncorrected), which is supported by a date of A.D. 1010 $\pm$ 150 (M-1144, uncorrected) from the upper part of the underlying Stratum B at this site. Probably the youngest example of Great Salt Lake Gray pottery found in eastern Idaho are the several rim and body sherds from a single jar recovered in 1962 from Layer 2 of 10-CL-100, a rockshelter at the foot of the mountain range forming the eastern margin of Birch Creek Valley (identification by R. Madsen; provenience data taken from the notebook of R. Bonnichsen, R. Powers, and D. Rice on file in the IMNH Division of Archaeology). Charcoal taken from an earth oven exposed in the underlying Layer 3 yielded a radiocarbon date of A.D. 1585 $\pm$ 80 (UCLA-253; Swanson, Butler, and Bonnichsen 1964).

As indicated earlier, all of the confirmed findings of Great Salt Lake Gray and other non-Shoshonean pottery in Idaho lie to the south of the Northern Rocky Mountains, between the Henry's Fork of the Snake on the east and

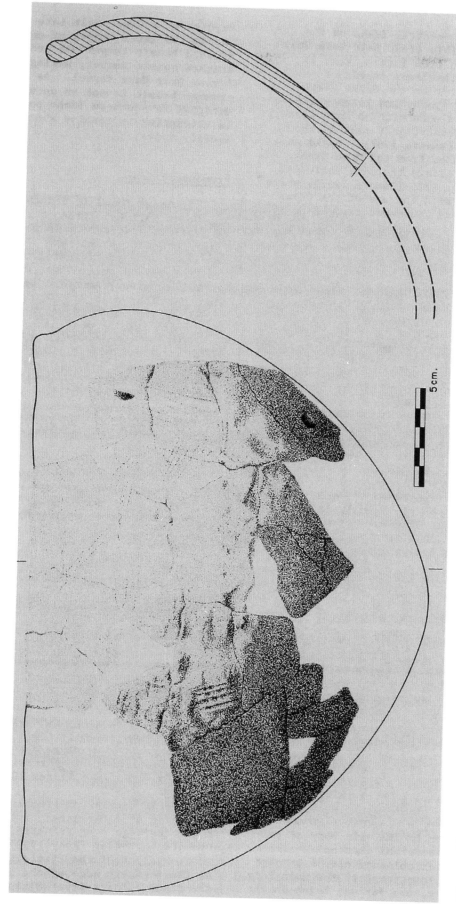

Figure 12. Reconstructed Great Salt Lake Gray bowl from below American Falls Reservoir (from Butler 1979a: Fig. 4, lower).

5 cm.

Butler

Clover Creek in south-central Idaho on the
west. However, possible Great Salt Lake Gray
sherds were recovered from further west in
southern Idaho from the lower levels of
10-AA-15, a rockshelter on the Snake River
below Swan Falls dam (Tuohy and Swanson 1960)
and from 10-WN-30, an open site on Mann Creek,
a tributary of the Weiser, just east of the
Idaho-Oregon border (Bowers 1967). Based on a
single radiocarbon date from the Mann Creek
site, the earliest pottery there is estimated
to date from ca. A.D. 1715 (Bowers 1967), which
would be consistent with the age of the Great
Salt Lake Gray pottery recovered from 10-CL-100
in eastern Idaho.

Other (?) Desert Gray Ware

The most outstanding example in this category is the large, nearly complete globular jar
with flaring rim shown in Figure 13. It was
recovered from a narrow slabrock niche along
the north side of the Snake River a few miles
below the town of American Falls in the winter
of 1982-1983 by a local trapper. When found,
the jar was upside down with the neck embedded
in a sandy silt deposit on the floor of the
niche and the bottom broken out. The trapper
brought the jar to me the following year, after
the opening of a Northern Fremont exhibit at
the Idaho Museum of Natural History. I asked
him if he would loan the jar for study and
exhibit. He was agreeable, and the jar went on
exhibit in the spring of 1984, at which time
David Madsen saw it and immediately identified
it as a typical Sevier Gray Ware vessel
(personal communication). Because I wanted to
make a more detailed analysis, I prevailed upon
the trapper to lead me to the site so that I
might search for bottom sherds. We recovered
several of the same configuration, color, and
finish as the main body of the jar. One of
these sherds was sent to R. Madsen for his
appraisal and analysis. Mainly on the basis of
the crushed quartz temper present in the sherd,
he concluded that this was a Great Salt Lake
Gray Ware sherd, an unexpected conclusion to
say the least. I encountered nothing in the
niche that would point to the possible presence
of a second vessel, and all of the sherds recovered from the niche were consistent with the
color, finish, and configuration of the main
body of the jar, as noted above. Therefore, in
June 1984, I took all of the remaining sherds,
along with the jar shown in Figure 13, to R.
Madsen for further study, which is still under
way at this writing. There is no doubt that
crushed basalt temper, a diagnostic of Sevier
Gray Ware, is present in the main body of the
jar. None is present in the "bottom" sherds.
On the other hand, variable amounts of crushed
quartz temper are also present in the main body
of the jar. Possibly, the jar was begun in the

fashion of a Great Salt Lake Gray Ware vessel,
but in the later stages of construction,
crushed basalt temper was added along with
crushed quartz temper, making it analytically a
Sevier Gray Ware vessel. As mentioned earlier,
crushed basalt is not an uncommon tempering
material in southern Idaho pottery. R. Madsen
is attempting to resolve whether this jar was
locally made.

Promontory Gray

Although found in and characteristic of
the Great Salt Lake Fremont region, this ware
is distinctly different from all of the other
Fremont (Desert Gray) wares; it may represent
an intrusive pottery-making tradition of
Plains-Woodland origin that did not coalesce to
any degree with Fremont pottery-making traditions (D. Madsen 1979). It is also the most
recent of the potteries characteristic of the
Great Salt Lake Fremont area, probably dating
no earlier than A.D. 1000 (R. Madsen 1977).
The type description below is from Rudy (1953)
as modified by D. Madsen (1979); another can be
found in R. Madsen (1977):

Construction: [Coiled.]
Core color: Predominantly black, occa-
    sionally brownish black to dark buff or
    tan (rare).
Temper: Coarse, angular calcite and
    medium quartz sand, occasionally minute
    flakes of mica.
Texture of core: Usually coarse, but
    ranging from medium to coarse; rarely
    fine.
Surface finish: Poorly smoothed or
    scraped; striations apparent on both
    surfaces; occasionally lightly polished,
    polishing marks visible. Surface is
    undulating.
Surface color: Black, rarely dark buff or
    dark gray.
Shapes: Jars; possibly bowls.
Rims: Straight, out-curved, occasionally
    in-curved. Lips rounded or flat and
    generally thickened. Average 10 mm in
    thickness and range from 9 to 12 mm.
    Decorated.
Wall thickness: Variable. Averaging
    4.5 mm; range, from 3 to 9 mm.
Decorative techniques: Incising
    [applique], fingernail impressions,
    punching. (Figures 10, 11.)

Small samples of Promontory Gray have been
collected at a disturbed cave site in the Bear
River drainage near Franklin, just north of the
Utah-Idaho border (Rudy 1953); from a site at
the lower end of the Little Lost River Valley
on the northern edge of the central section of
the Eastern Snake River Plain (Butler 1979b);

Figure 13. Nearly complete Fremont Gray Ware vessel found among boulders on north side of Snake River, between Eaglerock and Massacre Rocks. Typology is problematical as this vessel has been identified as Sevier, Uinta, and Great Salt Lake Gray by different ceramic analysts (Maximum diameter 33.6 cm; height from rim to broken bottom 26.5 cm).

and from one end of a series of dry-laid
masonry walls delineating rooms in an overhang
on the opposite shore of the Snake a few miles
upstream from the Clover Creek site mentioned
earlier (Butler and Murphey 1982). The largest
sample and youngest of the Promontory pottery
found in southern Idaho are the 450 or more
sherds representing a dozen or more vessels
recovered from the uppermost layers of the
Wasden site (Owl Cave) 18 miles west of Idaho
Falls. The associated projectile points are
mainly of the Desert Side-notched type,
possibly dating from after the introduction of
the horse, but certainly later than A.D. 1350.
Results of an analysis of a rim and a body
sherd from the Wasden site made at the
University of Colorado Museum by Joe Ben Wheat
and his associate, Priscilla Ellwood, are
quoted below, beginning with the letter of
transmittal dated May 19, 1983, from Wheat, who
refers to this pottery as Great Salt Lake Gray,
as does Ellwood. However, R. Madsen subsequently re-examined the entire collection and
concluded that it was mostly Promontory, rather
than Great Salt Lake Gray--hence, the inclusion
of the sample in question here. Madsen's
comments follow those of Wheat and Ellwood:

> I have finished my examination of the
> potsherds you sent from Idaho together
> with Mrs. Priscilla Ellwood, our spe-
> cialist on Plains pottery. We compared
> the sherds with a number of types, espe-
> cially the sherds and vessels from Hells
> Midden, Nantle's Cave, and other Fremont
> sites in Dinosaur National Monument. In
> vessel and rim form, surface treatment,
> color range, and temper they are nearly
> identical to the Great Salt Lake Gray
> ware sherds from the Dinosaur National
> Monument sites. I enclose Mrs.
> Ellwood's description of your sherds
> . . . [letter from Wheat, 1983].

Description of Sherds from Idaho State
by Mrs. Priscilla Ellwood
University of Colorado Museum, Boulder
May, 1983

Provenience: Central Idaho-Montana Area
   - B. Robert Butler (Wasden site--Owl
   Cave)
Culture: Fremont
Type: Great Salt Lake Gray [subsequently
   identified as Promontory ware by R.
   Madsen; see below]
Construction: Possible coiling
   construction-evidence slight
Finishing & Trimming: Scraping to thin
   and smooth, striations parallel to rim
   clearly evident interior and exterior
Firing method:
   Interior: indication of reducing
      atmosphere-dark color indicates

carbonaceous
   Exterior: light brown color indicative
      partial oxidation
Core:
   Clay - possible alluvial
   Color:
      Interior: Very dark gray to black
         Munsell 5YR - 3/1 to 3/2
      Exterior: Reddish brown - Munsell
         5YR - 5/3
   Temper: Identification based on fresh
      break
      Particles of milky quartz
      Minimal occurrences of Mica/Biotite
      No calcite - Hydrochloric acid test
   Shape & size: Based on Wentworth Scale
      angular particles, Pebble size 4.0 mm
      to Coarse 1.0 to .5 mm
      Percentage in vessel wall - 15%
   Texture: medium to fine, compact par-
      ticles ranging in 9.05 to 0.1 mm
   Thickness: 7.0 mm - slightly thicker
      than average
   Carbon streak: prominent from oxidized
      exterior to dark carbonized interior
Surface:
   Color: exterior - Reddish Brown
      (Munsell 5YR 5/3)
   Firecloud: Dark gray (Munsell 5YR -
      3/1) (2.5 cm x 1.5 cm)
   Sooting: No
   Finish: Smoothed, scraped and
      polished
      Interior and exterior -
      Striations visible -
   Slip: None, although wet polishing
      aligns clay particles -
   Weathering: not visible
Shape and Size: jar, indicated by finish
   and curvature of walls
   Rim: Squared and rounded with slight
      thickening at lip
Decoration: absent
Comment: Probably locally made Fremont
   pottery - fits description of Great Salt
   Lake Gray

As noted earlier, a short time after
receiving the Wheat-Ellwood analysis of a small
sample of the "burnished red ware" sherds from
the Wasden site, I prevailed upon R. Madsen to
re-examine the same sherds, along with the
other 450 to 500 sherds from the same levels at
the Wasden site. He did so and provided me
with a letter report dated August 10, 1983 (on
file IMNH), from which the quotations below are
taken. Along with several sherds of "classic"
Great Salt Lake Gray, there were "numerous
sherds of 'burnished red ware' and gray pottery
representing 9 or 10 different vessels,"
apparently mostly Promontory Gray; also present
were a few sherds of Great Salt Lake Gray and
one sherd of Shoshoni ware in the collection:

The gray samples in this collection, including several partially reconstructed vessel walls [Figures 10 and 11], have undulated surfaces characteristic of numerous samples of Promontory Gray from the Bear River sites in northern Utah. Some of the sherds exhibit fingernail impressions on the exterior surfaces. All of the gray sherds in this category are from vessels which were constructed by the paddle and anvil technique. As I explained to you during our recent meeting, my initial reaction was that the sherds in this category were Promontory Gray, although I could not give a definite opinion until I had carefully examined the sherds under a binocular microscope. Following such examination, I was able to conclude that these sherds are indistinguishable in paste and temper from numerous Promontory Gray sherds in University of Utah ceramic collections.

The "Burnished Red Ware" sherds pose a slightly different problem. All of the sherds in this category are also of paddle and anvil construction. However, many of the sherds are from vessels that were carefully constructed and polished on both exterior and interior surfaces. I realize that Joe Ben Wheat and Priscilla Ellwood have classified these sherds as Great Salt Lake Gray. However, due to the paddle and anvil construction and the considerable variation in tempering particle size in many of the sherds, I would classify these sherds as a polished variety of Promontory Gray, which was apparently manufactured by a small group of Fremont people in southern Idaho. If it were not for the polished surfaces, these sherds would be almost identical to many Promontory Gray sherds from northern Utah Fremont sites.

Several of the sherds from this collection are also Great Salt Lake Gray. These include samples 75889-1 and 76029 (which have small mica particles on their surfaces) and 75176-26, 75501-2, 75501-12 and 75282-3 (and other rim sherds glued to this specimen).

One rim sherd, No. 75423-1, closely resembles Shoshone pottery from the University of Utah collections. It contains large, angular tempering particles and has an extremely rough surface, both of which are characteristic of the Shoshone pottery that I have examined from northern Utah (R. Madsen 1983).

Generic Basin Ware

Included in this category, as indicated earlier, is the pottery made by the Numic-speaking peoples of the Basin and previously (Butler 1979a) referred to separately as "Shoshonean," "Paiute," or Owens Valley Brown wares. Vessel forms include conical jars with either rounded, pointed, or flat bases and bowls. Examples from the Upper Snake and Salmon River country are illustrated in Figures 10 and 11. Based on ethnographic accounts cited in Rudy (1953:97), all of these forms may have been made by the Shoshonean-speaking peoples of northern Utah and Nevada and southern Idaho (Figures 14, 15). However,

the descriptions available are of little utility in studying types, distributions or relationships of pottery. The shapes illustrated in the . . . ethnographic reports are based upon informants' memories; they indicate a range including small shallow bowls, vessels with constricted necks, jars with outflaring rims and conical jars. The most common shape, however, is the conical jar with a round, pointed, or flat, flanged base . . . (Rudy 1953:97).

The most common "Shoshonean" pottery in southern Idaho is the flat-bottomed, flanged base, flower-pot-shaped jar (Figures 16, 17) also referred to as "Intermountain Tradition" pottery (Tuohy 1956; Coale 1963). It occurs nearly everywhere in southern Idaho south of the east-west course of the Salmon River across central Idaho and dates from ca. A.D. 1450 (along the Idaho-Nevada-Utah border) into the early historic period, ca. A.D. 1820-1840. Coale's (1963) description of this pottery is one of the more detailed. With the exception of the vessel form (flat-bottomed, flower-pot-shaped), his description probably applies equally well to all pottery forms produced by Basin Shoshoneans, whether flat-bottomed, conical, or globular. His description (Coale 1963) is given below:

The most outstanding, and therefore perhaps the most diagnostic, characteristic of the ceramic ware under discussion [Shoshonean], is its shape. Normally, vessels of this ware are generalized truncated cones, flat-bottomed with straight walls which are flared out of the vertical plane at angles of from approximately five to twenty-five degrees. The form of the vessel may vary from this norm in two respects without falling outside of the ware shape range. First, the shoulder formed by the juncture of the bottom and wall may constitute a simple angle, or it may have an annular flange development. Secondly, the wall may be slightly inverted at the mouth so that the greatest diameter of the vessel may fall at a distance approximately one-third of the vessel height below the rim . . . .

Butler

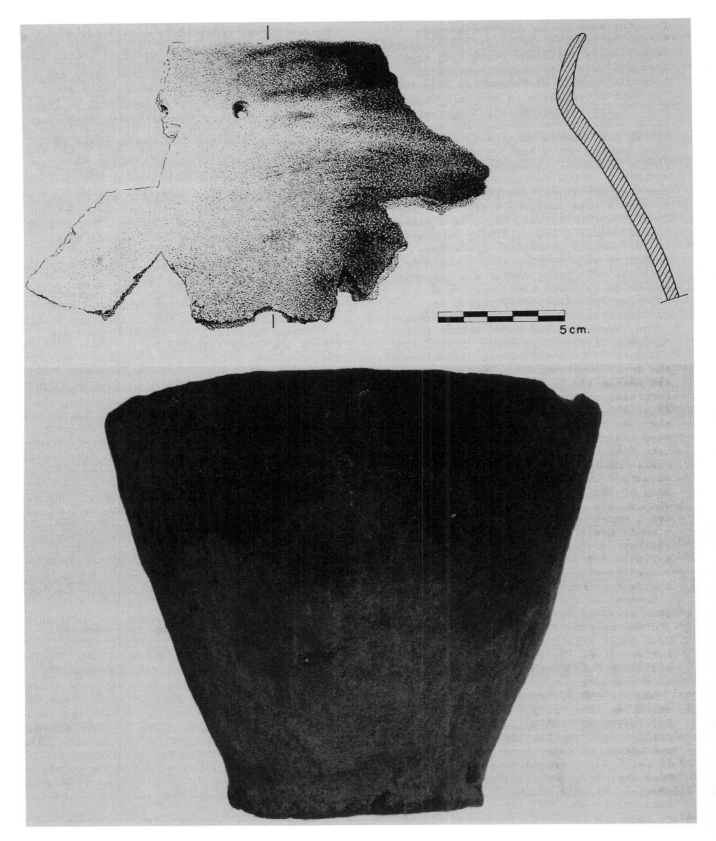

Figure 14. Examples of Generic Basin and Shoshonean ware. Upper, fragment of globular pot similar to Owens Valley Brown Ware but positively identified as Great Salt Lake Gray Ware from Snake River Plain in south-central Idaho. Lower, flat-bottomed pot from Corn Creek Campground on main Salmon River below Middle Fork.

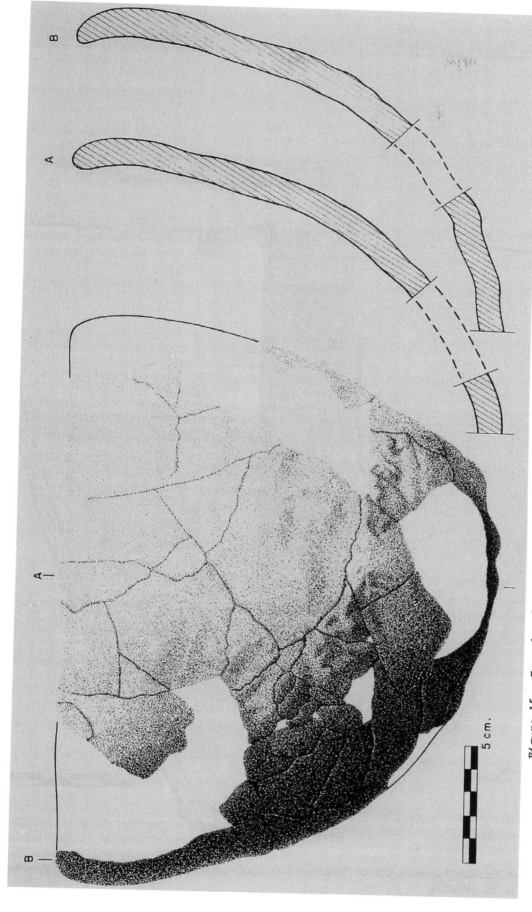

Figure 15. Example of partially reconstructed Generic Basin Ware from below American Falls Reservoir (similar to Southern Paiute Utility Ware) (from Butler 1979a: Fig. 3).

5 cm.

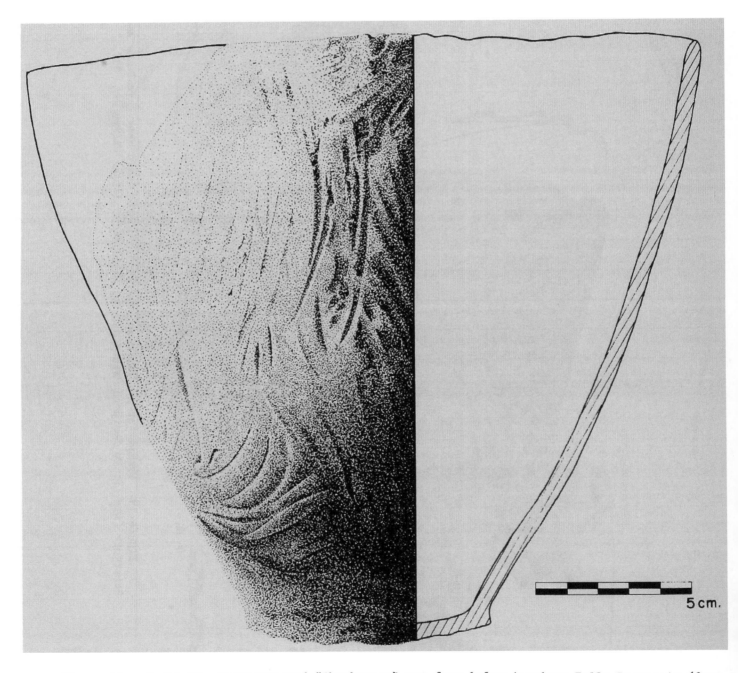

Figure 16. Partially reconstructed "Shoshonean" pot from below American Falls Reservoir (from Butler 1983c: Fig. 9, upper).

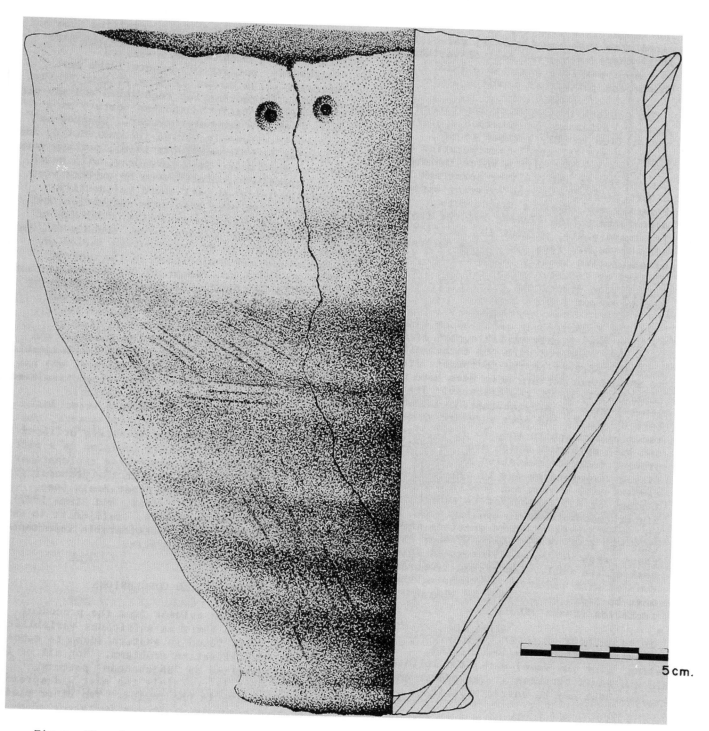

Figure 17. Complete "Shoshonean" pot from Snake River Plain just north of Blackfoot, Idaho (from Butler 1979a: Fig. 2).

5 cm.

Ranking next most important as a diagnostic feature is tempering material. The temper consists of grit, sand, or crushed rock. In case of grit and sand, the paste may not always have been intentionally tempered since aplastics occur naturally in sedimentary clays. Quartz fragments may also be natively present in imperfectly decomposed residual clays. The temper is ordinarily quite coarse compared with Puebloan [Anasazi] wares, but still there is a great deal of variability of temper-particle diameter within Shoshonean pottery as a unit . . . .

The surface treatment of Shoshonean pottery, evidenced by numerous sherds, varies from roughly scraped to well smoothed and "floated" (manipulation of the paste surface with a moist implement). The smoothing and floating operation occurs generally on the exterior surfaces. Floating may impart a pseudo-slip appearance to the finish, but the finish is always plain, without the addition of a slip or wash. Pots are seldom decorated, ornamentation usually being limited to incised or indented geometric designs in a narrow zone around the firm [rim], either inside or out . . . .

Firing temperatures and methods appear to have been highly variable, but it would seem that compared with the technically superior pottery of the Southwest, firing of Shoshonean pottery must have been at consistently lower temperatures. The general grey or greyish cast of large numbers of sherds and pots suggests that a reducing atmosphere was the rule. Brown and buff splotches which are frequently present indicate oxidation at higher firing temperatures due to two possible causes: (1) uneven and poorly controlled firing, or (2) subjection to subsequent, higher temperatures in cooking use. Even so, examination of sherd sections shows that the zone of oxidation present in these cases seldom penetrates the thickness of the wall. Low firing temperatures coupled with reduction atmosphere, then, must be added to our list of characteristics (Coale 1963:1-2).

As to methods of construction, Coale (1963) suggests that both coiling and "modeling" (for the base) were used followed by paddle-and-anvil treatment. The paddle-and-anvil treatment may be characteristic of pottery found at the southern end of the Basin, but I have seen no evidence of such treatment in the Shoshonean pottery of southern Idaho. However, an irregular, undulating surface is common in this pottery, particularly in eastern Idaho. I suspect that this is partly the result of another set of techniques employed in making this pottery, namely molding and patching, such as was used in making flat-bottomed pottery on the Northern Plain in the protohistoric and early historic periods (see Simon 1979). This set of techniques (molding and patching), along with coiling, was reportedly employed by the Lemhi Shoshoni and other horse-mounted, former Plains-dwelling Shoshoni in eastern Idaho and northern Utah (Steward 1943). Thus, much of the so-called "Shoshonean" pottery of eastern Idaho may represent a fusion or blending of late Plains and Basin pottery-making techniques and may not be typical of Basin Shoshonean pottery as a whole. By any account, however, "Shoshonean" pottery is extremely varied in construction and finishing techniques (Tuohy 1956), perhaps more so even than Great Salt Lake Gray, with which it is sometimes confused even by experts when handed an isolated wall sherd to identify.

There has even been some suggestion that the Shoshoni acquired extensive knowledge of Fremont material culture forms, techniques, and technology during an hypothesized period of interaction and competition in the eastern Great Basin (e.g., Keyser 1975), knowledge that led to the production of "Fremont" pottery by Shoshoni living in southern Idaho. As was pointed out in another paper (Butler 1983a), there are many problems with this line of reasoning. For example, if the Shoshoni who occupied the eastern Basin became knowledgeable producers of Fremont material culture, why has no evidence whatever been found of continuities in the material culture of the historic Shoshoni occupants of the eastern Great Basin and that of their immediate predecessors, the Fremont, except in the raw materials utilized (e.g., Steward 1937)? This question is a part of a much larger issue concerning explanations of the variability observed in the archaeological record of the eastern Great Basin (see, for example, O'Connell, Jones, and Simms 1982) and cannot be resolved here. Suffice it to say that the question is of considerable importance and worthy of serious pursuit.

SUMMARY AND CONCLUSIONS

It should be evident from the preceding discussion that there is sufficient variability in the pottery found in eastern Idaho to cause serious identification problems. Not all of it can be classified as "Shoshonean" pottery, although that is certainly the most widespread and recent ware in the region. Two other plain wares also occur here, though in lesser quantity and restricted to the southern half of the region: a Desert Gray ware characteristic of the Great Salt Lake Fremont called Great Salt

LATE PERIOD POTTERY SEQUENCE
IN SOUTHERN IDAHO

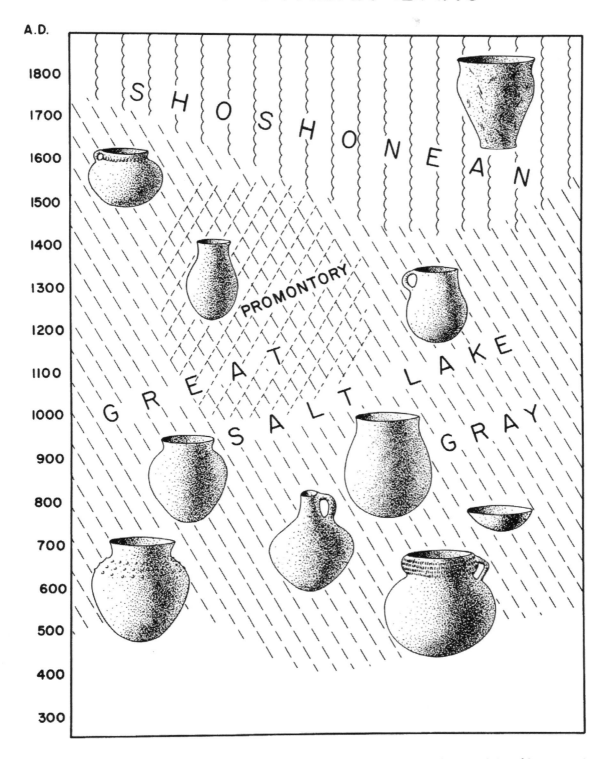

Figure 18. Reconstructed Late Period pottery sequence in southern Idaho (from Butler 1983c: Fig. 14).

Lake Gray and Promontory ware, a Plains-Woodland pottery distinctly different in certain respects from Great Salt Lake Gray, but also characteristic of the Great Salt Lake Fremont (Figure 18). The difficulty is that all of these wares overlap in various attributes to the degree that they cannot always be readily or easily distinguished from one another. This may simply reflect deficiencies in present analytical procedures or it may point to a complex set of processes at work in the eastern Great Basin during late prehistoric times that cannot be adequately treated in terms of existing research paradigms. Perhaps more light will be shed on these problems at future pottery workshops.

REFERENCES CITED

(Citations not listed here will be found in the Annotated and Indexed Bibliography of Ceramics at the back of this volume.)

Bowers, Alfred W.
  1967   Archaeological Excavations in the Spangler Reservoir and Surveys in Washington County, Idaho. Mimeographed report to the National Park Service and to the National Science Foundation. Copy on file at Idaho Museum of Natural History, Idaho State University.

Butler, B. Robert
  1968   An Introduction to Archaeological Investigations in the Pioneer Basin Locality of Eastern Idaho. *Tebiwa* 11(1):1-30.

  1978   *A Guide to Understanding Idaho Archaeology* (3rd Edition): *The Upper Snake and Salmon River Country*. The State Historic Preservation Office, Boise, Idaho.

  1982b   A Closer Look at the Clover Creek Site. Paper presented at the 10th Annual Conference of the Idaho Archaeological Society, Boise State University, October 16, 1982.

  1981   Late Period Cultural Sequences in the Northeastern Great Basin Subarea and their Implications for the Upper Snake and Salmon River Country. *Journal of California and Great Basin Anthropology* 3(2):245-256.

  1983   Shield-Bearing Warriors, Horned Figures and Great Salt Lake Gray Ware: Whither the Fremont after A.D. 1300? Paper presented at Annual Idaho Archaeological Conference, Boise, Idaho, October 8, 1983.

Butler, B. Robert, and Kelly Murphey
  1982   *A Further Delineation of Cultural Resource Loci within the Proposed Dike Hydroelectric Project Impact Area*. B.R. Butler Associates Report 82-2. Pocatello.

Cinadr, Thomas J.
  1976   *Mount Bennett Hills Planning Unit: Analysis of Archaeological Resources*. Idaho Museum of Natural History Archaeological Reports No. 6.

Epperson, Terrence W.
  1977   *Final Report on Archaeological Inventory of the Challis Planning Unit*. Idaho Museum of Natural History Archaeological Reports No. 9.

Harrison, Richard R.
  1972   The Inventory Survey in Modern Archaeology. MA thesis, Department of Anthropology, Idaho State University.

Keyser, James D.
  1975   A Shoshonean Origin for the Plains Shield Bearing Warrior Motif. *Plains Anthropologist* 20(69): 207-216.

Kingsbury, Lawrence A.
  1977   *Final Report on the 1976 Cultural Resource Inventory of the Little Lost River/Birch Creek Planning Unit*. Idaho Museum of Natural History Archaeological Reports No. 10.

Lister, Robert H.
  1959   *The Coombs Site* (with a chapter, *Pottery*, by Florence C. Lister). University of Utah Anthropological Papers No. 41.

Madsen, David B.
  1979   Great Salt Lake Ceramics. In *The Levee and the Knoll Site*, edited by G. Fry and G. Dalley. University of Utah Anthropological Papers No. 100.

Madsen, Rex E.
    1983   Letter to B. Robert Butler, August
            10, 1983, on file at the Idaho
            Museum of Natural History.

Murphy, Robert F., and Yolanda Murphy
    1960   *Shoshone-Bannock Subsistence and
            Society*. University of California
            Anthropological Records 16:7.

O'Connell, James F., Kevin T. Jones, and
Steven R. Simms
    1982   Some Thoughts on Prehistoric
            Archaeology in the Great Basin.
            In *Man and Environment in the
            Great Basin,* edited by J.F.
            O'Connell and D.B. Madsen. Society
            for American Archaeology Papers
            No. 2.

Roberts, Daniel G.
    1976   *A Final Report on the 1974-1975
            Camas Creek/Little Grassy Archae-
            ological Survey*. Idaho Museum of
            Natural History Archaeological
            Reports No. 5

Shields, Wayne F., and Gardiner F. Dalley
    1978   *The Bear River No. 3 Site*. Miscel-
            laneous Paper 22, University of
            Utah Anthropological Papers No. 99.

Swanson, E. H. Jr., B. Robert Butler, and
R. Bonnichsen
    1964   *Birch Creek Papers No. 2: Natural
            and Cultural Stratigraphy in the
            Birch Creek Valley of Eastern
            Idaho*. Occasional Papers of the
            Idaho State University Museum
            No. 14.

Tuohy, Donald R. and Earl H. Swanson, Jr.
    1960   Excavation at Rockshelter 10-AA-15,
            Southwest Idaho. *Tebiwa* 3 (1 and
            2):20-24.

Wheat, Joe Ben
    1983   Letter to B. Robert Butler, May 19,
            1983.

BROWN WARE POTTERY FROM
HONEY LAKE VALLEY, CALIFORNIA

Francis A. Riddle and Harry S. Riddle, Jr.

During a visit to archaeological site CA-Las-3 in the late 1930s three fragments of brown ware pottery were recovered. Franklin Fenenga, Garth Murphy, and the authors composed the field party. The pottery pieces Fenenga found constitute the only documented potsherds for the Honey Lake region of Lassen County, though verbal reports of other potsherds in the region have been made. Clyde Knox of Janesville reported a cord-marked sherd as having come from the north shore region of Honey Lake. Knox, a private collector, has family roots in Missouri and has other specimens from there. For this reason it seems prudent to view the specimen, now housed at the Lowie Museum, University of California, Berkeley, as having questionable provenience. It will, therefore, not be consdiered at this time. He also said he had seen potsherds at CA-Las-15, a very extensive multicomponent site area about one mile north of Wendel, thus nearly three miles from the shore of Honey Lake (Figure 19). Neither of us has seen these potsherds, however.

Site CA-Las-3 is located on a sandy terrace on the left bank of Baxter Creek about three miles before it flows into Honey Lake (Figure 19). The long-abandoned Eagle Lake irrigation canal bisected the site. Collections we made from the site beginning in the late 1920s are now at the Lowie Museum. This multi-component site has a late manifestation, and numerous manos and metates (or fragments thereof), basalt and obsidian debitage, projectile points, scrapers, core tools, mortars, pestles, drills, a tubular stone pipe, and knives have been recorded over a period of 50 years (F. Riddell 1950). Little evidence now remains. No potsherds were ever found on subsequent trips to the site, leaving one to assume that the pottery sherds are from a single "pot drop." A description of the three sherds from CA-Las-3 follows:

Type specimens: Three sherds, two of which fit together bear the Lowie Museum of Anthropology catalog number 1-103578.

Type site: CA-Las-3, on Baxter Creek, Lassen County, California.

Temporal placement: Unknown, but presumed to be protohistoric, possibly historic.

Construction: Not clear, but possibly molded in part. Some evidence of coiling, but not the use of paddle and anvil for thinning. The size and quantity of sherds prevent clear definition.

Fired: In oxidizing atmosphere.

Core color: Exterior yellowish-brown (Munsell 10YR 5/4) with interior a dark grey (Munsell 7.5YR 4/0).

Temper: Rounded quartz sand; mica is limited.

Carbon streaks: Not seen in this limited sample.

Texture core: Coarse.

Walls: Weak.

Fracture: Crumbling.

Surface finish: Smoothing appears to have been done with wet hands. There is no clear evidence of thinning by scraping as no striations occur on either the interior or the exterior.

Luster: Dull.

Surface color: Yellowish brown (Munsell 10YR 5/4).

Form: Wide-mouth bowl probably with flat bottom (see Figure 20).

Vessel size: The curvature of the single small rim sherd suggests the vessel may have had a mouth diameter of ca. 15 cm. A guess of a base diameter of ca. 12 cm seems about the best one can do with the two base/wall fragments available. The height of the vessel is only speculation based on a consideration of the estimated rim and base diameters and what would seem proportional relative to height: ca. 12 cm.

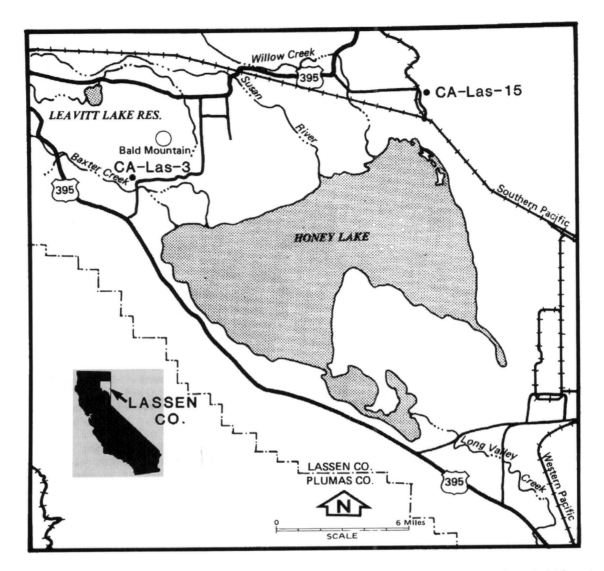

Figure 19.   Location of sites containing brown-ware sherds near Honey Lake, California.

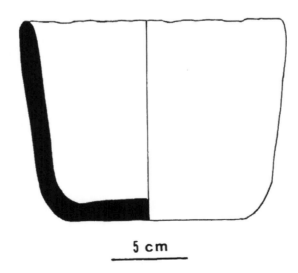

5 cm

Figure 20.   Postulated reconstruction of vessel shape of sherds found at CA-Las-3.

Base: Probably molded as a separate
piece upon which coils were banded.
Evidence of this is the form of one
sherd which has separated on a coil
line, but in addition has elements of
thickening on the inside. It is presumed to have been flat (see Figure 20),
but a round molded base is entirely
possible.
Thickness of vessel walls: 10 mm.
Rim: Uneven and rounding.
Handles or lugs: No evidence on the
limited sample.
Decoration: No evidence even though
enough of a rim fragment was preserved
to accommodate any evidence if rim
incising had been done.
Slip: None.
Paint: None.

Comparison

All the materials for this vessel are
readily available at the site, as well as in
the region. Because of the fragmentary nature
of the vessel no detailed comparison will be

attempted except to say that if these sherds
were found in Owens Valley they would not stand
out in contradistinction to what has been
described as Owens Valley Brown Ware (H.
Riddell 1951). If the attempt at reconstruction of the vessel form is close to the
fact, the vessel was similar to the open-mouth
bowls made by the historic Mono-Yokuts potters
(Gayton 1929; Kroeber 1925: Plate 51). In
fairness, however, it must be stressed that no
definite evidence exists to demonstrate clearly
that the vessel was flat bottomed as shown in
Figure 20. The use of mud by children to make
toys has been documented for the Honey Lake
Paiute in the ethnographic period by F.
Riddell (1978:90), and the antiquity of fired
clay figurines also has been demonstrated by F.
Riddell (1960).

REFERENCES CITED

All sources cited in this paper may be
found in the Annotated and Indexed Bibliography
of Ceramics at the back of this volume.

SISKIYOU UTILITY WARE AND THE DISTRIBUTION OF FIRED CLAY IN SOUTH-CENTRAL OREGON

Joanne M. Mack

INTRODUCTION

Siskiyou Utility Ware was first analyzed and named in 1978 (Mack 1978). All the analyzed potsherds came from archaeological sites in the Salt Cave locality on the upper course of the Klamath River and from two sites within the drainage system of the upper Rogue River in Oregon, the vast majority from Border Village, 35-KL-16, dated to A.D. 1400. This ware was also identified from 4-Sis-13, also within the drainage system of the upper Klamath River in south-central Oregon (Figure 21). In both river drainages Siskiyou Utility Ware was found in association with fired-clay ceramic figurines and figurine fragments and a high frequency of Gunther Barbed projectile points.

Recently, the author had the opportunity to examine potsherds from the Lorenzen site (4-Mod-250), located within the upper Pit River drainage, northeastern California. Visual inspection indicates the likelihood that the sherds from the Lorenzen site might also be included as examples of Siskiyou Utility Ware, but a more detailed study will be needed to confirm or deny the visual impression. The existence of these pottery-using late prehistoric period villages, as well as those recently reported on the Consumnes River in the lower Sacramento Valley (Johnson et al. 1976), will require a re-evaluation of the assumptions which were held, until recently, concerning the lack of ceramics in northern California and southern Oregon (Kroeber 1925). Clearly, pottery was used by some groups in northern California for some period of time in the recent past. It is also likely that the stimulus for these wares did not come from the Southwest.

DESCRIPTION

Siskiyou Utility ware is a very crude hand-modeled brown ware (Figures 22-23). Its surface color ranges from orange-buff (2.5YR 2/3) through brown (7.5YR 2/3) through light-brown (10YR 3/5-7), with the most common colors being 7.5YR 2/4, 7.5YR 4/5, 10YR 2/4, and 10YR 3/5 on the Munsell Soil Color Chart. The core color shows less variation and much of it comes close at 5YR 4/6 to the orange (5YR 6/6) which resulted when a sample of sherds were refired in a bisque kiln at 894°C. The luster is dull to matte. The apparent surface texture is grainy, the apparent paste texture medium to coarse. The sherds show rather sharp to crumbling fracture and have a hardness of 3 or 4 on the Mohs scale (Mack 1983:81-84).

Those sherds of Siskiyou Utility Ware which have been analyzed all had temper added. The temper appears simply to be dirt from the occupation area. A geologic analysis of the nonplastic inclusions in a sample of sherds supports this assertion (Mack 1983:84). The minerals observed would have been destroyed by the deep weathering which produces clay; therefore, it was added to the clay. An analysis of the dirt from an occupation area at Border Village (35-KL-16) showed the same suite of minerals (Kittleman 1964).

This ware has been fired in an uncontrolled firing atmosphere, leaving the clay incompletely oxidized and causing some surface smudging. The clay has apparently not been cleaned or kneaded before use, resulting in surface cracks in the outer walls (Figure 22b) and impressions of leaves and other plant parts within the walls. The ware is hand modeled commonly with finger impressions. Some sherds show evidence of wiping when the clay was still plastic (Figure 22b). The vessel walls range from 2-10 mm thick, usually 2-4 mm thick near the rim (Mack 1983:84).

Only two forms seem to be present: a shallow, wide-mouth bowl (estimated interior diameter 10-16 cm; and 5-6 cm depth) and a small cup (estimated interior diameter 3.5-5.0

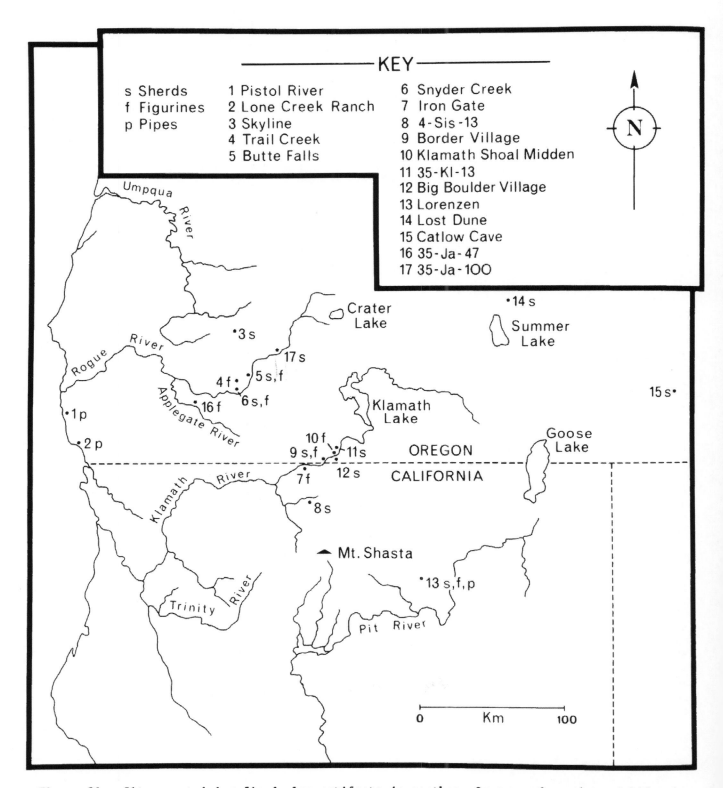

KEY

s Sherds
f Figurines
p Pipes

1 Pistol River
2 Lone Creek Ranch
3 Skyline
4 Trail Creek
5 Butte Falls

6 Snyder Creek
7 Iron Gate
8 4-Sis-13
9 Border Village
10 Klamath Shoal Midden
11 35-KI-13
12 Big Boulder Village
13 Lorenzen
14 Lost Dune
15 Catlow Cave
16 35-Ja-47
17 35-Ja-100

Figure 21. Sites containing fired clay artifacts in southern Oregon and northern California.

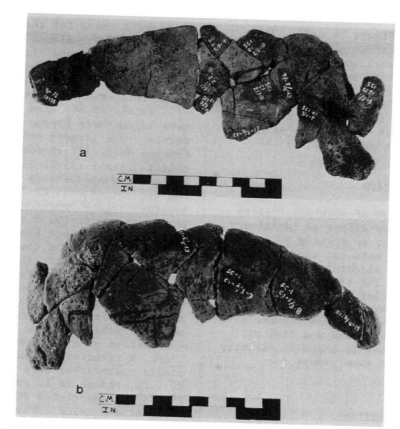

Figure 22. Siskiyou Utility Ware: Reconstructed bowl from 35-KL-16. (A) Interior, (B) Exterior (from Mack 1983: Plate VIIb and Plate VIIa).

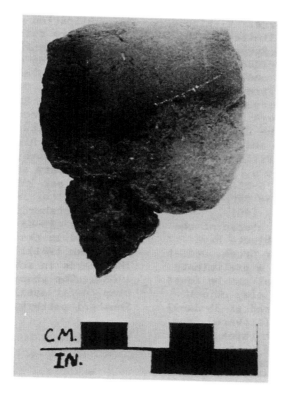

Figure 23. Weathered exterior of Siskiyou Utility Ware bowl rim fragment from 35-KL-16 (from Mack 1983: Plate VIIIa).

cm; and 3.0 cm depth) (Figure 24 c,d). The rims are irregularly rounded, slightly incurved and often uneven. No basal sherds have been recovered from a scientific excavation. One broken vessel from a private collection from the Rogue River Valley has a thick, flattened base. A few rim sherds from a Rogue River site show some fingernail impressions on the inner edge of the rim as decoration.

FUNCTION

The primary function of Siskiyou Utility Ware appears to have been either as containers for grease or fish oil or as serving or eating bowls. They apparently were not used for cooking, as there is no blackening on the outer surface of the sherds. The shape of the bowls appears to be quite similar to some of the steatite bowls used by various ethnographic groups along the Klamath and Rogue rivers. These were used to store grease and fish oil. The bowls are also similar in shape to basketry mush bowls used by these same groups for serving acorn mush.

DISTRIBUTION

Fired clay objects and potsherds are relatively rare in southern Oregon and northern California, but as the number of archaeological investigations increases, so do the incidences of fired clay objects and potsherds. Siskiyou Utility Ware at this time seems limited to the upper courses of the Klamath and Rogue rivers and their tributaries. If we include the potsherds from the Lorenzen site we could add the upper course of the Pit River. Fired clay objects including pipes and figurines have a somewhat wider distribution (Figure 21).

Along the upper course of the Klamath River several fired clay objects and figurines were recovered: 22 from Border Village (35-KL-16) (Figure 25 a-h, j-k, m-n, p-s); four from Klamath Shoal Midden (35-KL-21) (Figure 25 l,o); and two from Iron Gate site (4-Sis-326) (Mack 1983; Leonhardy 1961). Within the drainage of the upper course of the Rogue River similar fired clay objects have been found on Trail Creek, Snider Creek, and at Butte Falls on the Rogue River. A preliminary report on the Rogue River material can be found in Deich (1977). A single baked clay object with punctate designs was recovered at 35-JA-47 on the Applegate River. It was recovered from a late prehistoric component with three other baked clay fragments (Brauner and MacDonald 1983). Fired clay pipes were recovered from sites on the southern Oregon coast: the Pistol River site (Heflin 1966) and sites on the Chetco River (Berreman 1944). Historically, fired clay pipes were reported on the northern

California coast for the Wiyot by Loud (1918) and in the lower Klamath Basin for the Modoc by Spier (1930). Among the Chimariko, small bowls of unfired clay were used for catching grease drippings and unfired clay figurines were made as children's toys (Silver 1978).

Potsherds are also found in limited numbers in southern Oregon and northern California. The largest collection of Siskiyou Utility Ware, 417 sherds, was recovered from Border Village (35-KL-16) on the Klamath River. Two questionable sherds were recovered from Big Boulder Village (35-KL-18) (Mack 1983). In addition, three questionable sherds were reported for 35-KL-13, a rockshelter at Big Bend on the Klamath River (Newman and Cressman 1959). A single rim sherd was reported for 4-Sis-13, also within the Klamath River drainage (Wallace and Taylor 1952:28-29). Along the upper course of the Rogue River amateur collectors have recovered potsherds at a site on Snider Creek and at Butte Falls. In addition potsherds were recovered from the test excavations of a house pit at 35-JA-100, on Elk Creek, a tributary of the Rogue River. A single radiocarbon date for the site is 1150+ 85 B.P., though it is unclear whether the potsherds are associated with the dated sample (Brauner and Lelow 1983).

Within the drainage of the upper Pit River in northern California, the Lorenzen site also contained potsherds. Personal examination of 25 sherds leads me to suggest these might also be considered Siskiyou Utility Ware. The publication of their analysis hopefully will confirm this observation.

There are three other pottery sites in southern Oregon which should be mentioned, though they do not seem related to Siskiyou Utility Ware. On the divide between the South Umpqua and the Rogue rivers, five whole pottery vessels were recovered from a shaman's cache at the Skyline site by a collector. These pots date from the historic period and may be the work of the Reverend A. L. Todd who began making pottery at Looking Glass, Oregon, in 1855 (Corless 1982: personal communication).

Two sites in southeastern Oregon have also yielded potsherds: Catlow Cave and the Lost Dune site (35-HA-792). Only a few sherds were recovered in the upper strata of Catlow Cave (Cressman 1971). The Lost Dune site yielded 189 sherds in seven clusters (S. Thomas et al. 1983). The sherds from both these sites would seem to fit easily into the general category of Shoshoni pottery.

COMPARISONS

There are similarities between Siskiyou Utility Ware and the confusing group of wares known as Shoshoni pottery, but they are outweighed by differences. The similar charac-

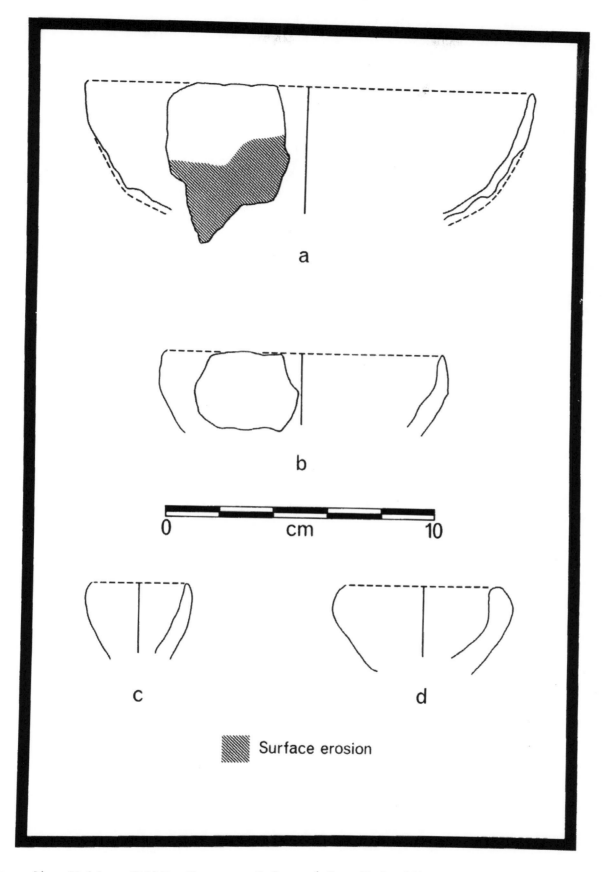

Figure 24.   Siskiyou Utility Ware vessel forms (after Mack 1983: Figs. 25, 26, 27).

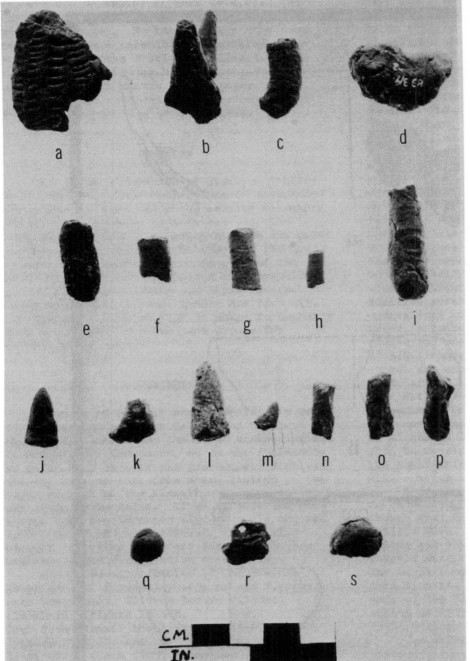

Key

a. Decorated Cone; Border Village; House Pit 1
b. Figurine; Border Village; House Pit 1
c. Broken Ring; Border Village; House Pit 1
d. Figurine; Border Village; House Pit 1
e-h. Elongated Cylinders; Border Village; House Pits 1 and 2
i. Decorated Elongated Cylinder; Klamath Shoal Midden; Stratum III
j-k. Cones; Border Village; House Pit 1
l. Cone; Klamath Shoal Midden; Stratum III
m. Cone; Border Village; House Pit 1
n. Angular Cylinder; Border Village; House Pit 1
o. Angular Cylinder; Klamath Shoal Midden; Stratum III
p. Angular Cylinder; Border Village; House Pit 1
q. Flattened Round; Border Village; House Pit 1
r. Perforated, Irregular Lump; Border Village, House Pit 1
s. Flat, Irregular Discoidal; Border Village; House Pit 2

Figure 25. Fired clay objects and figurines from sites along the Upper Klamath River (from Mack 1983: Plate VI).

teristics indicate a common level of technological development but not necessarily a
direct relationship. These characteristics
include the presence of a sand or grit temper,
vessel walls 5-8 mm thick, hardness of 3.5 to
4.0 on the Mohs scale, and firing vessels in
an uncontrolled atmosphere.

There are several differences between
Siskiyou Utility Ware and Shoshoni pottery,
Owens Valley Brown Ware, and pottery from the
Columbia Plateau. The incurved bowl shape of
Siskiyou Utility Ware is quite different from
the truncated conical vessels of Shoshoni
pottery (Steward 1943; Tuohy 1956; Coale 1963).
In shape the Siskiyou bowl resembles archaeological specimens of Owens Valley Brown Ware
and Wilson Butte Plain Ware (Gruhn 1961), but
they were made with a different technique. The
Rogue and Klamath River pots are hand modeled
and wiped. Owens Valley Brown Ware is coiled
and wiped. Owens Valley Brown Ware and
Shoshoni pottery occasionally have fingernail
decoration or incising on the outer surface.
Thirteen sherds from one of the Rogue River
sites have fingernail impressions on the inner
rim. There is also a difference in function.
The various Shoshoni wares and the Owens Valley
Brown Ware were used for cooking. Siskiyou
Utility Ware was apparently not put over a fire
but was used for storage or serving. Therefore, Siskiyou Utility Ware does not fit well
into the general category of Shoshoni pottery.
A more detailed comparison of Siskiyou Utility
Ware and its associated figurines to archaeological and ethnographic occurrences of pottery
and figurines from the northern and western
Great Basin, the Columbia Plateau, and California can be found in Mack (1983:84-89).

CONCLUSIONS

Siskiyou Utility Ware seems to be part of
an independent fired clay tradition which developed around A.D. 1400 and disappeared before
the protohistoric period in the southern
Cascades of Oregon and northern California.
Its distribution seems limited to the upper
courses of the Rogue and Klamath rivers and
their tributaries, with the possible extension
to the upper Pit River drainage system. It is
not found in the Klamath Basin just to the east
of the southern Cascades, nor does it appear to
be present west of the Western Cascade geological province. Its distribution falls roughly
within the ethnographic boundaries of the
Upland Takelma or Latgawa.

Chronologically, it is securely dated to
the Late Prehistoric Period in the Salt Cave
locality (Mack 1983). It is associated almost

exclusively with Gunther Barbed projectile
points in the upper Rogue River drainage and
other Klamath River sites, which would also
place it within the Late Prehistoric Period.

Mineral analysis of the figurine fragments
and potsherds from the Salt Cave locality supports the contention the pottery was manufactured within that area (Mack 1983). There are
several differences between Siskiyou Utility
Ware and Shoshoni pottery. The few similarities in technology indicate a common degree of
technological development but not necessarily a
direct relationship.

It seems, from the evidence, that Siskiyou
Utility Ware was an independent pottery tradition which developed out of a California Fired
Clay tradition. This is supported by the fact
that the figurines and other fired clay objects
from the Salt Cave locality and the upper Rogue
River show the strongest similarities to fired
clay objects from northern and central California (Mack 1983:89). In addition, the presence of steatite bowl fragments at Border
Village indicates a similarity in shape to
those made in northwest California and southwest
Oregon and also a similarity to the shallow
bowl shape of Siskiyou Utility Ware (Mack
1983:73). It is not unreasonable to predict a
group with knowledge of fired clay, which they
used in making figurines and other objects, to
transfer their technology to the production of
bowls similar in shape to those carved from
steatite. It is worth noting within the Rogue
River drainage near Center Point, Oregon at the
Saltsgaver Site (35-JA-15), 100 clay lined
pits, radiocarbon dated to 3360 160 B.P. were
excavated by Dr. LeRoy Johnson in 1968. The
pits were apparently used for cooking (Follansbee and Pollack 1978). The knowledge of baked
or fired clay seems to have considerable time
depth along the Rogue River.

It is also possible that this group with
knowledge of fired clay from the manufacture of
figurines and other objects was influenced by
pottery-making groups from the northern or
western Great Basin. This would be an example
of trait unit diffusion. At this time there is
not enough information on the development or
technology of Shoshoni or Owens Valley pottery
to determine whether trait unit diffusion is a
reasonable explanation. In addition, recent
evidence places another pottery-making group
within Plains Miwok territory, manufacturing
Cosumnes Brown Ware, also within the Late Prehistoric Period (Johnson 1976). Trait unit
diffusion from the Sacramento Valley to the
southern Cascades is also possible. For the
present, Siskiyou Utility Ware seems best
described as an independent pottery tradition.

REFERENCES CITED

(Citations not listed here will be found in the Annotated and Indexed Bibliography of Ceramics at the back of this volume.)

Berreman, Joel V.
1944   *Chetco Archaeology.* George Banta Publication Company, General Series Anthropology II.

Cressman, Luther S.
1971   *An Approach to the Study of Far Western North American Prehistory: Early Man.* University of Oregon, Museum of Natural History, Bulletin 20.

Deich, Lyman
1977   Aboriginal Clay Figurines from the Rogue River Area. Paper presented at Oregon Academy of Sciences, Annual Meetings, Eugene, Oregon.

Follansbee, J., and N. Pollock
1978   *Prehistory and History of the Klamath-Jackson Planning Unit: A Cultural Resources Overview.* Bureau of Land Management Class I Resources Inventory.

Heflin, Eugene
1966   *The Pistol River Site of Southwest Oregon.* University of California Archaeological Survey Reports 67:151-206.

Kittleman, Lawrence R.
1964   Appendix A: Comparisons of Potsherds and Soil from Site SC-1 HP-1. In *Excavations at Site SC-1,* by Adrienne Anderson and David Cole. MS on file, Museum of Natural History, University of Oregon.

Leonhardy, Frank C.
1967   *The Archaeology of a Late Prehistoric Village in Northwestern California.* University of Oregon, Museum of Natural History, Bulletin 4.

Loud, Llewellyn L.
1918   *Ethnogeography and Archaeology of the Wiyot Territory.* University of California Publications in American Archaeology and Ethnology 14(3).

Mack, Joanne M.
1978   A Ceramic Tradition from the Siskiyou Mountains of Southwestern Oregon. Paper given at the 43rd Annual Meeting of the Society for American Archaeology, Tucson, Arizona.

Newman, Thomas M., and Luther S. Cressman
1959   Final Report on Archaeological Salvage Program in the Big Bend Project of COPCO on the Klamath River, Oregon. MS on file, Museum of Natural History, University of Oregon.

Silver, Shirley
1978   *Chimariko.* In *Handbook of North American Indians*, Vol. 8: *California,* ed. R. Heizer, pp. 205-210. Smithsonian Institution, Washington, D.C.

Spier, Leslie
1930   *Klamath Ethnography.* University of California Publications of American Archaeology and Ethnology 30.

THE POTTERY OF MESQUITE FLAT, DEATH VALLEY, CALIFORNIA

WILLIAM J. WALLACE

Knowledge of pottery making came to the Death Valley region in the final prehistoric phase (A.D. 1000 – ca. A.D. 1870), seemingly concurrent with the appearance of Shoshonean-speaking Indians. Local potters, undoubtedly women, limited themselves pretty much to the production of cooking vessels. Broken pieces of these turn up at campsites all over the valley floor. By contrast, campsites in the surrounding mountains yield very few sherds. Evidently the Death Valley Indians did not like to carry easily broken clay receptacles with them on their seasonal jaunts into the high country to hunt and to harvest pine nuts.

Potsherds were the most numerous finds made during an archaeological survey of Mesquite Flat, the long northern arm of Death Valley (Figure 26). Four thousand eight hundred and thirty-four potsherds were collected from 193 camping places among the sand dunes. Included are 4,159 body pieces, 587 rim fragments, and 88 bases or parts thereof. A half dozen intact or partial vessels were also found.

MATERIALS AND CONSTRUCTION

Mesquite Flat potters looking for raw material did not have far to go, for the region is richly endowed with workable clay eroded from surrounding alluvial fans. Of good quality, the clay needed little preparation apart from initial sorting and grinding on a stone slab. Natural sand, containing rounded or angular bits of quartz and flecks of mica, served as tempering material. The quantity and coarseness of the temper varies considerably, and it is difficult to know whether it represents a natural inclusion or was deliberately introduced. In either case, pot-makers do not seem to have been too particular about its amount or uniformity.

The manufacturing process was simple. After a thick disk had been molded for a base, the pot was built up spirally by adding coils of clay. Bonding, done by pressing coils together with the fingers, was not always strong so that breakage often took place along juncture lines. Coils can sometimes be seen as faint ridges on the interior of a vessel and occasionally on the exterior as well.

Vessel walls were smoothed and thinned by hand rubbing and by scraping with a blunt tool such as a potsherd. Striations, generally vertical, from the scraping instrument are frequently visible, both inside and out. Surfaces are sometimes scored in such a way as to suggest rubbing with a sharp- or rough-bristled brush, rather than a scraping tool. No evidence of thinning by paddle and anvil could be detected on any of the sherds. Nor was there anything to suggest that pots were laid on their sides and tapped on the inside with a stone, a practice reported by a Death Valley Shoshoni (Driver 1937:122).

Normally, a pot baked to a deep brown, but, now and again, its color varied toward a paler or redder hue. These differences stemmed from variations either in firing or in the clay's composition. Interiors ranged from gray to a near black.

Baking was effected in an open fire, presumably fueled with mesquite branches. Conditions of firing do not appear to have been too well regulated, for some pots emerged insufficiently hardened. Black areas ("fire clouds") on others attest to uncontrolled firing.

FORM AND DECORATION

Only two standard forms of vessels were constructed. Favored was a bucket-shaped, thin-walled receptacle with a wide mouth

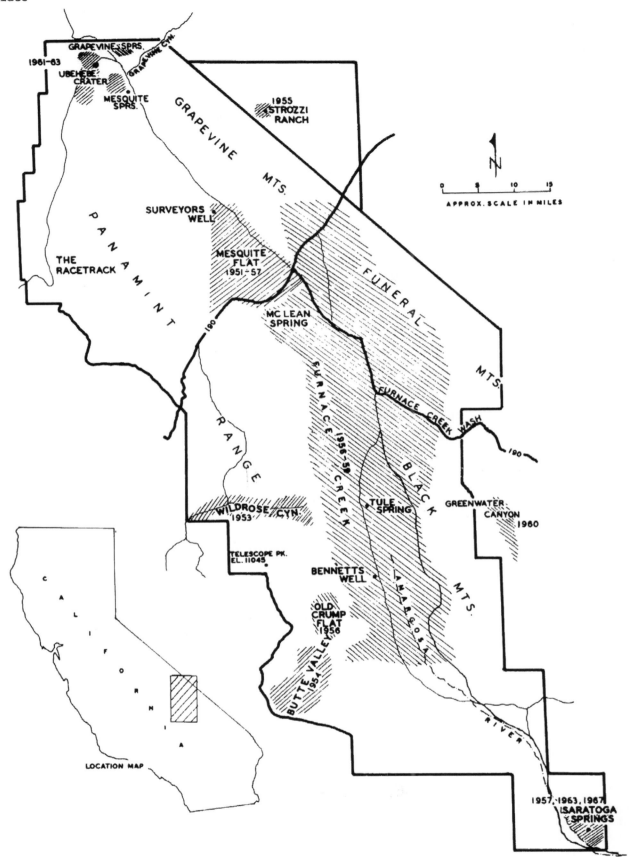

Figure 26. University of Southern California Archaeological Surveys, Death Valley National Monument, 1951-1967.

Figure 27. Vessel forms from Mesquite Flat, Death Valley. Photo by
Edith Wallace.

Figure 28. Miniature vessels from Death Valley. Photo by Edith
Wallace.

(Figure 27 a,c,d). The thickened base was flat, gently rounded, or indented. Rims were straight (or direct), with rounded, or more rarely, squared edges. Globular vessels with short, flaring necks were produced in lesser numbers (Figure 27 b). Also thin walled, these pots had everted rims with rounded edges. Bases were rounded or indented. Pointed-bottom containers that could be set in the ground and fire built around them for cooking are said to have been made (Steward 1941b:340). None such could be identified in the Mesquite Flat collection.

Most containers were left plain, without ornament of any kind. Of the more than 4,800 sherds, only 112, or slightly above 2 percent, bear decoration. Ninety-five of these are rim pieces. The usual decoration consisted of a row of slanting or curving lines incised or impressed on the lip or just below it with a stick or thumbnail. Infrequently, this was elaborated into a crude V-shaped design. Body ornament consisted of irregular scorings or punctates. Red ocher covered one potsherd.

Cracked rims were sometimes repaired by "crack sewing." This was achieved by drilling holes on either side of the break and binding it tightly together with fiber passed through the perforations. Among the sherds are six perforated rims, five drilled from one surface, one from both.

OTHER CERAMIC PRODUCTS

Potters occasionally made things other than culinary vessels. These included miniature containers, most often made by modeling rather than coiling (Figure 28). Three whole examples resemble carrying baskets in form. Four fragments, two with incised edges, came from shallow bowls. Whether the tiny receptacles served as toys or had some other purpose remains unknown.

Highly stylized human figurines were occasionally made of fired clay. They duplicate the more numerous unbaked specimens (A. Hunt 1960:229-233; Wallace 1965:436-439). A broken animal image appears to represent a fox or coyote. An unusual find was a nicely molded elbow pipe.

CONCLUDING REMARKS

Although the ceramic materials display diversity in physical composition, color, and quality of manufacture and finish, they seem to belong to a single ware. Interestingly enough, archaeological sites situated around the salt pan in the central part of Death Valley contained a much wider range of wares (A. Hunt 1960:193-224). Twenty-five percent of approximately one thousand potsherds collected by Hunt came from vessels thinned by the paddle-and-anvil technique. Three separate wares--Lower Colorado Buff, Tizon Brown, and Southern Paiute Utility--are represented. Among the remaining sherds, derived from pots smoothed by scraping, are examples of Shoshoni, Southern Paiute Utility, and Owens Valley Brown wares.

The Mesquite Flat pottery is much like that fashioned in late prehistoric and historic times by Indians living in the Owens Valley. Individual sherds from the two regions are often indistinguishable in appearance and fabric. Shared vessel forms and modes of decoration serve further to emphasize their community of tradition and to argue for derivation from a common source. Pottery of this kind also has a wide distribution in areas formerly inhabited by Western Mono (Monache), Tubatulabal, and Foothill Yokuts (Lathrap and Shutler 1955:237-238). Local variations are evident but tend to be rather minor in nature.

But there are insufficient data by which to trace this pottery labeled Owens Valley Brown Ware (Riddell 1951:20-23) to a precise source or center of dispersal. It does not relate to any Southwestern wares, but it does show affiliations to those of the Great Basin. Steward (1941b:242) has suggested an ultimate origin in the north.

Nor is it possible at this time to trace the evolution of the ceramic ware over the 900 years that it was made in Death Valley and Owens Valley. On the whole, local artisans seem to have been tenaciously conservative, content to stick to traditional forms and techniques. Innovations must have crept in, but these could hardly have been revolutionary.

Pottery-making was one of the first native handicrafts to succumb to Western civilization, apparently becoming defunct before the close of the 19th century. Earthenware containers gave way so quickly to metal pots, buckets, and tin cans frequently salvaged from mining camp rubbish heaps, that ethnographic information regarding their production remains scanty and in some instances contradictory (Driver 1937: 80, 122; Steward 1941b:294-295, 339-340).

Early in the present century, a Death Valley Shoshoni, hoping to profit from the tourist trade, attempted to revive that art (Steward 1933a:268). His crude vessels--thick walled and unevenly burnt dark gray or even black--had little appeal to valley visitors, however, and his enterprise soon collapsed.

REFERENCES CITED

All sources cited in this paper may be found in the Annotated and Indexed Bibliography of Ceramics at the back of this volume.

NOTES ON THE PRODUCTION, USE AND DISTRIBUTION OF POTTERY IN EAST-CENTRAL CALIFORNIA

RICHARD A. WEAVER

The occurrence of pottery in east-central California has been noted consistently by researchers for over five decades. To date, however, no comprehensive regional analysis of its distributional patterns has been undertaken. Based upon such an analysis it is apparent that there are substantial intra-regional differences in the prehistoric patterns characterizing pottery production and use.

BACKGROUND

The pottery distribution data for east-central California that serve as the basis for this presentation were derived from a larger distribution concordance (Weaver 1983) prepared specifically for dissemination at the 1983 California Great Basin Pottery Workshop. The intent of that document was to provide interested researchers with a synthesis of both obscure and readily available pottery distribution data which might assist and encourage future research efforts in the region.

The original distribution concordance relied heavily upon data contained in the Site Record Index Sheets for Inyo and Mono counties, California, which are maintained by the Eastern Information Center of the California Archaeological Inventory (EIC/CAI). These indices list general artifact and feature attributes for Inyo County sites 1 to 2500 and Mono County sites 1 to 1680, included in the regional files as of June 22, 1983. These index sheets do not, however, include all known archaeological loci within the subject counties since the EIC/CAI currently uses an artifact density criterion--15 or more artifacts per 10 contiguous square meters--to determine which loci will be assigned permanent trinomial designations. Those archaeological sites that do not meet the density criterion are considered to be

"isolate" evidence. Although the EIC/CAI retains copies of all isolate records, only those from lands administered by the Inyo National Forest were examined and included in the concordance due to pragmatic constraints. This review revealed one additional pottery site in Inyo County and four more Mono County sites.

Several means were used to assess the accuracy of the EIC/CAI Site Record Index Sheets. First, all records for archaeological sites within the Inyo National Forest were reviewed. This resulted in the identification of 16 pottery-bearing sites not so indicated in the index sheets. Of these sites, seven are located in Inyo County and nine in Mono County. A review of excavation reports for the region (Weaver 1983:73-75) identified four pottery sites in each county that were not properly classified in the indices. Finally, all site records from the Wallace (1958) and A. Hunt (1960) surveys in the Panamint Valley-Death Valley area of eastern Inyo County were examined since the EIC/CAI has deleted this information from the official regional files. In summary then, it may be stated that the index sheets are, at best, only a generally accurate indicator of the known distribution of pottery-bearing sites in either Inyo or Mono counties.

In addition to the above records, the original pottery distribution concordance also included a partial listing of Inyo and Mono county pottery sites recorded by Mr. and Mrs. Rollin Enfield and Norm Weller of Bishop, California. Their records, which are currently being incorporated into both the Inyo National Forest (INF) and EIC/CAI data bases, contain information on a total of 927 sites located in Inyo and Mono counties. A review of those records already submitted to the INF indicate pottery as a site attribute at 18 Inyo and 151 Mono County sites. Undoubtedly their files note other pottery-bearing sites in the two counties, but until their records have been fully integrated into the INF and EIC/CAI files it will be impossible to determine how many and which of the Enfield/Weller records duplicate previously recorded information. It is because of this limitation that only a few of their indicated pottery sites are discussed in any detail in subsequent portions of this presentation. For the moment, other investigators should at least be aware of the existence of the Enfield/Weller data and note that both the site records and associated artifact collections are available for study through arrangement with the Inyo National Forest.

DISTRIBUTION DATA

Inyo County

Of the 2,500 official Inyo County site numbers listed in the EIC/CAI Index Sheets, 839 have not been assigned to specific archaeological properties. Most of these unassigned trinomials, it should be noted, stem from the deletion of the Wallace and Hunt site records from the official county files. Of the remaining 1,661 sites, 233 (14 percent) contain pottery (Table 1).

TABLE 1. Inyo and Mono County Pottery Distribution Data

Data Source	Sites with Pottery	Total Sites	Pottery-bearing Percent
Inyo County			
Official Records	233	1,661	14.0
Wallace/Hunt Records	318	1,024	31.1
Total	551	2,685	20.5
Mono County			
Official Records	32	1,678	1.9
Inyo-Mono Counties TOTALS			
Official Records	265	3,339	7.9
Official and Wallace/Hunt	583	4,363	13.4

In spite of their deletion from the official files, the Wallace and Hunt records do provide a substantial data base for the eastern portion of Inyo County. Collectively, their efforts document a total of 1,024 sites of which 318 (31.1 percent) contain pottery. The definition of "pottery" used in categorizing these sites, however, varies from the definition used in the EIC/CAI Index Sheets since the Wallace and Hunt records make frequent reference to such objects as "unfired coil pots," "clay figurines," "pottery cones," and "clay cylinders." For present purposes, all sites containing these types of objects were classified as pottery-bearing since their production involved technological processes similar to those required for the manufacture of utilitarian ceramic vessels. Further, these types of artifacts appear to co-occur consistently with the more traditionally defined type of pottery in the area. The addition of these 318 sites to the previous county total (233 sites) yields an aggregate sum of 551 pottery-bearing sites (20.5 percent) in Inyo County.

Due to the incomplete data bases from which the isolate and Enfield/Weller data for Inyo County were obtained, no relative pottery-bearing percentages can be calculated. In turn, this precludes any direct comparison or incorporation of these data with the county totals presented above. All that can be confidently stated at present is that these data collectively indicate at least 19 additional pottery occurrences in the county.

Mono County

In comparison to Inyo County, the data base for Mono County is substantially smaller. Of the 1,680 site numbers listed in the EIC/CAI Index Sheets, two have not been assigned to specific sites and only 32 (1.9 percent) are known to contain pottery. As is the case with the isolate and Enfield/Weller data for Inyo County, neither of these information sources can be directly added to or compared with the pottery-bearing sites noted in the official files. They do, however, note the existence of 155 additional pottery sites in the county.

COMMENTS, OBSERVATIONS, AND INTERPRETATIONS

Before proceeding to data analysis and interpretation, it is first appropriate to briefly summarize various problems inherent in the data base. Collectively these data result from the efforts of many individuals over a period of almost 40 years. Considering this and the changes in professional norms and standards over time, it is not surprising that there is an extremely high degree of variability in the quantity, quality, and types of information recorded for a particular site or survey effort. Such a lack of consistency makes any statistical analysis of the distribution data for Inyo and Mono counties unlikely to yield either reliable or quantitatively meaningful results. Despite these limitations, however, a number of qualitative observations and interpretations can be made concerning prehistoric patterns of pottery production and use in the two counties. In most cases these data may be sufficient to permit the formulations of substantive explanations for observed differences. In other instances, however, the observations made here should be regarded as tentative and subject to further investigation.

Pottery Distribution Analysis

First of all, the total number of pottery sites in the two counties suggests that the manufacture and use of this cultural item was more substantial and widespread than indicated in the ethnographic literature. For example, given the quantity of data from Owens Valley, which has resulted from the survey of only a small percentage of the total land area, it seems certain that Steward (1933:266) was either misinformed or mistakenly inferred that pottery manufacture was a specialized art practiced by only a few women.

The second and more complex point to be discussed relates to the distributional variations within and between the counties. These variations appear to reflect very real differences in the aboriginal patterns of pottery manufacture and use. Unless otherwise noted, all archaeological pottery loci herein are referred to as sites, including those noted in the isolate and Enfield/Weller data. Since pottery-bearing percentages cannot be calculated for these two data sources, the reader can determine when they have been combined with the EIC/CAI records in the course of discussion by the absence of cumulative pottery-bearing percentages.

Mono County

In relation to the rest of the study area, Mono County exhibits the lowest number and percentages of pottery sites: 32 sites (1.9 percent) as opposed to 551 (20.5 percent) for Inyo County as a whole. This pattern appears to hold even if the gross totals of all site records are compared (see Table 1). Similarly significant variations also occur within the county.

Of the known Mono County occurrences, only six pottery sites have been recorded within the coniferous forests dominated by Jeffrey pine (*Pinus jeffreyi*). Four additional sites are also recorded in areas immediately adjacent to this biotic association. This sparse representation of pottery sites is all the more dramatic considering that roughly one-half (ca. 100,000 acres) of this environmental stratum has been intensively surveyed within the last eight years. It should also be noted that these examinations, completed in blocks of land ranging from 500 to 10,000 acres, have primarily been conducted by only three sets of personnel and that each contained several surveyors from the preceding group. This would seem to minimize potential data errors resulting from the use of different personnel, differences in survey strategy and coverage, and other similar factors affecting the regional data base. Further, recorded ethnographic data appear to substantiate the validity of this distribution pattern.

Late prehistoric and early historic settlement-subsistence activities within the Jeffrey pine forests of the region focused upon the procurement of three resources discussed below. Although pottery may have been incidentally used in these contexts, it is not recorded as either a critical or necessary material element in such land-use activities.

The first pattern to be examined relates to the procurement of *piuga* (the larvae of the pandora moth, *Coloradia pandora*), a relatively well-documented food source for both the Mono Lake and Owens Valley Paiute groups. Major infestations of this forest defoliator generally occur at about twenty-year intervals and span a period of two to eight years. The larvae, however, were only collected when they descended from the host trees to pupate, a fact limiting procurement activity to two to three weeks during late June and early July in alternate years of the outbreaks (Steward 1933a:256; Carolin and Knopf 1968:1-2). Normally, nuclear or extended family task groups dug trenches around the bases of a number of trees to facilitate collection of large quantities of the caterpillar during the brief harvest period. Once collected, the larvae were initially processed by parching them in baskets, or alternately by mixing them with hot earth and subsequently separating them from the soil using winnowing baskets or sieves. After this, they were dried and stored in a cool place for future use (Steward 1933a:256). Steward (1933a:256) also noted that the dried *piuga* were boiled in either baskets or pots before being eaten.

Since five of the six known pottery-bearing sites within the Jeffrey pine forests of Mono County are located within or adjacent to ethnographically or archaeologically recorded *piuga* collection areas, it seems likely that they are related to on-site consumption of *piuga*. A precise calculation of the percentage of Mono County sites these occurrences represent cannot be made since only two of the sites are included in the EIC/CAI records. By themselves, these represent 6.3 percent of the total number of officially recorded pottery sites in the county, 0.1 percent of all the official sites. It must also be noted that two of the five sites are located at or adjacent to known obsidian quarries and therefore might be associated with this economic activity. For reasons outlined below, however, this seems a less likely association.

The second major ethnographic use of the Jeffrey pine forest was for the hunting of ungulates, primarily Inyo mule deer, *Odocoileus hemionus inyoensis*, although in the past bighorn sheep, *Ovis canadensis californiana, O. c. nelsoni* may have been present in particular locales. As noted by Steward (1933a:252-253), these game were usually pursued by individual males or by small male hunting parties during brief trips away from more permanent settlements.

Only one of the six pottery sites in the Jeffrey pine forest environment might be characterized as a possible hunting camp. Since pottery was produced and presumably used by females (Steward 1933a:266), a direct correlation with male-dominated or exclusive hunting camps would offer an unlikely explanation for the occurrence of pottery within the forested areas of the county. However, inasmuch as hunting forays may also have been undertaken incidental to *piuga* collection or obsidian quarrying, there may be some indirect, though seemingly unlikely, correlation between hunting and the distribution of pottery within the region generally.

The quarrying of obsidian for either trans-Sierra exchange or local consumption is the final major land-use pattern for the Jeffrey pine forest noted in the ethnographic literature (Steward 1933a:257. 262). Since this was also an exclusively male activity, the relative absence of pottery at quarry sites is not unexpected. In addition, the lack of pottery at other major sites in and immediately adjacent to the Jeffrey pine forested areas of the county (e.g., in the vicinity of the town of Mammoth Lakes) may also be partially explained by this activity given the pattern of quarrying and lithic reduction noted by Basgall (1982:117-124), Hall (1983:130, 140-148), and Weaver, Bouscaren, and Wilke (1984). Based upon the results of these site excavations, it appears that the pattern of obsidian procurement generally involved obtaining raw nodules and doing only preliminary reduction at the actual quarry location. Most reduction, as well as the production of bifaces, blanks, and finished tools, appears to have been completed at obsidian stoneworking camps located some distance from the actual obsidian source.

As previously noted, only two occurrences of pottery (both isolates) can be tentatively associated with quarry locations. Even these,

however, are also located within known *piuga* collection areas. Given that quarrying appears to have been an exclusively male activity and brief periods of time seem to have been spent at the quarry locations, the presence of pottery at these two sites would seem most likely attributable to the consumption of *piuga*. In addition to these two sites, pottery is also noted at five sites located in areas immediately adjacent to the Jeffrey pine forest. All of these are noted in the EIC/CAI records and therefore represent 15.6 percent of the known pottery sites, or 0.3 percent of all officially recorded sites in the county. These sites, which can be characterized as primarily obsidian stoneworking camps, are also all located adjacent to water sources. The more varied and substantial amounts of food resources available in such locations, and the fact that producing tools is more time-consuming than quarrying nodules, would seem to argue for a greater likelihood of long-term and possibly family-group occupation. Such an inference is supported by the more extensive and relatively varied cultural deposits exhibited by these sites.

Recent geologic investigations by Miller (personal communication 1984) suggest a maximum age for Owens Valley Brown Ware within the Jeffrey pine forest of Mono County. Based upon his analysis of the pattern of eruptive episodes involving the Inyo Craters volcanic chain, much of the area was blanketed by pumiceous deposits from a series of magmatic eruptions dating ca. 600 B.P. By inference then, this constitutes a maximum age for pottery found atop volcanic deposits in these settings although not necessarily a maximum age for the inception of pottery manufacture and use in general within the region.

In summary, the sparse representation of pottery sites within and immediately adjacent to the Jeffrey pine forest in Mono County appears to reflect actual patterns of ethnographic use. When pottery is found in these locales, it appears to be associated with *piuga* collection sites or with obsidian stoneworking camps located near water sources. Even in these instances, pottery seems incidental rather than essential to the indicated procurement activities.

In contrast to the sparse occurrence of pottery within or immediately adjacent to vegetation areas dominated by Jeffrey pine, the available data do indicate one apparent concentration of pottery sites in Mono County. A total of 19 (59.4 percent) of the pottery-bearing sites noted in the EIC/CAI files (1.1 percent of all sites in the county) are located within an approximately five-square-mile area centered some 17 miles northwest of Bishop, California, in the vicinity of Casa Diablo Mountain. The Enfield/Weller data indicate an additional 30 pottery sites in this same area.

Further, if all pottery sites within a 10-mile radius of the center of this apparent concentration are considered, another five EIC/CAI sites (cumulatively representing 75 percent of all the pottery sites in the county) and 29 Enfield/Weller locations must be added to the previous figures.

A closer examination of the collective site records for this apparent cluster, however, seems to indicate that it reflects sampling factors rather than aboriginal manufacture and use patterns. Specifically, all but four of these sites were recorded in intensive surveys of the area conducted by the Enfields and Weller. As is apparent, the failure to control for overrepresentation of a particular environmental stratum or locale skewed the data base. Given that no comparable data from similar environmental settings in either Inyo or Mono counties are available, it cannot be quantitatively determined whether the pottery distribution data from the Casa Diablo Mountain area is representative of other portions of the study area. It would certainly seem reasonable to expect that valley floor areas would exhibit relatively high although not necessarily equal densities. The data from Inyo County seem to substantiate this last premise.

Inyo County

Several observations and inferences can also be made regarding the distribution of pottery-bearing sites in Inyo County. The combined EIC/CAI and Wallace/Hunt records for Inyo County indicate a much greater proportion of pottery sites (20.5 percent) than did the Mono County data (1.9 percent). Some of the difference between the two counties seems attributable to the fact that the Riddell and Riddell (1956), Wallace (1958), and A. Hunt (1960) surveys appear to reflect an overrepresentation of sites on valley floors, in canyons, and adjacent to drainages. In Owens Valley, these were areas where more permanently occupied villages and clay sources were located (Bettinger 1982: 49-51; Steward 1933a:266-267). Therefore, it would be expected that these areas would exhibit a greater density of both nonpottery-bearing and pottery-bearing sites. By analogy, the Panamint Valley-Death Valley area of eastern Inyo County could reasonably be expected to exhibit a similar pattern.

Another consideration that seems to account for at least a portion of the percentage and numerical differences between the counties is that a very large portion of the Mono County site data comes from the inventory of Jeffrey pine forest where pottery sites are scarce. While the total number of pottery-bearing sites in this environmental stratum is quite low, the total number of recorded sites

constitutes a large portion of the total number of sites recorded in the county to date. Collectively, these two factors effectively decrease the overall percentage of Mono County pottery sites.

Even compensating for the above considerations, however, would not seem to account for all of the observed difference in the relative pottery percentages. For example, if the data from the Casa Diablo Mountain area of Mono County is compared with the Inyo County data excluding the Wallace and Hunt records (since they do not document a contiguous area), there is still over a tenfold difference indicated: 1.1 percent (19 sites) compared to 14.0 percent (233 sites). Considering that these percentages are similar to those resulting from a comparison of the respective countywide data, and that the areas are both contiguous and generally similar in environmental characteristics, the apparent differences may in fact be culturally significant. It should be pointed out here, however, that the exclusion of the Wallace and Hunt data from the balance of the Inyo County records provides only a crude approximation of the actual number of pottery sites in Owens Valley since it erroneously includes some sites from other parts of Inyo County. Nonetheless, this means of arriving at an approximate comparative figure seems acceptable for present qualitative purposes, especially since no exact statistical analysis can be attempted. That this figure reflects the real situation to some reasonable degree is supported by the fact that the preponderance of the recorded sites in Inyo County are from the Owens Valley.

In summary, all factors considered, it would appear that the overall higher percentage and numbers of pottery sites in Inyo County do reflect different patterns of cultural use. Further investigations are necessary to substantiate this tentative conclusion and, if supported, to develop explanatory models.

The pottery distribution data from within Inyo County appear to reflect differences in cultural manufacture and use patterns. In contrast to Owens Valley where approximately 14 percent of the sites contain pottery, the Panamint Valley-Death Valley area exhibits a much higher frequency of pottery sites (31.3 percent or 318 sites). Initially these figures seem inconsistent with the fact that population densities in the Owens Valley were substantially higher (Bettinger 1979:43-48). A closer evaluation of both the ethnographic and archaeological data for these areas offers several explanations that, either singly or collectively, seem to account for this apparently real difference.

The occupation of permanent villages located on the valley floor, especially near watercourses, seems to have characterized the late prehistoric and early historic Paiute settlement pattern in Owens Valley. This pattern, which Bettinger (1978) termed Desert Village strategy, stands in sharp contrast to the more ephemeral and transitory settlements of a Desert Culture strategy (Bettinger 1978; 1982)--the latter being similar to Jennings's (1957) Desert Culture concept--that was characteristic of Shoshoni groups in eastern Inyo County. Given the more stable population centers in Owens Valley, and their proximity to clay sources, it appears reasonable to infer that pottery would tend to be present at a fewer overall number of sites and that these sites would also tend to be more localized in the vicinity of permanent villages than would be the case in the Panamint Valley-Death Valley area. This does not, however, imply that pottery had greater or fewer functional applications in the respective areas. Such an issue is beyond the scope of this presentation, regardless of the fact that the available data appear insufficient to address such a premise. In any event, the relative restriction of pottery to more permanently or frequently used occupation areas--a pattern also noted for the Chemehuevi groups in the eastern Mojave Desert (Steward 1933a:269)-seems to explain at least a portion of the apparently lower proportion of pottery-bearing sites in Owens Valley in comparison to the Panamint Valley-Death Valley area.

Similar considerations offer another possible explanation for the apparent higher incidence of pottery sites in eastern Inyo County. Given the more ephemeral and highly mobile character of the Shoshoni settlement subsistence strategy, if pottery vessels were carried along during settlement relocation it would be reasonable to expect a relatively higher incidence of breakage. In turn, this should be reflected in the archaeological record by the relatively frequent occurrence of sites containing either only pottery or pottery in association with a few other portable items that may have been transported in the vessels.

As previously noted, biases in synthetic data bases might be assumed generally to preclude most analytical efforts. In this instance, however, such does not appear to be the case on a qualitative level. As was common to many of the early investigations in the Inyo-Mono region, the Wallace and Hunt survey documentation does not clearly indicate how survey areas were selected, precisely what locales were examined, nor what proportions of the various environmental strata within the study area were examined. Based upon the available information it does appear as though both the Wallace (1958) and A. Hunt (1960) investigations primarily focused on the examination of valley floors, canyons, and areas adjacent to drainages. These localities, as is the case in Owens Valley, are more likely to contain a preponderance of the evidence of past

human activity in the area since they tend to be the most resource productive and/or provide access to more productive locales. Therefore, while the sampling fractions may preclude statistical analysis of the settlement and subsistence activities within and between various environmental strata, more intensive coverage would seem to result in an accurate characterization of the various types of aboriginal activities undertaken in the area. This would also seem to include evidence of both vessels broken during transport as well as sites where pottery was produced.

A reexamination of both the Wallace and Hunt site records revealed only nine isolated, exclusively sherd sites (7.4 percent of the pottery sites or 0.9 percent of all recorded sites), all from the Hunt records. By itself this situation seems to reflect either some cultural differences between the Panamint Valley and Death Valley areas or some type of sample error. A detailed examination of this question, however, will not be attempted here. A tally was also made of those sites containing only minimal amounts of portable cultural material in addition to pottery. For example, this count included those sites which contained pottery in association with several manos, flaked stone tools, and similar transportable items, but excluded those exhibiting evidence indicative of more permanent or long-term occupation such as hearths, house floors, metates, and mortars. This effort identified 40 sites constituting 12.6 percent of the recorded pottery sites, or 3.9 percent of all recorded sites. Collectively, these two categories of pottery sites include a total of 49 pottery-only or essentially pottery-only sites that represent 15.4 percent of all the pottery sites, or 4.8 percent of all sites recorded by the Wallace and Hunt surveys.

In light of the vaguely defined site categories, as well as inherent data-base problems, the above figures must be viewed as only rough indicators. Despite these considerations, the level of resolution as well as the overall numbers and percentages seem to suggest that pottery tended not to be transported during moves to new occupation/procurement areas. Such a pattern, to this point, is consistent with the inference that pottery in the Owens Valley tended to be most heavily present in the vicinity of more permanent occupation sites. In the case of the Shoshoni groups, however, such a conclusion also implies that: (1) pottery vessels were cached at or near repeatedly used occupation/procurement locales and (2) that if previously cached vessels were broken after abandonment, or if new vessels were needed for some other reason, pots would have to have been produced on site. Both of these inferences seem consistent with the archaeological record, especially the apparent abandonment of both fired and unfired whole pots. The frequency with which such occurrences are noted in the Wallace and Hunt site records argues that they resulted from an intentional cultural practice rather than accidental factors. A more intensive pattern of on-site/on-demand pottery production would have been facilitated by the presence of optimum occupation and resource procurement locales along drainages and in canyons providing readily available clay sources, as they did in Owens Valley (Steward 1933a:266-267).

In summary, it is suggested that the higher percentage of pottery-bearing sites in the Panamint Valley-Death Valley area, in comparison to Owens Valley, results from the fact that pottery in both areas tended to be most intensively produced and used in the vicinity of major occupation sites and resource procurement locales. In the case of the Shoshoni groups of eastern Inyo County, however, the relatively limited number of more optimum procurement locales, their more widely distributed nature, and the more mobile nature of the settlement/subsistence strategy resulted in the more frequent caching of vessels and also a more intensive pattern of on-site/on-demand pottery production.

SUMMARY

Evaluation of the distribution of pottery-bearing sites in east-central California reveals substantial intraregional variability in prehistoric pottery production and use patterns. It is suggested that these observed differences resulted from a combination of differing settlement/subsistence strategies and functional contexts within the region in late prehistoric and early historic times.

ACKNOWLEDGMENTS

The support, suggestions, and criticisms of several friends and colleagues contributed significantly to this effort. I am especially indebted to M. C. Hall and T. Beth Snyder for their insightful comments and constructive criticisms on earlier drafts of this paper as well as their support throughout the effort. Rollin and Grace Enfield, Norm Weller, and Daniel McCarthy all deserve special thanks for their efforts on my behalf. Robert L. Bettinger and Suzanne Griset also provided useful comments and suggestions during various stages of the project. Finally, my wife, Karen, and son, Jeromy, deserve my most sincere appreciation for their patience, understanding, and support throughout this endeavor.

Any errors in facts, judgment, or interpretation are, of course, my own.

REFERENCES CITED

(Citations not listed here will be found in the Annotated and Indexed Bibliography of Ceramics at the back of this volume.)

Basgall, Mark E.
1983   Archaeology of the Forest Service Forty Site (CA-Mno-529), Mono County, California. Manuscript on file at the Inyo National Forest, Bishop, California.

Bettinger, Robert L.
1978   Alternative Adaptive Strategies in the Prehistoric Great Basin. *Journal of Anthropological Research* 34(1):27-46.

1982   *Archaeology East of the Range of Light: Aboriginal Human Ecology of the Inyo-Mono Region, California.* Monographs in California and Great Basin Anthropology, Number 1.

Carolin, V. M., Jr., and J. A. E. Knopf
1968   *The Pandora Moth.* U.S. Department of Agriculture Forest Pest Leaflet 114.

Hall, M. C.
1983   *Late Holocene Hunter-Gatherers and Volcanism in the Long Valley-Mono Basin Region: Prehistoric Culture Change in the Eastern Sierra Nevada.* Ph.D. dissertation, University of California, Riverside.

Weaver, Richard A., Stephen Bouscaren, and Philip J. Wilke
1984   Test Excavation and Comparative Analysis of Site CA-Mno-1654, near Mammoth Lakes, Mono County, California. Manuscript on file at the Inyo National Forest, Bishop, California.

ANALYTICAL APPROACHES

The four papers in this section present four varied approaches to
ceramic analysis. The first by Tuohy and Strawn presents thin-section
data from 36 sherds collected from central Nevada and adjacent
regions, including two from Baja California. An introduction to the
problem and description of the sample is set forth by Tuohy, followed
by Strawn's petrographic analysis. Tuohy concludes the paper with a
discussion and conclusion of the results.

Bettinger presents a statistical approach to ceramic typology.
In contrast with other authors in this volume, he does not think a
general term should be used for Basin brown wares until the intuitive
grouping of these ceramics has been tested and proven statistically
verifiable. He presents a method for quantifying descriptive attributes of brown wares so that they may be compared statistically for
significant differences that would justify creating "wares" or
"types." He examines surface treatment of sherds from three excavated
sites in central Owens Valley. By comparing statistical differences
between and among these sets of data he argues for attributes that may
be significant in Owens Valley and suggests the applicability of the
technique for other areas of the Basin.

James takes a functional approach to vessel morphology as a means
of interpreting ceramic assemblages and site function. This, in turn,
is used as evidence to argue whether Fremont peoples occupied areas of
what he terms the "Western Periphery"--the western edge of Utah/
eastern edge of Nevada. Using ethnographic analogy he postulates
functional uses of reconstructed vessel shapes from archaeological
collections. He then proposes three hypotheses as to the kinds of
ceramic vessels he predicts would be used at villages or temporary
camps. These are compared to the archaeological data and to the
hypothesized differences in settlement systems of the Fremont and
Paiute peoples.

Griset details an overview of analytical approaches. She examines two phases of ceramic analysis, description, and interpretation,
and reviews the literature for approaches applicable to the small
assemblages of undecorated sherds found at sites in the Basin and
surrounding areas.

A COMPARATIVE ANALYSIS OF THIN SECTIONS
FROM PLAIN BROWN POTTERY VESSELS
FOUND IN THE DESERT WEST

Donald R. Tuohy and Mary B. Strawn

INTRODUCTION

Thin-section analysis of plain-ware ceramics has long been regarded a useful tool in determining comparative and possible generic relationships among prehistoric ceramic traditions in the Desert West. Painted and textured ceramics found mainly in the eastern Great Basin have their origins in southwestern culture area pottery traditions. Native people of the Great Basin, on the other hand, tended to reject ceramic vessels for use as containers, choosing instead a variety of finger-woven vessels to meet the bulk of their container needs. Nevertheless, Numic speakers did make aboriginal pottery, usually a plain brown ware, sometimes decorating it with "fingernail" incisions. This plain brown ware pottery usually postdates earlier Fremont and Anasazi ceramic types whenever they are found together, but nowhere does the brown ware seem to be older than about A.D. 800.

As archaeological research has increased over the past 50 years, so, too, has knowledge of the distribution of plain brown-ware ceramics. The only ethnographic subregion in the Great Basin where it is scarce to absent is the Northern Paiute area of northwestern Nevada (Tuohy 1973). Elsewhere, plain brown-ware ceramics subsumed under a variety of names such as "Shoshoni Ware" (Rudy 1953), "Southern Paiute Utility Ware" (Baldwin 1950a), "Owens Valley Brownware" (Riddell 1951), and "Intermountain Ware" (Kehoe 1959; Mulloy 1958; Wedel 1954), have been reported from southwestern Montana and western Wyoming, southern Idaho, western Utah, Nevada, Oregon, and parts of central and southern California.

As many researchers have pointed out, the nomenclature and typology of these plain brown-ware ceramics have confounded rather than clarified cultural and historical relationships among them. This confusion particularly abounds in geographic regions where ceramic distributions overlap, such as western Utah, central and southern Nevada, and Death Valley, California. Thin-section analysis of plain brown-ware ceramics may help resolve some of these questions of ceramic variability.

When the present thin-section study was completed, only a handful of similar studies of Great Basin brown wares were underway (Butler 1983a) or had been published. Among the latter were: the first Great Basin thin section study by C. Hunt (C. Hunt 1953:101); and his study of Death Valley thin sections (C. Hunt 1960: 193-224); studies of Idaho thin sections by Coale (1963:1-11), by Plew (1982:9-13), and by Butler (1983a); and studies of Nevada thin sections by Williams (Williams in Prince 1959:9) and by Olson (1978, 1979).

As Shepard (1956:157-158) has noted, the use of a petrographic microscope and a binocular microscope in thin-section analysis is superior to examination of sherds in powdered form, particularly in attempts to identify temper. Thin sections not only show the texture of the paste, but the proportions of the inclusions and the size and shape of the grains. They also show the relationship, proportion, and texture of different constituents, mineral components of rocks, and the structure and texture of clay inclusions. These attributes are particularly important in comparative studies of plain brown-ware ceramics.

Procedures

In order to conduct the present study, 28 potsherds recovered from various parts of Nevada were subjected to thin-section analysis (Figure 29). In addition to the Nevada samples seven potsherds from California, Baja California, and Idaho also were thin-sectioned (Figure 30). All except the Mission Period

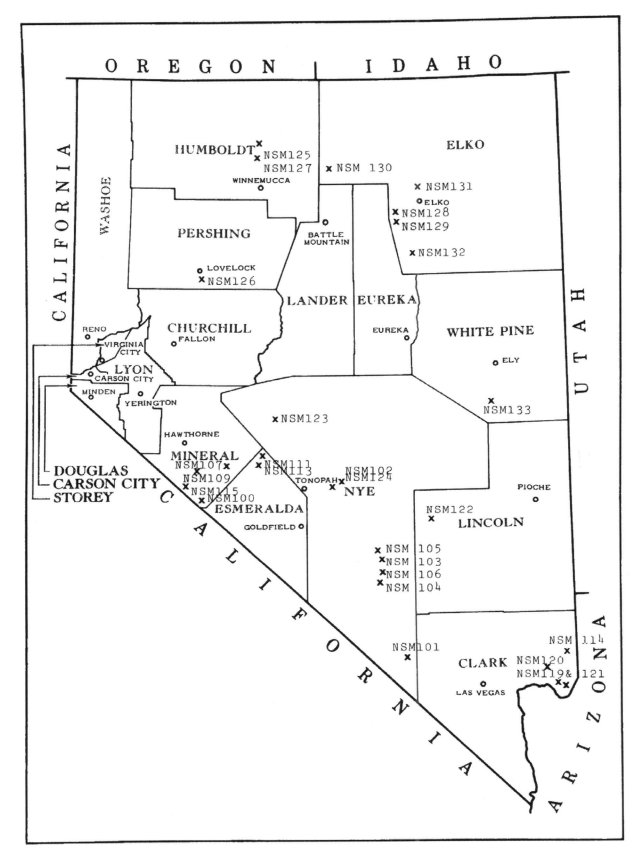

Figure 29. Map of Nevada showing the counties in which the 28 thin section samples were taken and the approximate find spots of the vessels and sherds.

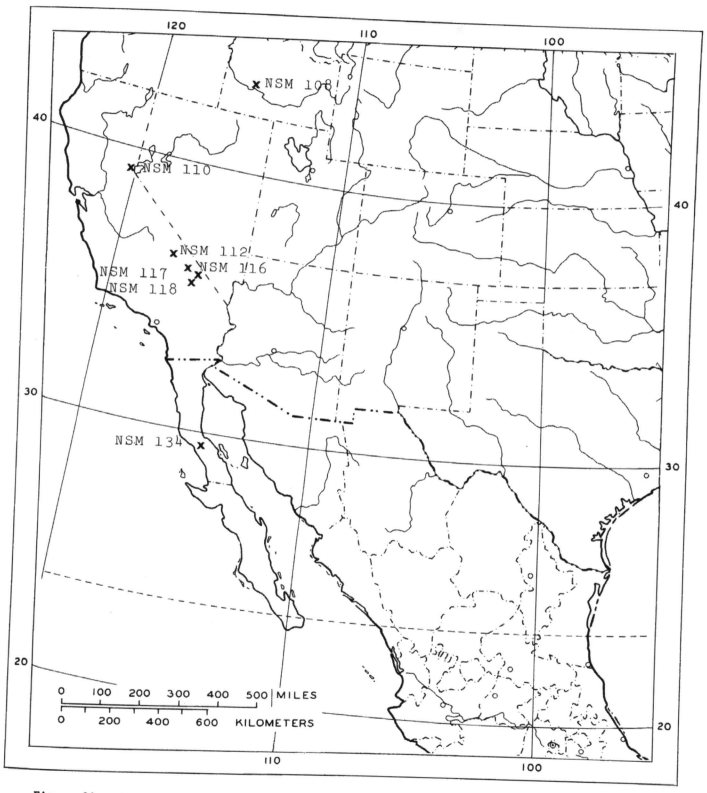

Figure 30. A portion of western North America showing the locations outside of Nevada where plain brown ware potsherds were recovered and later became part of the thin section sample.

TABLE 2. Descriptive Data for Potsherds Comprising the Thin-Section Sample

Cat. No.	Provenience		Vessel Type	Av. Thickness (cm)	Core Color	Ext. Color	Notes
100	Alkali Spr	Nye Co., NV.	flat, flanged	base 1.9 wall 0.88	2.5YR4/0	5YR5/4	base diameter 8.1 cm
101	Rainbow Spr	Nye Co., NV.	rounded bottom	base 1.6 wall 0.85	2.5YR2.0	10YR6/4	base sherd only
102	Tonopah	Nye Co., NV.	flat, no flange	base 1.4 wall 0.7	7.5YR2/0	2.5YR6/2 2.5YR4/0	base diameter 9.0 cm coiled and scraped
103	Ammonia Tanks	Nye Co., NV.	flat, no flange	base 1.0+ wall 0.77	2.5YR2/0	5YR5/3	base diameter 7.0 cm coiled and scraped
104	Big George Cave area	Nye Co., Test Site, NV.	concave, no flange base	base 1.0 wall 0.8	2.5YR2/0	7.5YR5/2	base diameter 9.0 cm coiled and scraped
105	Paiute Mesa	Nye Co., Test Site, NV.	bowl?	wall 0.7	2.5Y2/0	10YR4/1 to 10YR5/4	coil junctures not obliterated (found in pine nut cache)
106	Big George Cave area	Nye Co., Test Site, NV.	flat, flanged	base 1.4 wall 0.8	2.5YR2/0	10YR4/2	base diameter 7.4 cm coiled and wiped
107	Rattlesnake Vly	Mineral Co., NV.	jar form; everted rim	base 0.73 wall 0.73	10YR4/1	10YR5/3	decorated (incised and punctate)
108	Glenn's Ferry	Idaho	cooking pot	wall 1.0	10YR2/2	10YR4/1	rim and wall sherds only
109	R39E,T3S,S6	Esmeralda Co., NV.	wall sherd	wall 0.88	10YR2/1	10YR4/1	wall sherd only
110	NW Lake Tahoe	Placer Co., CA.	jar	--	--	--	returned to finder; described by Tuohy and Jerrems (1972)
111	Cedar Mts.	Mineral Co., NV.	wall sherd	wall 0.86	10YR5/1	10YR5/3	coiled and scraped
112	Panamint Vly	Inyo Co., CA.	jar, everted rim	wall 0.7	10YR3/1	10YR4/1 2.5YR5/2 5YR6/4	
113	Dry lake west of Cedar Mtn	Mineral Co., NV.	wall sherd	wall 0.76	5YR4/1	5YR5/3	
114	Mesquite	Clark Co., NV.	wall sherd	wall 0.76	5YR4/1	5YR5/3	olivene phenocrysts as temper
115	26Mn114	Mineral Co., NV.	wall sherd	wall 0.6	5YR3/1	5YR4/1	punctate design on shoulder
116	"WC" site	Inyo Co., CA.	jar, everted rim	wall 0.8	5YR5/1	10YR5/4	pebble smoothed
117	Crowley Lake	Inyo Co., CA.	jar, everted rim	wall 0.7	5YR3/1	10YR5/3	coiled with junctures obliterated
118	Benton	Inyo Co., CA.	jar, everted rim	wall 0.7	10YR5/1	10YR5/2	punctate designs below neck

Cat. No.	Provenience	Vessel Type	Av. Thickness (cm)	Core Color	Ext. Color	Notes
119	Shutler site 63, Clark Co., NV.	incurving rim	wall 0.6	10YR4/1	10YR4/3	vertical, diagonal and horizontal scrape marks from pebble
120	Shutler site DD:7:67, Clark Co., NV.	pointed base	base 1.97	2.5YR3/0	10YR4/2	basal sherd, pointed bottom
121	Shutler site 23, Clark Co., NV.	wall sherd	wall 0.7	10YR4/1 Interior 7.5YR3/0	5YR5/3	
122	R47E,T10S,S32, Lincoln Co., NV.	wall sherd	wall 0.9	7.5YR4/0	2.5YR5/2	scraped vertically across coils
123	26Ny22, Nye Co., NV.	wall sherd	wall 0.7	7.5YR4/0	7.5YR6/2	carbon in vugs, coiled and scraped
124	Nye Co., NV.	wall sherd	wall 0.8	7.5YR4/0	7.5YR6/2	everted rim
125	Paradise Vly, Humboldt Co., NV.	wall sherd	wall 0.69	10YR7/2	7.5YR4/0	core lighter in color than rim
126	Lovelock area, Pershing Co., NV.	wall sherd	wall 0.78	10YR4/2	10YR3/4	has mending hole
127	Paradise Vly area, Humboldt Co., NV.	wall sherd	wall 1.0	10YR6/1	10YR4/1	scraped vertically across coils
128	26Ek1671/440, Elko Co., NV.	wall sherd	wall 0.9	10YR3/2	10YR5/3	scraped vertically across coils
129	26Ek1672/129, Elko Co., NV.	rim sherd	wall 0.88	10YR3/1	10YR5/2	normal rim, coils not obliterated
130	26Ek514, Elko Co., NV.	flat-bottom flanged	wall 0.7 base 1.35	10YR3/1	10YR5/2	incurvate rim, wipe marks vertical outside; inside horizontal
131	no prov., Elko Co., ? NV.	whole vessel, pointed bottom	rim 0.7	10YR2/1	10YR2/2	184-G-1, normal rim, coiled
132	Ruby Mts., Elko Co., NV.	whole vessel flanged, flat	wall 1.0	10YR2/1	10YR3/3	288-L-1 coiled, crack mended with pitch
133	R60E,T18N,S27, White Pine Co., NV.	whole vessel, pointed bottom	wall 0.7	2.5YR6/6	10YR4/3 to 10YR3/1	11-G-1 coils incompletely obliterated – wipe marks vertical on exterior
134	Mission San Fernando Velicata, Baja Calif.	wall sherd				
135	Mission San Juan Londo, Baja Calif.	wall sherd				

(Baja California) potsherds could be classified as Great Basin brown ware pottery, neither painted nor slipped, but with a few containing linear incisions in bands or in geometrical forms, commonly called "fingernail" impressions. An attempt was made to obtain sherds from whole or nearly whole "Shoshoni Ware" vessels, and from those sherd collections where the shape of the vessel or the base could be reconstructed, or at least inferred from basal sherds. In some cases, wall sherds alone were thin sectioned as they comprised the only available sample from the particular locality or site (Table 2).

All thin sections and mounts containing them were produced at the Rudolph von Huene Thin Section Laboratory located in Pasadena, California. The 36 newly prepared slide mounts together with the original 17 slide mounts reported previously by Coale (1963) were then sent to Mary B. Strawn, Professor Emeritus in Geology, Idaho State University Museum, Pocatello. Strawn has had extensive experience in petrographic analysis as a geological consultant in Idaho. The inclusion in the sample of the 17 slide mounts analyzed by Coale (1963) presumably would allow comparisons between the old and new samples. So as not to bias the comparison, I left to Strawn's judgment the reporting of similarities and differences among the mineral constituents contained as temper in the samples.

To facilitate her analysis and comparison of the 36 NSM specimens with the original 17 reported by Coale (1963), I sent her a catalogue of the pots and potsherds that were thin-sectioned and notes on their original find spots (see Table 2). She also was provided with a copy of Charles B. Hunt's study of the petrography of Death Valley ceramics (1960: 195-224). A brief summary of her methods of analysis follows.

PETROGRAPHIC ANALYSIS

Methods of Analysis

Both black-and-white microphotographs and 35 mm color slides were made of each thin section. In some cases 35 mm slides were made under polarized light as well. The mineral constituents comprising the temper were then recorded on five-by-eight-inch cards. This "temper composition" category was followed by notation as to whether the temper was very angular, angular, subangular, subrounded, rounded, or very rounded following Powers's (1953) chart for visual estimation of roundness. The second entry recorded temper size in millimeters, while the third noted the percentage of temper. The latter estimate was made utilizing a comparison chart for estimating

percentage composition by Terry and Chilingar (1955). This chart is similar to the "Percentage Density Chart--Filler Particles" in Bennett (1974:105) except that the latter illustrates densities of up to 80 percent, while the Terry and Chilingar chart ends with densities of 50 percent. Thus, none of the entries exceeds a 50 percent estimate.

The final entry on the cards forming the data base for the thin-section analysis is Strawn's notation on the nature of the mineral inclusions visible in the microphotos, with references to the microphotos themselves. Copies of these data cards and microphotos are on file at the Nevada State Museum.

Temper Composition

A list of all the mineral constituents found in the sample is provided in Table 3. In classifying the temper of the Nevada State Museum and Coale potsherds, C. Hunt's (1960:194) categories were used as much as possible for the sake of comparison. Nearly half of the potsherds in the Coale and Nevada State Museum (NSM) collections had temper from volcanic materials. Sherds with nonvolcanic temper were divided into those with granitic temper and those with temper other than granite.

I. *Sherds with Volcanic Temper*.
   A. Devitrified glass and rounded to subrounded vitrophyre together with lesser quartz, feldspar, and mafic minerals (Death Valley Brown Ware, NSM #106, 124, 133; Snake River Ware, NSM #108, 130, 131; Owens Valley Brown Ware, NSM #113, 117; and Southern Paiute Utility Ware, NSM #120, 121).
   B. Devitrified volcanic glass, associated with quartz, potash feldspar, plagioclase, and mica. The temper in these sherds is most similar to Hunt's Shoshoni or Southern Paiute Utility Ware (C. Hunt 1960:201, Fig. 53f), but rarely shows perlitic texture (Death Valley Brown, NSM #100, 104, 105, 123; Snake River Ware, NSM #128, 129; Owens Valley Brown, NSM #111, 116; Southern Paiute Utility Ware, NSM #119, 122; Deep Creek, Coale #22658-2, 22658-6).
   C. Clear undevitrified volcanic glass with plagioclase and biotite (West Warren Paiute, Coale "no number" and #206550-6).

II. *Sherds with Granitic Temper*. These were differentiated on the presence or absence of quartzite, on the presence of perthitic intergrowths (microcline) and on the degree of argillization of the feldspars.
   A. Finely divided microcline and only slightly argillized feldspars. These

TABLE 3. Mineral Constituents of the Potsherds (modified from Coale 1963)

Specimen No.	Q	Qc	Qz	P	Pk	Ps	B	VG	VGd	Ma	Mu	Chert	H	Mk	D	Mi	Ho	Sc
100	X	X		X			X											
101	X			X			X					X	X					
102	X			X			X			X						X		
103	X			X														
104	X	X		X				X	X									
105	X			X				X	X				X					
106	X			X			X	X				X						
107				X			X	X	X								X	
108	X		X	X			X			X							X	
109	X			X				X	X				X					
110	X		X	X	X		X	X	X									
111	X	X		X			X	X	X								X	
112	X			X			X	X	X	X							X	
113	X			X				X										
114	X		X	X			X	X	X									
115	X		X					X									X	
116	X		X				X									X		
117	X	X		X				X	X	X							X	
118	X		X	X				X	X	X								
119	X	X		X			X			X							X	
120	X		X					X	X									
121	X	X					X	X								X	X	
122	X	X		X			X	X	X	X			X				X	
123	X	X		X				X	X									
124	X	X		X			X	X	X	X								
125		X						X	X									
126	X			X			X			X			X					X
127	X		X	X									X			X		
128	X	X		X			X	X										X
129	X	X		X			X	X		X								
130		X	X	X			X	X	X								X	
131	X			X				X	X				X				X	
132	X		X	X	X	X	X											
133	X			X				X										
134	X	X	X	X			X											
135	X		X	X													X	
																	X	

Key to Symbols:

Q – Quartz
Qc– Quartz (chalcedony)
Qz– Quartzite
P – Plagioclase
Pk– Kaolinized plagioclase
Ps– Saussuritized plagioclase
B – Biotite
VG– Volcanic glass
VGd–partially devitrified volcanic glass

Ma– Magnetite
Mu– Carbonate
H – Hematite
Mk– Mica
D – Diopside
Mi– Microcline
Ho– Hornblende
Sc– Schist

sherds possibly correlate with Hunt's Owens Valley Brown Ware (1960:201, Fig. 53b). (Death Valley Brown, NSM #101, 115, 107; Southern Paiute Utility Ware, NSM #114; Deep Creek, Coale #22658-3; Snake River Shoshoni Ware, Coale #A; Owens Valley Brown, Coale #1-202479, 1-202568); NSM #112, 118, 132, 135).

B. Granitic temper with little or no quartzite and with slightly argillized feldspars (Lake Tahoe Brown, NSM #110; Snake River Ware, NSM #126; Death Valley Brown, NSM #102, 103; Owens Valley Brown, Coale #1-202721; Deep Creek, Coale #18420-25, 18420-63; NSM #109, 134).

III. *Sherds with Temper other than Volcanics or Granite*. Only two sherds fall into Hunt's schist with quartzite category (1960: 201, Fig. 53e); (Snake River Ware, NSM #125, 127).

Further Analysis of These Categories

I. *Sherds with Volcanic Temper*. Nearly half of the sherds studied had temper from volcanic rocks, primarily felsic vitrophyre and volcanic ash. Quartz, feldspars, and mafic minerals were usually found associated with the volcanics, but the temper was dominated by subrounded-to-angular devitrified ash or glass, with or without vitrophyre. In some thin sections, the glass was pumiceous and rare sherds of pumice were present (NSM 123).

Some of the devitrified glass sherds were associated with radiating fibers of chalcedony suggestive of a spherulitic structure in the original glass. In other glass fragments, devitrification resulted in the formation of chert (NSM 105). The chalcedony and chert occurred within the glass sherds and as discrete particles.

In only two thin sections, Coale's West Warren Paiute sherds, was the volcanic glass clear and unaltered.

The temper of the sherds mentioned in this discussion is similar to that of Hunt's Shoshoni or Southern Paiute Utility Ware (C. Hunt 1960:200-F and 201, Fig. 53f) except that perlite is rarely found and Hunt did not specify that the volcanic glass was devitrified.

II. *Sherds with Granitic Temper*. Potsherds in the Nevada State Museum and Coale collections having granitic temper were differentiated on (1) the presence or absence of quartzite, (2) the presence of perthitic intergrowths (microcline), and (3) the degree of argillization of the feldspars. This classification follows Hunt's to some extent, as he used the presence of microcline and the slight amount of alteration in the feldspars to distinguish temper from younger Cretaceous

granite and that from Precambrian granite.

Sherds with granitic temper containing finely divided microcline and unargillized or slightly argillized feldspars have temper most similar to that of Hunt's Owens Valley Brown Ware (1960:200B, and 201, Fig. 53b). Only a few microcline crystals were noted in the NSM thin sections and several of the sections showed devitrified glass as well.

Granitic temper with quartzite and strongly argillized feldspars is most closely related to that of Hunt's Southern Paiute (1960:200C and 201, Fig. 53c). Particles of temper that are identified here as quartzite may be what Hunt called "quartz intergrowths," as they have a similar aspect under the microscope.

Granitic temper with little or no quartzite and only slightly argillized feldspars did not appear to have a counterpart in the temper of sherds from the Death Valley salt pan.

III. *Sherds with Temper other than Volcanics or Granite*. This temper consists of relatively large laths of a quartzose schist with associated quartzite. Only two sherds had this temper, NSM 125 and 127, both called Snake River Ware. The temper correlates closely with Hunt's Death Valley Brown Ware (1960:201, Fig. 53e) except that Hunt describes the schist as rounded; in the NSM thin sections, it appears to be angular.

Coale Collection

A comparison of the temper composition of the potsherds Coale (1963) studied and those of the Nevada State Museum shows that their tempers are, in most cases, significantly different.

Four sherds of Coale's pottery (Eskimo) have a distinctive basaltic temper; no basalt temper was observed in the NSM thin sections.

Coale's Owens Valley sherds have granitic temper but little or no volcanic glass is associated with it, whereas NSM Owens Valley Brown Ware, with the exception of NSM 118, have glass in varying amounts. The unaltered glass temper of Coale's West Warren Paiute sherds is unique among the thin sections studied.

Coale's Snake River Shoshoni Ware A and B contain quartzite, but only a small amount of devitrified glass. In contrast, five thin sections of NSM Snake River Ware showed considerable amounts of the glass. NSM 126 and NSM 132, both called Snake River Ware, have the greatest similarity to the Snake River Shoshoni wares.

The petrographic analysis of the Nevada State Museum and Coale potsherds demonstrated that the temper of the sherds was derived from only a few sources, i.e., rhyolitic glassy rocks and tuffs, granitic rocks, quartzite and schist, or reworked deposits of these materials. Their use appears widespread over the Great Basin and adjoining areas so temper composition alone would not suffice to differentiate among pottery types. Other temper characteristics such as size, roundness, and relative percentages in the sherd can also be used to distinguish the various types of brown wares.

DISCUSSION AND CONCLUSION

Virtually every observer who has attempted thin-section studies of plain wares in the Desert West has come to the same conclusion: no single attribute measured or described for plain brown wares is diagnostic. Several attributes, often including temper, must be considered together in order to separate analyzed collections into types. A common conclusion derived from thin-section studies of plain brown ceramics is that the materials used in manufacture appear to reflect the local geology.

As noted, problems also arise in analyzing collections of plain brown potsherds on the basis of gross morphological characteristics alone. The sherd collections appear to share physical characteristics, such as exterior wiping or obliteration of coils by scraping, all the way from Muddy River examples to examples from Elko. In other words, from known Virgin Branch Anasazi or Southern Paiute plain ceramics to known or suspected Snake River Shoshoni vessels.

As Olson (1978) has noted for Lost City plain gray wares, none of the individual attributes for that ceramic series was diagnostic. However, by choosing two arbitrary attributes, temper and exterior color, she separated her plain wares into types. Of all the individual attributes noted for the vessels in this comparative sample (Tables 2 and 3) no such combination seems apropos. What may be more appropriate for our purposes is a review of the geographical distributions of similar morphological types in the hope of discovering concordances between or among them and the temper groups.

Perhaps the most important need at this juncture in Nevada Shoshoni ceramic studies is for thin sections of Grass Valley Shoshoni pottery (Beck 1981; Wells 1983) to be made and reported. The Grass Valley region has produced large quantities of plain brown ware Shoshoni pottery diagnostic of the Late Period (A.D. 1000 to A.D. 1860) there. Magee (1964, 1967) and later Deatrick (1978:137-140) first reported whole pottery cooking pots for Grass Valley. One nearly complete vessel Magee (1964:97) reported was recovered at an historic site--Grass Valley Tom Village. A second vessel, recovered from another historic

village, had a flat bottom and was decorated with spiral grooves evidently following the coil junctures. The vessel Deatrick (1978: 137-140) reported lacked basal sherds so its entire form could not be determined. Also recovered during these studies of Grass Valley archaeology were clay animal figurines, first reported by Magee (1967:204-207) and later by Ambro (1978:106-118; 1972). The well-controlled data base on Shoshoni ceramics recovered in central Nevada is superior to that known from any other area in Nevada where Shoshoni ceramics are found. Indeed, Beck's (1981:1-29) study of the 3,513 Shoshoni ware potsherds from 57 archaeological sites represents the largest substantive sample of Nevada Shoshoni ceramics yet studied.

Beck's analysis of temper in Grass Valley pottery, however, was done by magnification, not by thin-section (1981:15). She believes the clay used for pottery construction was obtained at local sources and some vessels contained plant material or no temper at all (Type 0). Other types of temper in pottery from Grass Valley included:

Type 1, mica; Type 2, small sand particles; Type 3, coarse sand particles; Type 4, mica, quartzite; Type 5, mica, quartzite, and coarse sand; Type 6, small granitic particles; Type 7, medium granitic particles; and Type 8, coarse granitic particles (Beck 1981:12-13, Table 3).

"Small" (Type 6) and "coarse" (Type 8) granitic particle tempered potsherds were the most numerous, appearing in sherds from 26 sites, while potsherds from 12 sites lacked any temper at all (Type 0). Thin-section analysis of these eight temper types from Grass Valley pottery surely would make Beck's data much more comparable than they are now.

The inclusion of granitic rock derived tempering minerals in "Shoshoni" pottery was among the first thin-section observations made. Charles B. Hunt did the first thin-section analysis of a western Utah "Shoshoni Ware" sherd:

The sherd of Shoshoni ware (14901) has temper of crushed granitic rock or subangular sand that was derived from granitic rock; probably the latter because a few grains are subround. The minerals of the temper are perthite or orthoclase, quartz, oligoclase, and biotite. The paste is moderately micaceous, and the fine grain part has properties suggestive of hydromica (C. Hunt 1953:101).

As previously mentioned, outside of the above study and Hunt's later study of thin sections of Death Valley ceramics (1960), Coale's (1963) pioneering thin-section analysis, and

Strawn's study reported here, the only other thin-section studies of "Shoshoni Ware" published or in progress known to me are those by Plew (1982:9-16), Butler (1983a), Williams in Prince (1959, and this volume), and Dean (1983:60-66).

Plew's (1982:9-16) thin-section analysis of 13 potsherds, five Snake River Shoshoni sherds, and eight "Southern Idaho Plain" sherds from south-central Idaho yielded results no other thin-section study has yet reported. While there was ample evidence that quartz, sand, and mica were used as temper in Plew's "Shoshoni Ware," basalt was also present as temper in three of the five sherds. As we have noted, basalt was not observed in any of the NSM thin sections. If basalt is regularly found to be a constituent of Snake River Shoshoni pottery, then a possible means for differentiating between some Snake River Brown Ware and some Nevada Shoshoni Ware may be in the offing.

Perhaps Butler's (1983a) recent "thin-section analysis of a geographically stratified sample consisting of some 50 different sherds from 40 different sites or site locations in the 24 county area" he calls the "Upper Snake and Salmon River Country" will help resolve whether basalt was commonly used as temper on Snake River Brown ceramics. Butler's preliminary report indicates that the mineral composition of the temper only reflects the mineralogy of the areas (the Snake River Plain and the Idaho batholith) where Idaho "Shoshonean" pottery was produced. As we have noted, for Nevada "Snake River Ware" (NSM 125 and 127) large laths of quartzose schist with associated quartzite are used as temper. Schist commonly occurs in that portion of Humboldt County, Nevada, where the vessels were found (Figure 29), so local manufacture is strongly suspected.

The question of local manufacture also is broached with respect to geographical groupings of the samples. For example, there is no doubt that NSM 114, 119, 120, and 121 were recovered in the Virgin and Muddy River subarea of the Colorado River. Thus, such brown wares should relate either to "Southern Paiute" brown ware or to "Virgin Branch" Anasazi ceramics. Three of these samples fall into the category having essentially volcanic temper (NSM 119, 120, and 121) while the fourth (NSM 114) has essentially granitic temper. The latter sample more than likely travelled some distance, as volcanics are more readily available in the vicinity of Grand Wash where the potsherd was collected. Petrographic analysis of temper constituents obviously does not insure identification of the ethnic identity of the vessel makers, even when site proveniences are known and morphological characteristics of the vessel can be reconstructed.

Manufacturing techniques may yet have some utility in differentiating brown wares. Pippin (1984:98) notes the rarity of paddle-and-anvil constructed pottery on the Nevada Test Site in south-central Nevada and the preponderance of coiled-and-scraped brown ware pottery there. Virtually all of the pottery reported here lacks paddle-and-anvil marks and exhibits the coil-and-scrape technique. Patch-coiling and modeling is noted for the Upper Snake River area by Butler (1983a:16) who also suggests that all of the brown ware from southern Idaho lacks evidence of paddle-and-anvil treatment. Paddle-and-anvil pottery, therefore, appears to be rare everywhere outside of the Colorado River and its tributaries in Nevada, the Southern Paiute area, and possibly the eastern Great Basin (Dean 1983:61).

The thin-section work by Tomtem (1983) in the eastern Great Basin on Northern Shoshoni and Salt Lake Gray pottery suggests some interesting possibilities. Carbon-covered clay was noted in thin sections of Black Rock Cave pottery. Dean (1983, 1984) suggests that the carbon can be dated using a linear accelerator/mass spectrometer. Since a number of Numic tribes tempered pottery with organic materials, the potential for future direct dating of brown ware is greatly enhanced. Dean also notes certain manufacturing techniques are shared by the northern Numic peoples and northern Fremont peoples. These include the addition of carbonaceous material to unfired clay, paddle-and-anvil construction, straight-rimmed vessel forms, and the addition of chert temper to clays. This last attribute was not common among the Nevada samples reported here, but chert was more frequently found as part of the temper among the pottery grouped under "Owens Valley Brown" in our sample, than in any other. Still, nowhere in the NSM samples did it approach the 40 percent levels Dean found in the plain wares of the Great Salt Lake region (Dean 1984).

Thus, particular minerals or rock particles such as chert or basalt may be key indicators of manufacturing localities. They must be used with caution, however, and Coale (1963:9) has already made mention of this possibility. He suggested the presence or absence of such minerals as quartz, carbonate, or micaceous materials were meaningful. The West Warren Paiute sherds in his study lacked quartz, Owens Valley Paiute sherds lacked mica, and the Deep Creek potsherds possessed carbonates. Likewise, Hunt's analysis of thin-section minerals in Death Valley plain ware allowed him to conclude that most of the pottery found there was imported from other areas, as grains of limestone and dolomite were abundant in Death Valley, but not present in his thin sections (C. Hunt 1960:195-224). The nature of the particular mineral or rock found within a thin section may also help in sourcing problems. As we have noted, even when an identical rock type is used as temper, such as the schist found in our provisional Snake River group (NSM 125 and 127) and in Hunt's Death Valley Brown Ware, it may have been subjected to different weathering processes. Hence, Hunt's Death Valley Brown with schist temper had rounded grains, while the schist in our samples was essentially angular.

In conclusion, it is clear from this study that much new knowledge will be gained by continuing with thin-section studies of the enigmatic brown wares found throughout the Desert West.

REFERENCES CITED

All sources cited in this paper may be found in the Annotated and Indexed Bibliography of Ceramics at the back of this volume.

INTERSITE COMPARISON OF GREAT BASIN BROWN WARE ASSEMBLAGES

ROBERT L. BETTINGER

More than any other artifact category commonly found in Great Basin sites, brown-ware ceramics have resisted attempts at systematic classification and analysis. Proposed here is such a method for classifying Great Basin ceramics, illustrated by its application to the ceramic assemblages from three recently excavated sites in central Owens Valley: Pinyon House, Two Eagles, and Crater Middens.

Owens Valley Brown Ware was originally described by Riddell (1951). He defined it as a simple brown ware made of residual clays containing quartz and mica inclusions, shaped by coiling and scraping, and fired in an uncontrolled, oxidizing atmosphere. Vessel forms included bowls and jars with flat or rounded bottoms, and decoration was limited to rare examples with thumbnail punctations near the rim.

Subsequent research in Owens Valley (e.g., Bettinger 1975) has shown that a great deal of variability in paste, thickness, and surface finish exists within sherd collections traditionally identified as Owens Valley Brown Ware. To date no comprehensive treatment of this variability has been undertaken. There are similar shortcomings in the published descriptions of late prehistoric ceramics from adjacent parts of the western Great Basin and eastern California. Because of this, it is unclear whether sherds that have been previously identified as Owens Valley Brown Ware —chiefly on the basis of geographical location—differ in any significant way from late prehistoric ceramics found in adjacent parts of central eastern California and the western Great Basin. The impression of such differences, however, might easily result from a comparison of ceramics from a single site in Owens Valley to those of a single site in another region, partly owing to the problem of sampling, partly to differences in site function, and partly to geologic idiosyncracies.

Certainly, much of the variability evident in paste, aplastic inclusions, and wall thickness reflects differential access to raw materials. There being no evidence that temper was ever intentionally added in Owens Valley Brown Ware (but see Steward 1933a:266)—or in all probability, any other late prehistoric Great Basin ceramic ware—differences in size and kind of inclusions are largely the result of the sedimentary facies from which clay was obtained; and there is sufficient diversity in most clay-bearing localities to produce material that varies from finely sorted to coarsely sorted. In turn, wall thickness is partly a function of the size of inclusions; large walls are needed to accommodate large inclusions, while fine inclusions are accommodated by either thin or thick walls. Wall thickness is also closely dependent on vessel size and function and therefore may be more reflective of site function or settlement pattern than stylistic tradition.

Interior, exterior, and core colors are of even less value as a defining characteristic in these ceramics if for no other reason than because they are severely affected by weathering. To cite a specific case relevant here, two fitting sherds from Pinyon House (0-34, 0-1455) are distinctly different in surface and core color. One appears to have been fired in an oxidizing atmosphere (10YR 3/3), the other in a reducing atmosphere (10YR 3/1). Use subsequent to manufacture—for instance in cooking—might also alter differentially the color of various parts of a vessel. As a more general consideration, the uncontrolled atmosphere used to fire nearly all late prehistoric Great Basin ceramics produces substantial color variation even within individual vessels. The traditional distinction between vessels fired upside down, with the interior in a reducing atmosphere and the exterior in an oxidizing atmosphere, and vessels fired standing up, with both interior and exterior in an oxidizing atmosphere, is also suspect in that the degree to which this distinction holds is subject to vessel size and shape, which affect air circulation during the firing process.

It is not implied here that the variables discussed above are meaningless archaeologically. Distinctions in clay source or wall thickness, for instance, may provide important evidence regarding a variety of interesting patterns, including trade and site function. Nevertheless, the definition of specific ceramic wares entails the identification of certain culturally meaningful attributes that distinguish the ceramics of one folk from those of another, apart from those deriving solely from circumstance, e.g., access to raw materials and function. With this in mind it should be recognized that the accepted definition of Owens Valley Brown Ware (Riddell 1951) describes adequately nearly all late prehistoric Great Basin ceramics. Simply put, whatever intuitive impressions might exist to the contrary, as far as can be now demonstrated when site function and location are taken into account, the differences between ceramics found in Owens Valley--Owens Valley Brown Ware--and those found in any other Great Basin locality are no greater than those that might separate any two ceramic assemblages from within Owens Valley.

To alter materially the present state of Great Basin ceramic studies two things need doing. First, it must be understood and acted upon that the currently accepted type definitions for the three major late prehistoric ceramic wares, i.e., Owens Valley Brown Ware, Shoshoni Ware, and Southern Paiute Utility Ware, carry no specific informational content except that of ethnogeographical location. The continued use of these terms seems permissible as a working hypothesis that there are three distinct variations in late prehistoric ceramics. It would be a serious mistake, however, for investigators to persist in the accepted practice of describing particular ceramic assemblages in terms of the type definition of any one of these wares as though it contained distinctive meaning in the usual sense of a type definition.

Throughout this paper the term Owens Valley Brown Ware is used because the sherds in question here are by definition of that ware. The problem at hand is to present basic data toward an understanding of what this term actually means archaeologically. This, of course, will only partly resolve current ambiguities. Similar analyses need to be undertaken elsewhere. The results of this work would then provide a basis for revision of the current ceramic typology. If, for example, upon careful examination, ceramics from the remainder of the western, central, or eastern

Great Basin turn out to be no different from those found in Owens Valley, it would greatly clarify the situation if the term Owens Valley Brown Ware were applied to them as well. Any designation would do, of course, but this one has chronological priority in the literature and to devise a new one would add needless complication to an already complicated situation. Southern Paiute Utility Ware was named earlier, but appears to consist partly of paddle-anvil vessels, thus distinguishing it from nearly all other Great Basin brownware ceramics. Terminology aside, the point is that emphasis on local ceramic idiosyncracies is likely to lead nowhere. The tracing of broader regional distributions of wares and varieties of wares, on the other hand, offers a viable opportunity to draw Great Basin ceramic studies into a position where they can contribute to problems of general archaeological interest, particularly those related to culture history and prehistoric ethnolinguistic distributions.

The second thing that needs doing in Great Basin ceramic studies is to improve description. It is not so much that past description has been shoddy--many detailed descriptions exist. What has been lacking, however, is systematic description in a standard format that permits meaningful comparison in terms of the attributes most likely to vary between assemblages. The lack of quantification is especially noteworthy here.

The above discussion resolves few questions but it does make clear that future attempts to distinguish Owens Valley Brown from other western Great Basin ceramic wares are most likely to meet success if the more gross characteristics, e.g., paste, color, aplastic inclusions, which apparently reflect functional and geological variability within a large areal ceramic tradition, are given less attention than more subtle distinctions within functionally equivalent vessel forms, including variations in bottom form, rim form, decoration and surface finish. With regard to many of these the problem of sampling is nearly insurmountable. Rims, bottoms, and decoration are only rarely found in Great Basin ceramic assemblages; normally, all that is available for analysis is a box of unremarkable body sherds. Nevertheless, these are the data at our disposal, and there are a variety of straightforward procedures for extracting useful information from them.

The simplest of these--and preferable for that reason--is to quantify (rather than merely list as present) the frequency with which modes of surface treatment occur individually on sherd interiors and exteriors and jointly on the interior and exterior of the same sherd. These data can be put in matrix form as is done below (p.100) with the exterior modes as columns and the interior modes as rows. Thus,

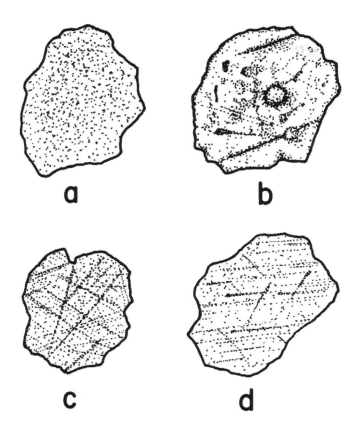

Figure 31. Modes of surface treatment for Owens Valley Brown Ware: (a) smooth; (b) rough; (c) random-brushed; and (d) parallel-brushed.

each body sherd tallies one count for the exterior mode it displays, one count for the interior mode it displays, and one count for its specific combination of exterior and interior modes.

Examination of the ceramic assemblages from the three sites considered here and those collected from surface sites in Owens Valley (Bettinger 1975) and review of published descriptions of late prehistoric ceramics from the Great Basin indicates that the vast majority of brown-ware sherd interiors and exteriors can be adequately described in terms of five more or less discrete modes of surface treatment: smooth, rough, random-brushed, parallel-brushed, and tooled (Figure 31). Although the meanings of these terms seem relatively clear, the tendency for different treatments to intergrade makes it useful to provide at least a brief definition of each one. Smooth interiors and exteriors have been finished by wiping, presumably with a moistened hand, to remove surface irregularities. The surface may be uneven in the sense of showing gentle undulations, but never to the point that it feels rough to the touch. Rough surfaces, by contrast, both feel and look rough. Minor

imperfections including cavities, partially unobliterated coil joints, spatters, scrapes, and lumps characterize these surfaces. Random-brushed surfaces are matted by brush marks that intersect each other and show no obvious direction of orientation. Parallel-brushed surfaces, on the other hand, are covered by brush marks that in the main conform to a single line of orientation. Among all the vessel sherds examined from the three sites considered here, in nearly all cases where the orientation of a parallel-brushed sherd was clear (generally from a coil break) the interior parallel brushing was horizontal, running with the coils, and exterior parallel brushing was vertical, running across the coils. Thus, when both the interior and exterior of a sherd are parallel-brushed, the orientation of the brushing on one surface is generally perpendicular to the orientation of brushing on the opposite surface. Tooled surfaces are those in which a stick or very fine hard brush has left relatively deep gouge marks. Most commonly these occur as a series of parallel channels but in some cases the pattern is essentially random. Tooled surfaces are relatively rare in our collections and are found only on vessel interiors.

Notice that the classification of body sherds by interior and exterior surface treatment does not imply that the vessel from which each originated is uniformly characterized by the same attributes. Indeed, in our collections many of the larger sherds and vessel fragments formed by conjoining sherds exhibit two or more modes of treatment on the same surface; for the purpose of this analysis such sherds were classified according to the treatment characterizing the majority or plurality of the surface in question. The mixture of different treatments on the same vessel surface complicates analysis, but the frequency with which specific modes appear on sherd interiors and exteriors and co-occur in specific combinations on opposing sides of the same sherd provides perhaps the most concrete basis upon which ceramic assemblages can be compared.

The lack of independence between individual sherds, many of which will usually derive from the same vessels, precludes statistical tests routinely used to ascertain the probability of the pattern observed (cf. Spaulding 1953) within a single ceramic assemblage. Two different assemblages, however, can be meaningfully compared by use of Robinson's index of agreement (Robinson 1951), IA, though this statistic does not avoid the lack of independence inherent in data of this kind. This simple statistic is used here to quantify separately for exterior mode of surface treatment, interior mode of surface treatment, and joint combinations of exterior and interior modes of the same sherd the degree of similarity between

Bettinger

two ceramic assemblages. The index is easily calculated as:

$$IA_{jk} = 200 - \left(\sum_{i=1}^{m} \left| X_{ji} - X_{ki} \right| \right)$$

where IA_{jk} is the index of agreement between assemblages j and k, and X_{ji} is the proportion of i--a particular mode (exterior or interior) or combination of exterior and interior modes (depending on the case)--in assemblage j, and X_{ki} is the proportion of same mode or combination of modes in assemblage K. Put in plain words for the case in which it is being calculated for exterior modes, the index of agreement is obtained by finding for each exterior mode represented in at least one of the two sites being compared the difference in the percentage of sherds with that mode at one site and the percentage with the same mode at the second site. The sum of these differences, all taken as positive or absolute values, is subtracted from 200. Thus, should two sites show exactly the same percentages for every mode present, there would be no differences at all and the index of agreement would be: IA = 200 - 0 = 200. On the other hand should two assemblages share no modes in common--as for example when one site shows only one mode and a second site shows only a different mode--the sum of the differences would be 200 (100 for the percentage of the mode at the first site and 100 for the percentage of the mode at the second site) and the index of agreement would be: IA = 200 - 200 = 0. The same procedure would be used for calculations based on interior modes or joint exterior-interior combinations.

It is likely that computation of such agreement indices for the Great Basin ceramic assemblages already in hand would resolve many nagging problems surrounding the presumed distinctions between different late prehistoric Great Basin wares.

In the following analysis of the ceramics from Pinyon House, Two Eagles, and Crater Middens, indices of agreement are presented comparing each ceramic assemblage to those of the other two sites in terms of the frequency with which exterior modes, interior modes, and joint combinations of exterior-interior modes of surface treatment are represented. These analyses, thus, can be taken as examples of the approach advocated here for future Great Basin ceramic studies.

PINYON HOUSE

In keeping with their identification as Owens Valley Brown Ware, all 62 of the body sherds and the two rim sherds in the Pinyon House collection appear to represent vessels manufactured of residual clays shaped by coiling and scraping.

Wall thickness is variable:

	$\overline{X}$	S	Maximum	Minimum	n
wall thickness (cm)	0.61	0.16	0.9	0.3	64

The sherds large enough to be reliably classified exhibit the following composition with respect to surface treatment.

	EXTERIOR				
INTERIOR	Smooth	Rough	Random-Brushed	Parallel-Brushed	Total
Smooth	1	6	0	0	7(12%)
Rough	0	10	0	2	12(20%)
Random-Brushed	0	5	3	0	8(14%)
Parallel-Brushed	0	14*	12	4*	30(52%)
Tooled	0	1	0	0	1(2%)
TOTAL	1 (2%)	36 (62%)	15 (26%)	6 (10%)	58

*Note: each includes 1 rimsherd.

It is clear by inspection that rough exteriors, parallel-brushed interiors, rough and random-brushed exteriors in combination with parallel-brushed interiors, and rough exteriors in combination with rough interiors dominate this assemblage.

The following indices of agreement compare the body sherds from Pinyon House to those of Two Eagles and Crater Middens (see below) in terms of the distribution of exterior, interior, and joint exterior-interior modes of surface treatment.

Attribute	Pinyon House-Two Eagles IA	Pinyon House-Crater Middens IA
exterior	194	175
interior	146	169
exterior-interior	117	150

In comparison to both, Pinyon House shows the greatest resemblances in exterior surface treatment and the least resemblances in joint exterior-interior surface treatment. The strongest similarity is that between Pinyon House and Two Eagles in exterior surface treatment, the two being virtually identical in this respect. The similarity between Pinyon House and Crater Middens in exterior surface treatment is somewhat lower but still strong. On the other hand, in interior surface treatment and joint exterior-interior surface treatment Pinyon House is substantially more similar to Crater Middens than Two Eagles, although these values, especially for joint exterior-interior surface treatment, are uniformly lower than those noted for exterior surface treatment.

TWO EAGLES

There are 119 body sherds in the Two Eagles collection. Of these, 116 are thought to derive from a single vessel. Each of the remaining three is thought to represent one additional vessel. Without reference to the vessels they may represent, the Owens Valley Brown Ware body sherds large enough to be confidently classified from Two Eagles display the following composition with respect to modes of surface treatment. To reduce the lack of independence, conjoining fragments are treated as single sherds.

	EXTERIOR				
INTERIOR	Smooth	Rough	Random-Brushed	Parallel-Brushed	Total
Smooth	0	1	0	2	3(3%)
Rough	2*	1	0	0	3(3%)
Random-Brushed	0	3	9*	0	12(13%)
Parallel-Brushed	1	51++	14	6+++	72(78%)
Tooled	0	2*+	0	0	2(2%)
TOTAL	3 (3%)	58 (63%)	23 (25%)	8 (9%)	92

Notes: Entries marked by asterisks (*) denote categories that contain one sherd not belonging to the large group of sherds thought to represent a single vessel. Entries marked by (+) denote for each such mark one rim sherd.

For this same combined group of body sherds measured thickness for each sherd, including those within conjoining groups, yields the following summary statistics.

	$\overline{X}$	S	Maximum	Minimum	n
wall thickness (cm)	0.69	0.05	1.0	0.5	111

These data disclose substantial homogeneity within the Two Eagles ceramic assemblage, at least with respect to interior and joint exterior-interior surface treatment and thickness. The full range of surface treatments noted for Owens Valley Brown Ware is present in the collection, but 78 percent of the sherds exhibit parallel-brushed interiors and 55 percent exhibit the joint combination of rough exterior and parallel-brushed interior. Likewise, thickness, although it displays a substantial gross range from 0.5 cm to 1.0 cm varies within exceptionally narrow limits in that fully 66 percent of the specimens can be expected to fall between .64 cm and .74 cm.

The decided lack of variation among these sherds is consistent with the suspicion expressed that with only three exceptions they derive from a single vessel. If so, these data provide at least a rough approximation of the minimal variation to be expected in any collection of Owens Valley Brown Ware sherds. For this reason, it is hardly surprising that when the body sherd data from Two Eagles are compared to those previously presented for Pinyon House, the Two Eagles assemblage is found to be by far the more homogeneous with respect to interior surface treatment, joint exterior-interior surface treatment, and wall thickness. For the same reason, a nearly identical pattern is obtained when the Two Eagles body sherds are compared to those from Crater Middens, which are described subsequently. Here again, the Two Eagles collection exhibits substantially less variation in these attributes than does the Crater Middens collection. As a consequence of its greater homogeneity in interior surface, when measured by the Robinson index of agreement the Two Eagles ceramic assemblage shares little affinity with those of either Pinyon House or Crater Middens in these attributes.

Attribute	Two Eagles-Pinyon House IA	Two Eagles-Crater Middens IA
interior	146	127
exterior-interior	117	101

Given the distinctive character of the Two Eagles ceramic collection and the differences separating it from the collections from the other two sites, it is remarkable that in terms of the distribution and diversity of exterior surface treatment modes the body sherds from Two Eagles are virtually identical to those of both Pinyon House and Crater Middens (see below). In all three cases, rough exteriors constitute a substantial majority, followed by random-brushed exteriors, and either parallel-brushed exteriors (Two Eagles and Pinyon House) or smooth exteriors (Crater Middens). The Robinson index of agreement for exterior surface treatment underscores the similarities Two Eagles shares with Pinyon House and Crater Middens in terms of this attribute.

Attribute	Two Eagles-Pinyon House IA	Two Eagles-Crater Middens IA
exterior	194	175

A preliminary conclusion drawn from the above is that at least in central Owens Valley, exterior surface treatment of Owens Valley Brown Ware sherds is invariant. This is not meant in the sense that only one mode is present but rather in the sense that individual vessels appear to display the same modes in the same proportions as larger assemblages comprising many vessels. This further implies that diversity of exterior surface treatment is an unreliable measure of the number of vessels represented in any particular ceramic assemblage. Interior surface treatment, and consequently joint exterior-interior surface treatment, and thickness, on the other hand, appear to vary between individual Owens Valley Brown Ware vessels at least to the degree noted for these attributes in the Pinyon House and Crater Middens. They are, thus, useful in describing the variability within a collection as well as in determining the number of vessels it contains.

CRATER MIDDENS

The 472 undecorated body sherds from Crater Middens display the full range of exterior and interior modes of surface treatment. Those large enough to be classified reliably exhibit the following composition with respect to these modes.

	EXTERIOR				
INTERIOR	Smooth	Rough	Random-Brushed	Parallel-Brushed	Total
Smooth	33	47	2	1	83(26%)
Rough	2	65	2	1	70(22%)
Random-Brushed		11	7	5	23(7%)
Parallel-Brushed	5	60	42	29	136(43%)
Tooled		5		1	6(2%)
TOTAL	40 (13%)	188 (59%)	53 (17%)	37 (12%)	318

For this same group of sherds, measurements of wall thickness yield the following summary statistics.

	$\bar{X}$	S	Maximum	Minimum	n
wall thickness (cm)	0.64	0.14	1.1	0.4	318

It is apparent from the tabulation of surface treatment that the assemblage of body sherds from Crater Middens is in all respects more heterogeneous than the assemblages previously described from Pinyon House and Two Eagles; that is, sherds in this collection are more evenly distributed between different modes of exterior, interior, and joint exterior-interior surface treatment. Detailed inspection of these data in conjunction with Robinson's index of agreement comparing Crater Middens to Pinyon House and Two Eagles, however, indicates that the differences between these three assemblages are not substantial when differences in their nature and size of each assemblage is taken into account nor are they of uniform magnitude for all attributes. The Robinson's indices of agreement are presented below.

Attribute	Crater Middens-Pinyon House IA	Crater Middens-Two Eagles IA
exterior	175	175
interior	169	127
exterior-interior	150	101

It is evident first that regardless of the differences that separate the ceramic samples from these sites, the distribution of exterior surface treatment observed in the Crater Middens assemblage is comparable to that observed in both the Pinyon House and Two Eagles assemblages--which are themselves virtually identical in this respect. As noted earlier, this suggests that exterior surface treatment is rather stable both between vessels and between assemblages in the Owens Valley Brown Ware of central Owens Valley.

Second, there are strong similarities in interior and joint exterior-interior surface treatment between the Crater Middens assemblage and the Pinyon House assemblage despite the substantially smaller size of the Pinyon House collection. The Two Eagles assemblage, on the other hand, shows no strong resemblance to that of Crater Middens in these respects, just as was shown earlier it does not bear much resemblance to the assemblage from Pinyon House. This makes sense if it is understood that the body sherds from Two Eagles probably represent a single shattered vessel. Thus the close similarity between Crater Middens and Pinyon House in terms of interior and joint exterior-interior surface treatment of body sherds is between assemblages consisting of multiple vessels; the differences in these respects between these two sites and Two Eagles is that between assemblages consisting of multiple vessels and an assemblage consisting of one vessel. It seems reasonable to propose on this basis that interior and joint exterior-interior surface treatment vary between individual vessels of Owens Valley Brown Ware--either as the result of functional differences between vessels or the stylistic predilections of their makers--but at the same time these attributes are stable with respect to distribution and diversity between assemblages.

Comparison between the Crater Middens assemblage and the Pinyon House assemblage, both consisting of multiple vessels, shows that the two differ most markedly in the more frequent presence at Crater Middens of sherds with smooth exteriors and sherds with smooth interiors, frequently but not exclusively in joint combination, and the less frequent presence of sherds with random-brushed exteriors and sherds with random-brushed and parallel-brushed interiors. Sherds with rough exteriors and sherds with rough interiors occur in about the same proportion at both sites. On this basis it might be suggested that these are alternative methods of surface treatment in the sense that they seem to vary inversely: smooth exteriors increase at the expense of random-brushed exteriors and smooth interiors increase at the expense of random-brushed and parallel-brushed interiors, and conversely. This might represent stylistic preference, although given the differences in settlement between Pinyon House--an upland pinyon camp, and Crater Middens--a lowland occupation site, there is also the possibility that it is due to functional differences between these settlement categories. Whatever these differences are, it is clear that they do not affect the frequency with which rough exteriors and rough interiors are represented, though it is not clear whether the observed stability of these attributes is a matter of function or style.

Comparison of the summary statistics for sherd wall thickness from all three sites leads to essentially the same conclusions as that based on surface treatment. In this case, sherds from Crater Middens are distinctly thicker than those from Pinyon House, but the differences between these two sites in terms of this attribute are less than the differences separating either one from Two Eagles. Further, the standard deviations of wall thickness from Crater Middens and Pinyon House are virtually identical and substantially greater than that of the Two Eagles assemblage. This also suggests that, like interior and joint exterior-interior surface treatment, wall thickness is more variable between than within individual vessels--a conclusion not intuitively obvious by casual inspection of complete Owens Valley Brown Ware vessels, which often appear excessively lumpy and irregular.

CONCLUSIONS

It remains to be demonstrated what these differences in attribute variability mean with regard to the definition of Owens Valley Brown Ware. It may be, on the one hand, that the observed stable patterning of exterior surface treatment distinguishes this ware from others in the Great Basin. In this case, variation in interior surface treatment, joint exterior-interior surface treatment, and thickness would presumably reflect phenomena crosscutting, i.e., at work within, the cultural system responsible for and reflected by Owens Valley Brown Ware. Variability as a consequence of vessel function--and in turn site function and

settlement pattern--and stylistic variation as a consequence of social, political, or ritual organization might reasonably be expected to be among the more important of these.

On the other hand, the pattern of exterior surface treatment observed on Owens Valley Brown Ware sherds from central Owens Valley may be duplicated in brown-ware collections from throughout the western Great Basin or even the whole of the Great Basin. If so, surface treatment would obviously not be a defining characteristic for Owens Valley Brown Ware. In this case, Owens Valley Brown Ware might still qualify as a legitimate ware, distinct from other Great Basin ceramics, if it could be shown that it displays some distinctive pattern of composition with respect to interior surface treatment, joint exterior-interior surface treatment, or thickness, either alone or in conjunction with each other. The residual variation in these attributes--that is, the variability remaining when the pattern taken to define the ware is excluded from consideration --would then constitute the various functional, social, political, and ritual phenomena mentioned earlier.

Finally, Owens Valley Brown Ware would be invalid in a typological sense if either of two circumstances is found to apply. First, if the stable patterning in exterior surface treatment characterizes the whole of Great Basin ceramics and the pattern observed in interior and joint exterior-interior surface treatment and wall thickness also characterizes all Great Basin ceramics or the pattern observed in these latter attributes characterizes only central Owens Valley. In the former, there would be one Great Basin ceramic type--a term for which would be needed although Owens Valley Brown Ware would do--and no variability accounted for by local variations, ritual, political, and social organization or settlement pattern. In other words a very rigidly defined type. In the latter, the type would also be defined for the Great Basin as a whole, but within this would exist functional, social, political, and ritually related variations.

Second, Owens Valley would cease to be a viable typological designation if the invariant pattern of exterior surface treatment and the variation in interior and joint exterior-interior surface treatment and wall thickness all were unique to central Owens Valley. In this instance, the patterning in these attributes would be entirely the result of local variations of function and political, social, and ritual organization.

Implicit in the above is the notion that it would be premature to dismiss as invalid the Great Basin wares presently recognized without ever actually having put their validity to the test. Granted, there is every temptation to do so. The suggestion by some contributors to this volume that all ware designations at once be dropped and replaced with a single "Generic Great Basin Brown Ware," for instance, has the advantage of simplicity: with only one ware to contend with, archaeologists could continue to present brief, qualitative descriptions of ceramics, in the content belief that they <u>knew</u> what they were. But if anything is certain about Great Basin ceramics, it is that with regard to intersite and interregional variation we know next to nothing. If this statement rings true, then it follows that to classify all Great Basin ceramics under a single typological designation is no more justified than the current system of ware designation (unless it is meant merely as a morphological designation in which case the simple term "ceramics" is clearer and more correct). In fact, reclassification along these lines is worse because it implies that something new has been learned to justify this—which it obviously has not.

The basic problem in Great Basin ceramic studies is not one of nomenclature and it cannot be resolved by innovations in nomenclature. The problem lies in the degree to which ceramics vary between sites and regions, and it can only be resolved by undertaking tedious comparisons between ceramic assemblages from different sites and different regions.

REFERENCES CITED

(Citations not listed here will be found in the Annotated and Indexed Bibliography of Ceramics at the back of this volume.)

Bettinger, Robert L.
1975   Surface Archaeology of Owens Valley, Eastern California: Prehistoric Man-Land Relationships in the Great Basin. Ph.D. dissertation, Department of Anthropology, University of California, Riverside.

Robinson, W. S.
1951   A Method for Chronologically Ordering Archaeological Deposits. *American Antiquity* 16(4):293-301.

WHAT MEAN THESE SHERDS? A FUNCTIONAL APPROACH TO FREMONT CERAMICS IN THE WESTERN PERIPHERY

Steven R. James

INTRODUCTION

Recently, Madsen (1979) has stated that after 50 years of research the Fremont remain a perplexing problem. Since Madsen was referring to the Fremont heartland, their presence in peripheral regions such as eastern Nevada is even more enigmatic. We do not know, for instance, what Fremont ceramics and other Fremont traits in the western periphery indicate. Did the Fremont occupy the region or are their ceramics the result of trade or exchange with Prenumic or Numic hunter-gatherer populations?

Part of our inability to understand the Fremont in the western periphery stems from a lack of in-depth research on this problem. But beyond this, it is a matter of how the existing Fremont data have been examined. While other Fremont traits could be examined, their ceramics are the most diagnostic cultural indicators found in the region and, thus, provide a reliable means for assessing their presence.

The orientation of this paper is twofold. First, a summary of the Fremont ceramic evidence in the western periphery is presented. Second, a model is developed and several hypotheses examined which could account for the distribution of Fremont ceramics in the region.

HISTORY OF RESEARCH

The western periphery of the Fremont consists of western Utah and eastern Nevada where Fremont ceramics have been recovered (Figure 32). Most of this region lies in the eastern Great Basin, but a portion of southeastern Nevada, i.e., Meadow Valley Wash, White River, and Pahranagat Valley, is within the Colorado River drainage.

The presence of the Fremont in the western periphery was noted initially during the 1920s (Harrington 1926, 1928; Judd 1926:11-12, 60-61; Steward 1933b:5). On the basis of a few handfuls of sherds, Harrington (1926, 1928) outlined the western extension of "pueblo" (now Fremont and Virgin Branch Anasazi) groups in eastern and southern Nevada. Harrington's pottery boundary ran from Cobre, Nevada, about midway between the towns of Wells and Wendover, south through Steptoe Valley to Ely (Figure 32). The line then followed the present route of Highway 6 southwest from Ely and turned south toward California before reaching Tonopah. Harrington's pottery boundary has been depicted over the years by other researchers with few changes (Grosscup 1957; Shutler 1961: Plate 1; Hester 1973: Fig. 12; Tuohy 1973: Fig. 1).

Archaeological investigations by Harrington and his associates during the 1930s yielded further, albeit sketchy, data on the Fremont in eastern Nevada, which they generally referred to as an Early Pueblo or Pueblo II culture (Harrington 1932, 1932a; Wheeler 1936, 1938, 1942). Unfortunately, they did not describe the ceramics or relate them to contemporary descriptions of Fremont pottery (i.e., Steward 1936). Osborne (1941) also described three Fremont sherd types collected in eastern Nevada by amateurs from Ely.

Teams from the University of Utah collected more detailed data on the Fremont of the region in the 1940s and 1950s from sites along the Nevada-Utah border. These included survey and excavations in the Deep Creek Mountains (Malouf 1940, 1946; Malouf et al. 1940); survey and test excavations at sites in western Utah and extreme eastern Nevada (Rudy 1953); excavation of Pine Park Shelter in southwestern Utah (Rudy 1954); and excavation of the Garrison site, a Fremont village in Snake Valley on the Nevada-Utah border (Taylor 1954). Rudy's (1953:79-94) work in western Utah included a detailed analysis of Fremont ceram-

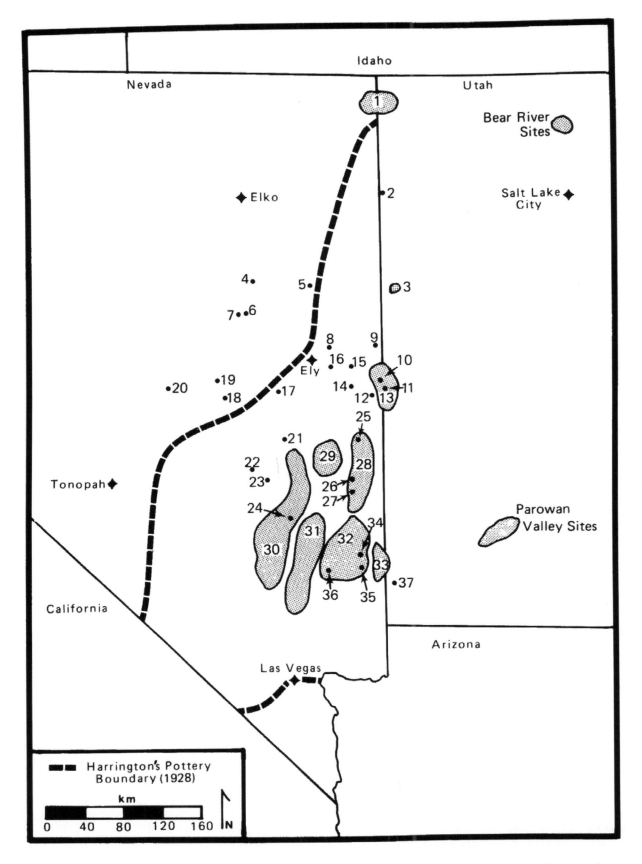

Figure 32. Location of Fremont ceramic sites in the western periphery. Site numbers are discussed in Table 4.

ics which became the basis for subsequent studies (e.g., D. Madsen 1970; R. Madsen 1977). In his analysis, Rudy (1953:79) placed the Fremont pottery of western Utah and eastern Nevada within what he called the Desert Gray Ware series. He also established a new type, Snake Valley Gray, which reclassified Steward's (1936:11-16) Sevier Black-on-gray and Sevier Corrugated as Snake Valley types.

Since the 1960s, a number of excavations and surveys have been conducted in eastern Nevada (see James 1981 for a complete summary). Major sites which have yielded evidence of Fremont occupations include O'Malley Shelter, Conaway Shelter, and the Scott site in south-eastern Nevada (Fowler et al. 1973), and Swallow Shelter and other sites in the Goose Creek-Grouse Creek area of extreme northeastern Nevada and northwestern Utah (Dalley 1976).

CERAMIC EVIDENCE

Archaeological investigations in the western periphery have yielded at least 94 Fremont pottery-bearing sites. Table 4 summarizes the pottery types and sherd counts from these sites; site locations are depicted in Figure 32. There are more Fremont ceramic sites in eastern Nevada, for the table is compiled mainly from published sources, and no attempt was made at a comprehensive listing of all recorded sites reported to contain Fremont pottery. Data from early workers such as Harrington and Wheeler could not be used since their pottery descriptions are vague.

As indicated in Table 4, a total of 5,639 Fremont sherds has been reported from 86 of the 94 sites listed. Most sites contained fewer than 25 sherds. In contrast, the Fremont village at Garrison in Snake Valley yielded the highest count with 1,992 sherds (Taylor 1954), representing 35 percent of the total. Rudy (1953) also reported another 848 sherds from nine Snake Valley sites, including sherds from the Garrison site. When combined with the sherds recovered from the Garrison site excavations, 50 percent of the Fremont sherd collection in the western periphery is from Snake Valley. Oddly enough, nearby Kachina Cave and Amy's Shelter had few Fremont ceramics. O'Malley Shelter, Conaway Shelter, and the Scott site in southeastern Nevada produced a total of 1,442 sherds, or 26 percent. In sum, 76 percent of the collection is derived from several sites in two areas.

The ceramic data reveal another interesting aspect with respect to Harrington's (1928) "pueblo" pottery boundary. An examination of Figure 32 shows that over a dozen sites containing Fremont ceramics have been reported in recent years west of Harrington's boundary. Thus, the limit of Fremont ceramics can be extended farther west. With the exception of the Goose Creek-Grouse Creek area, most of these sites had few Fremont sherds (see Table 4). The small number of Fremont sherds along this pottery boundary is suggestive of trade, as discussed later in this paper.

The majority of Fremont ceramics in the western periphery consists of Snake Valley Gray, with 3,191 sherds or 57 percent of the collection listed in Table 4. Snake Valley Black-on-gray is the second-most common ware (785 sherds, 14 percent), followed closely by Great Salt Lake Gray (747 sherds, 13 percent). Snake Valley Corrugated and Sevier Gray constitute 8 percent and 7 percent of the collection, respectively. The remaining types in the Other category, Sevier Black-on-gray, Ivie Creek Black-on-white, and Promontory Gray, are represented by only 15 sherds or 0.2 percent.

The ceramic data clearly indicate the extent of the Fremont in the western periphery. The presence of Fremont pottery alone, however, is insufficient to demonstrate that they occupied the entire region. Although the Fremont are generally considered to be horti-culturalists (contra Madsen 1979), some areas in eastern Nevada are unsuited for growing maize due to the limited number of frost-free days. The pottery could have been discarded during hunting-gathering forays from established Fremont villages or could have been the result of trade or exchange with neighboring non-Fremont groups. But how do we differentiate between these alternatives on the basis of pottery?

One way is to develop a model based on the function pottery vessels served among the Fremont as a means of assessing their occurrence in the archaeological record. The rest of this paper is devoted to developing and testing such a model.

THE MODEL

In many prehistoric societies the form of a pottery vessel often determined its function. Vessel shape, therefore, can provide a clue to the functions different vessel types may have served. Using this information, certain assumptions about the function of Fremont vessels can be proposed from their shape. Once the functions of the Fremont vessels have been postulated, these data can then be used to test several hypotheses regarding the nature of Fremont occupation in the western periphery.

Vessel shapes for the Fremont wares have been described by Madsen (1977), data summarized in Table 5 for the pottery types which have been reported from the region. Jars are the predominant shape for Snake Valley Gray, Snake Valley Corrugated, Great Salt Lake Gray, Sevier Gray, and Promontory Gray. The majority of these consist of vertical neck and flaring

TABLE 4. Distribution of Fremont Ceramics in the Western Periphery

Site	Map No.*	SVG	SVCor.	SVB/G	GSLG	Sev.G.	Other	Total	Reference
Swallow Shelter	1				131			131	Dalley 1976
Thomas Shelter	1				25			25	Dalley 1976
Kimber Shelter	1				8			8	Dalley 1976
Beatty Springs	1				20			20	Dalley 1976
Remnant Cave	1				24			24	Berry 1976
Danger Cave	2				117			117	Jennings 1957; Madsen 1970
Juke Box Cave	2					2		2	Jennings 1957
Coal Shovel Shelter	3				24			24	Lindsay and Sargent 1979
Scribble Rockshelter	3				54	10		64	Lindsay and Sargent 1979
Deep Creek Area: 9 sites	3	2			10	8	5	25	Lindsay and Sargent 1979
Bronco Charlie Cave	4	1						1	Casjens 1974
26WP1437	5				1			1	James 1978
Newark Cave	6			1				1	Fowler 1968b
26WP1578	7	X						X	Emslie 1982
26WP1435	8	X	X	X		X		X	James 1978
Amy's Shelter	9	1	1					2	Gruhn 1979
Kachina Cave	9				15			15	Tuohy 1979
26WP200 and 201	10	X	X	X				X	Fowler 1968a
Garrison Site	11	1033	185	330	311	133		1992	Taylor 1954
Wh-44	12	1						1	Shutler 1961
Snake Valley: 9 sites	13	350	131	133	7	227		848	Rudy 1953
26WP1244	14	6		1				7	James and Zeier 1981
26WP880	15					2		2	James 1977a
26WP882	15	12						12	James 1977a
26WP737	16	X						X	Fowler 1975, 1976a, 1976b
26WP903	17	3						3	James 1977b
Park Range: 1 site	18	X	X	X				X	Robert Crabtree, p.c.
26NY3684	19		?					?	Site form
26NY3685	19			9				9	Site form
26NY3683	19	41				X		41	Site form
Monitor Valley	20					?		?	Thomas 1982:161

Site	Map No.*	SVG	SVCor.	SVB/G	GSLG	Sev.G.	Other	Total	Reference
26NY556	21			?				?	York 1977
Slivovitz Shelter	22	15	9	13				37	Busby 1979
Avocado Shelter	22	5		5				10	Busby 1979
Civa Shelter II	23	14		2				16	Busby 1979
Mariah Site	24			4		46		50	Brooks et al. 1977
26LN2028	25	10						10	Site form
26LN2903	26	1						1	James 1979
26LN2902	27	10	10					20	James 1979
Upper Meadow Valley: 7 sites	28	180	34	22				236	Fowler and Sharrock 1973
Fairview Range: 5 sites	29	69	2	25				96	Fowler and Sharrock 1973
Pahranagat Valley: 6 sites	30	9	1				10	20	Fowler and Sharrock 1973
Delamar Valley: 2 sites	31	5	1	3				9	Fowler and Sharrock 1973
Middle Meadow Valley: 11 sites	32	133	6	10				149	Fowler and Sharrock 1973
Beaver Dam Wash: 3 sites	33	36	7					43	Fowler and Sharrock 1973
Scott Site	34	422	70	84				576	Fowler et al. 1973
O'Malley Shelter	35	457	6	104		2		569	Fowler et al. 1973
Conaway Shelter	36	264	8	25				297	Fowler et al. 1973
Pine Park Shelter	37	111		14				125	Rudy 1954
TOTAL: 94 sites		3191	471	785	747	430	15	5639	

* Map No. corresponds to locations in Figure 32

Pottery abbreviations

SVG: Snake Valley Gray
SVCor.:   Snake Valley Corrugated
SVB/G: Snake Valley Black-on-gray
GSLG: Great Salt Lake Gray

Sev.G: Sevier Gray
Other: other Fremont types
X: sherd count not reported
?:   questionable identification

TABLE 5. Fremont Vessel Shapes

Type	Vertical Neck Jars	Flaring Neck Jars	Pitchers	Bowls
Snake Valley Gray	+	+	o	o
Snake Valley Black-on-gray	o	o	-	+
Snake Valley Corrugated	o	+	-	o
Great Salt Lake Gray	+	+	o	o
Sevier Gray	+	+	o	o
Promontory Gray	+	+	-	o

+ = present; o = occasional; - = absent.

TABLE 6. Vessel Shapes Represented in the Western Periphery

Site	Site Type	SVG	SVCor.	SVB/G	GSLG	Sev.G.	Sev.B/G	Reference
Swallow Shelter	camp				jar (9)			Dalley 1976
Thomas Shelter	camp				jar (2)			Dalley 1976
Kimber Shelter	camp				jar (1)			Dalley 1976
Beatty Springs	camp				jar (1)			Dalley 1976
Scribble Rockshelter	camp				jar (2)			Lindsay and Sargent 1979
42JB3	village?	jar (1)					bowl (1)	Lindsay and Sargent 1979
42JB154	camp						bowl (1)	Lindsay and Sargent 1979
Amy's Shelter	camp	bowl (1)	jar (1)					Gruhn 1979
Garrison Site	village	jar (+)	jar (+)	jar (+) bowl (+)		jar (+) pitcher (+)		Taylor 1954
26WP1244	camp			bowl (1)				James and Zeier 1981
26NY3685	camp			bowl (1)				Site form
Slivovitz Shelter	camp		jar?(1)	bowl (2)				Busby 1979
Avocado Shelter	camp	bowl (1)		bowl (1)				Busby 1979
Civa Shelter II	camp	jar (1)		bowl (1)				Busby 1979
O'Malley Shelter	camp	jar (+) bowl (+)		bowl (+)				Fowler et al. 1973

Pottery abbreviations are contained in Table 4.

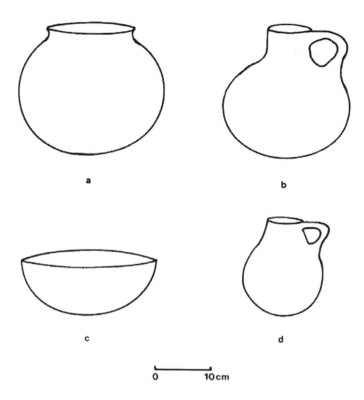

Figure 33. Outlines of Fremont vessel shapes: (a) flaring neck jar, (b) vertical neck jar, (c) bowl, and (d) pitcher (after Dodd 1982).

neck jars although several other neck shapes also occur in a few types. Flaring neck jars generally have wide mouths with short flaring or everted rims; in contrast, vertical neck jars have smaller openings and high, straight rims (Figure 33a, b). Vertical neck jars in Snake Valley Gray, Great Salt Lake Gray, and Sevier Gray almost always have loop handles, whereas they are generally absent on flaring neck jars. The differences between these two jar neck shapes appear to be functional as discussed below.

Pitchers and bowls are the other vessel shapes in Fremont wares (Table 5, Figure 33c, d). Pitchers are not a common shape and occasionally are represented in Snake Valley Gray, Great Salt Lake Gray, and Sevier Gray. They are virtually absent in the other types. Bowls are the predominant shape of Snake Valley Black-on-gray and occasionally occur in the other types. Both small (< 20 cm diameter) and large (> 20 cm diameter) bowls were manufactured.

Since analyses of Fremont ceramics have been mostly descriptive, vessel function has not been discussed in any detail. Madsen (1977) did briefly note that most Fremont wares were probably used for cooking and storage and that bowls were for serving and possibly

storage. Their functions need to be elaborated upon, however. In order to do so, we have to draw upon the work of other researchers for a comparative basis.

Hill (1970:49-52) has provided a good discussion of vessel shape and function as it related to ascertaining room function at Broken K Pueblo in eastern Arizona. From ethnographic Hopi and Zuni data, Hill inferred the uses of various vessels. Cooking vessels were usually textured utility pottery. Bowls were used in the preparation and serving of food. Jars with small mouths were probably used for transport and storage of water, whereas food was generally stored in large jars. The function of these vessel shapes generally is consistent with worldwide ethnographic data (Henrickson and McDonald 1983).

Vessel functions among the Fremont were probably quite similar to Southwestern vessels. Cooking appears to have been performed in Fremont jars with flaring necks. This was also the most common shape for Snake Valley Corrugated vessels, a type inferred to heat faster than noncorrugated wares (Dodd 1982:103; see also Gifford and Smith 1978:6; McGregor 1965: 282), and thus, would have been well suited for cooking. The vertical neck jars with loop handles would have functioned as containers for transport and possibly water storage (cf. Henrickson and McDonald 1983). Fremont jars would also have been used for storage of plant foods. Several jars containing a variety of seeds were recovered, for example, from Evans Mound in southwestern Utah (Dodd 1982:49).

Fremont bowls were used primarily in the preparation and serving of food, functions analogous to Southwestern bowls. The most common Fremont bowl type is Snake Valley Black-on-gray. Since painted vessels would probably have been more costly to make in terms of time invested than unpainted Fremont wares, some Snake Valley Black-on-gray bowls may have served more important functions in the society. Evidence for this comes from the Evans Mound where a number of these sherds were drilled along broken edges for the purpose of repairing cracked vessels (Dodd 1982:52). Leather thongs or pieces of cordage were tied through the holes to make the bowls last longer, suggesting that these bowls had a high curation rate and were probably held in higher esteem than plain gray vessels. If Snake Valley Black-on-gray bowls were, indeed, the most prestigious of the Fremont wares, then they may also have been important as trade items with neighboring Fremont groups or other peoples.

HYPOTHESES AND TEST IMPLICATIONS

Archaeological investigations have generated, in part, three hypotheses which have been proposed to explain the Fremont in the western periphery. They are reviewed here, and test implications using vessel shape and function and other ceramic data are discussed.

Hypothesis 1. The Fremont utilized the western periphery on a seasonal hunting-gathering basis coming from established villages at Garrison, in Parowan Valley, and along the eastern shores of Great Salt Lake.

Many researchers have suggested that the Fremont seasonally occupied the region west of known villages in the eastern Great Basin (Aikens 1970:195; Dalley 1976:161; Fowler et al. 1973:72; Jennings 1978:234; Madsen 1975).

> Although Fremont peoples occupied the study area [southeastern Nevada] and practiced some horticulture, they apparently did not build pueblos. The presence of horticulture but no village sites may indicate a seasonal occupation of the area, with small groups moving in from the north or east during the spring and summer and returning to those areas in the fall (Fowler, Madsen, and Hattori 1973:72).

Dalley offered a similar explanation for extreme northwestern Utah and northeastern Nevada:

> Logically, and on the basis of similarities in some artifact types, the Fremont peoples were coming into the area from the east, probably from the numerous villages clustered along the lower Bear River.... It is, however, a little surprising to find so much evidence of occupation at such distance from the nearest known permanent settlements (Dalley 1976:161; emphasis added).

Madsen (1975) goes even further in proposing that Numic groups occupied the same temporary hunting-gathering sites of the Fremont in the eastern Great Basin and that competition between them may have led to the eventual demise of the Fremont.

There are, however, several drawbacks to a seasonal Fremont occupation of the western periphery by Utah villagers. With the exception of the Garrison village site, one wonders why Fremont groups from the Bear River and Parowan Valley areas would forage so far west from their villages when the local environment contained all the plant and animal resources needed. Moreover, the Bear River Fremont would have had to travel around the north end of Great Salt Lake and across a portion of Great Salt Lake Desert to reach the Goose Creek-Grouse Creek area, a distance of about 160 km. Yet, within 16 km east of their villages is the Wasatch Range. A similar situation holds for the Parowan Valley villages nestled at the base

of the Hurricane Cliffs. In contrast, the distance to O'Malley Shelter and other areas in southeastern Nevada from the Parowan villages is at least 130 km. Only if population increases or other mechanisms depleted nearby resource areas would these villagers have possibly journeyed into eastern Nevada.

If the Fremont did occupy the western periphery on a seasonal basis, the pottery data can provide one way of testing this hypothesis. As a seasonal Fremont settlement pattern should be that of temporary camps, only certain types of pottery vessels should be represented. We would expect to see vertical neck jars used for water containers, cooking vessels such as flaring neck jars, and perhaps a few bowls for food preparation and serving. The temporary nature of these camps would suggest that the number of sherds and vessel types represented in the archaeological record would be limited. Further, we would not expect evidence of pottery manufacture at temporary camps, since this activity would have been conducted at village sites and not by seasonal Fremont groups.

Hypothesis 2. Pottery-using Fremont groups who relied mainly on a hunting and gathering economy occupied the western periphery.

Fowler, Madsen, and Hattori (1973:72) have suggested that as an alternative to seasonal use, the Fremont may have occupied the region on a permanent basis. To take their suggestion a step further, the western periphery Fremont could have been part-time horticulturalists who relied even more on hunting and gathering than the Sevier Fremont villages to the east (cf. Madsen 1979; Madsen and Lindsay 1977:91). During their annual hunting-gathering round, these Fremont people could have planted maize at springs and along drainages and returned later in the fall in much the same manner as the Southern Paiute on the Colorado Plateau (Kelly 1964). Such Fremont peoples could be seen as buffering groups between the Sevier Fremont to the east and the Prenumic or Numic hunter-gatherers to the west. Exchange of goods, ideas, and perhaps intermarriages could have occurred between these Fremont and non-Fremont groups.

If Fremont hunter-gatherers resided in the western periphery, we should expect to see a full range of site types—habitation, field camps, and task sites. The Fremont ceramics should reflect this range of site types. Major habitation sites should contain the full range of vessel types represented in Fremont ceramics, including both types of jars, bowls, and pitchers. Evidence of pottery manufacture should also be represented at the habitation sites. Temporary camps should contain the same types of vessels as discussed in the first hypothesis. Task sites would have very little pottery, only one or two broken vessels, depending upon whether pottery was used in the activity.

Hypothesis 3. Fremont ceramics in the western periphery represent pottery traded with Prenumic or Numic peoples to the west.

The possibility that Fremont ceramics in peripheral regions represent trade wares has been suggested at one time or another (Fowler and Sharrock 1973:135; Madsen 1970:68; Rudy 1953:74, 81). Fowler and Sharrock (1973:135) mentioned that "the apparent contemporaneity of Shoshonean and Fremont peoples in the area suggests that Shoshonean peoples living in Pahranagat Valley may have obtained some Puebloan pottery in trade."

Trade or exchange of Fremont ceramics probably did occur with Prenumic or Numic groups unless, of course, the region just west of the Fremont was vacant prior to the Numic expansion, a situation which seems doubtful. The problem is in discerning what types of vessels or other items were traded. For our purposes it is assumed that vessels which were highly regarded by the Fremont would have been preferred trade wares. One such vessel appears to have been Snake Valley Black-on-gray bowls which show evidence of considerable repair and hence curation in the Parowan Valley sites (cf. Dodd 1982:52).

If trade did occur with Prenumic or Numic groups in the western periphery, and Snake Valley Black-on-gray bowls were one of these trade items, then we would expect to find these bowls on the edge of Fremont territory in higher proportions than plain gray wares.

APPLICATIONS OF THE MODEL AND HYPOTHESES TESTS

Data on Fremont vessel shapes recovered from sites in the western periphery are presented in Table 6. Unfortunately, vessel shapes could be determined for only 15 of the 94 western periphery sites listed in Table 4. Since most researchers did not report this information, data on vessel shapes from the region are relatively limited. Nevertheless, we can make some preliminary tests of the three hypotheses proposed above based on the model.

Four excavated sites in the Goose Creek-Grouse Creek area in the north produced data on vessel shapes. The vessels from Swallow Shelter consist of wide-mouthed, short-necked Great Salt Lake Gray jars with straight or out-curving rims. According to the model, the Fremont used jars of this shape for cooking. Extensive blackening of the sherds and the presence of a probable organic residue on the insides of several sherds (Dalley 1976:56)

suggest some support for this function. It was estimated that at least nine jars were represented in the collection from the shelter.

Thomas Shelter in the nearby vicinity yielded a similar Great Salt Lake Gray jar as well as one with a high vertical neck (Dalley 1976:88). The latter was probably a water container as indicated by the model. While one Great Salt Lake Gray jar each appears to be represented at Kimber Shelter and Beatty Springs, the function of these was not apparent from the descriptions (Dalley 1976:106, 143).

Three sites in the Deep Creek Mountains provided evidence on vessel shapes. Two Great Salt Lake Gray wide-mouthed jars with estimated 30-cm diameter openings were represented among the Fremont sherds from Scribble Shelter (Lindsay and Sargent 1979:53). The jars probably functioned as cooking vessels; they may also have been used to store wild plant seeds. A Sevier Gray vessel of unspecified shape was present as well. One Snake Valley Gray jar with a small neck (6.5-7.0 cm diameter) and straight sides was estimated from a rim sherd recovered at 42-JB-3. Two Sevier Black-on-gray bowls were each represented at 42-JB-3 and 42-JB-154. Although site 42-JB-3 is considered a possible village (Lindsay and Sargent 1979), the small number of Fremont vessels and sherds point to a temporary campsite. The pottery data are, however, only from the surface and excavations may disclose a different picture.

The ceramics from the Goose Creek-Grouse Creek area and the Deep Creek Mountains indicate that the sites were temporary seasonal camps. Hypothesis 1, that of seasonal occupation by Fremont villagers from the east, seems the least likely since these temporary camps are a considerable distance from Fremont villages along Great Salt Lake as discussed earlier. On the other hand, Hypothesis 2 is more plausible suggesting that a hunting-gathering Fremont occupied this portion of Nevada and that nearby major Fremont habitation sites have simply not been located. In support of this hypothesis, Madsen (1982:218-219) recently has suggested that the Deep Creek Mountains sites represent a portion of the hunting-gathering seasonal round of a less-settled Fremont similar to Steward's Shoshonean pattern. The Deep Creek sites, however, could also have been occupied on a seasonal basis by Fremont peoples from the Garrison site. Or perhaps 42-JB-3 is, indeed, a village site. Either of these alternatives would still be in accord with Hypothesis 2.

The widest variety of vessels occurred at the Garrison site, the only definite Fremont village in the western periphery (Taylor 1954). Vessel shapes include Snake Valley Gray and corrugated jars, Snake Valley Black-on-gray bowls and jars, and Sevier Gray jars and pitchers. These vessels would have served various functions in the everyday lives of the

Fremont inhabitants, and, as predicted by Hypothesis 2, the site would have been a major occupation area.

The highest number of vessels at any site in southeastern Nevada came from O'Malley Shelter (Fowler et al. 1973). Snake Valley Gray and Black-on-gray bowls were the most common vessels based on the recovered rim sherds. Snake Valley Gray jars included both wide-mouthed types (15-20 cm diameter necks) with recurved rims and narrow-necked (10-15 cm diameter) jars with vertical rims. The bowls probably functioned in the preparation and serving of food. Cooking and water containers are indicated by the jar shapes. Another interesting aspect of the Fremont occupation at O'Malley Shelter is that local pottery-making may have been carried out as suggested by several unfired gray ware sherds and numerous pottery scrapers (Fowler et al. 1973:17-19).

Although O'Malley Shelter was classified as a temporary camp by the investigators, both the variety of vessel shapes and evidence of local pottery manufacture indicate the site may, instead, have been a major habitation area. Thus, this evidence tends to conform to the test implications for Hypothesis 2, suggesting a hunter-gatherer Fremont may have resided in the region.

Closer to the western Fremont pottery boundary in southeastern Nevada, vessel shapes have been discussed for the small quantity of Fremont ceramics recovered from three excavated rockshelters. The vessels consisted of a Snake Valley Gray jar (15 cm neck diameter) and a Snake Valley Black-on-gray bowl from Civa Shelter II; two Snake Valley Black-on-gray bowls (ca. 26-35 cm diameter) from Slivovitz Shelter; and one Snake Valley Gray bowl and one Snake Valley Black-on-gray bowl from Avocado Shelter (Busby 1979). In addition, at least one Snake Valley Corrugated jar may probably be inferred on the basis of body sherds from Slivovitz Shelter since this is the most common form for this pottery type (see Table 6).

The Fremont ceramic evidence from these three rockshelters suggests that the sites were temporary camps under Hypothesis 2. The sites do not fit well as seasonally occupied camps described in Hypothesis 1, since it is highly unlikely that Parowan Fremont groups would travel this far west from the Parowan Valley. It is possible that the Fremont from the Garrison site could have occupied these shelters, but even a journey between these two areas would be rather distant.

There is also the possibility of trade with Prenumic or Numic groups in this area. As suggested by Hypothesis 3, Snake Valley Black-on-gray bowls may have been a primary trade item on the fringes of the western Fremont realm, in which case these items might outnumber plain gray wares. If we examine the ratio of estimated vessel shapes at Civa,

Slivovitz, and Avocado Shelters, there are four Snake Valley Black-on-grey bowls to three Snake Valley Gray and Corrugated vessels. While not much difference is indicated by this ratio, Snake Valley Black-on-grey bowls or sherds have been reported from three other sites in the extreme western edge of the pottery boundary: Newark Cave, 26-NY-3685, and a site in the Park Range (see Table 4). The evidence in support time.

CONCLUSIONS

This paper has attempted to develop a model correlating vessel shape and function in order to explain the distribution of Fremont ceramics in the western periphery. The pattern that emerges from the vessels recovered at over a dozen sites suggests that Hypothesis 2 holds for most of the region. That is, less-settled hunter-gatherer Fremont groups occupied the western periphery.

The shapes and inferred functions of vessels lead to the identification of most sites in the sample as temporary camps. The Fremont occupations at these sites, however, cannot be economically accounted for under the hypothesis that the sites were seasonally occupied by Fremont groups from permanent villages in the Bear River and Parowan Valley areas. Temporary Fremont campsites around the Garrison site, perhaps even as far north as the Deep Creek sites, were more than likely seasonally used by the Garrison villagers. While several other possible villages (e.g., 26-WP-200 and 42-JB-3) have been noted, these have not been confirmed nor does the reported pottery evidence support this. Beyond perhaps a 75-km radius from the Garrison site, temporary camps in the western periphery appear to have been occupied by other local Fremont groups revolving around less-permanent habitation loci than the Garrison site. O'Malley Shelter in southeastern Nevada seems to be one such major habitation area as suggested by the Fremont ceramic evidence. Other similar sites have yet to be identified, which may, in part, be due to the limited nature of the data on vessel shapes from the region.

The conclusions reached by the present analysis are tentative and should be tested by a larger data set. Trade or exchange of Fremont pottery, particularly Snake Valley Black-on-gray, may still be a possible explanation for the presence of Fremont ceramics on the western edge of the region. The mechanisms for this trade network have yet to be worked out, however. Sourcing of western Fremont ceramics should be conducted in the future to determine if the pottery is trade ware from Utah villages or locally manufactured as suggested by the O'Malley Shelter evidence.

Obviously, the direction I have taken in this paper is not the only manner in which to analyze the Fremont evidence. The ceramic data presented should be combined with other cultural indicators to assess the Fremont presence. I have emphasized pottery to the exclusion of other data in order to demonstrate that more can be done with Fremont ceramics than has been done in the past. Investigators need to reconstruct vessel shapes and sizes when possible and attempt to determine the function these vessels served in Fremont society.

The model itself has several weaknesses which need to be tested by further research. First, there are other more reliable methods for ascertaining the function of pottery vessels than just shape. These consist of residue and pollen analyses of vessels and sherds (cf. Briuer 1976; Loy 1983). With one or two exceptions (see Madsen and Lindsay 1977:83), these analytical techniques have not been applied to Fremont ceramics to determine vessel function.

The second drawback with the model is that I have assumed that the several shapes of Fremont vessels usually served a single function. This is not always the case, for a single vessel may have served multiple functions throughout the life of the vessel. However, I think that each of the major Fremont vessel shapes probably had a primary function which can be correlated with a specific shape. Residue and pollen analyses could help verify this assumption.

Although these problems do exist with the model, future work can resolve them. More important, the approach presented here has implications beyond the Fremont ceramics of the western periphery. The model can be applied to other Fremont ceramic studies and to ceramic studies in general. For example, a similar approach recently has been published by Shapiro (1984) for Mississippian ceramics since I first wrote most of this paper. Another appropriate application within the Great Basin would be in determining the function of Intermountain Brown wares (cf. Pippin, this volume), a matter which has received very little attention.

ACKNOWLEDGMENTS

I am grateful to Suzanne Griset for general suggestions and editorial remarks. Eugene Hattori, Kathryn Pedrick, and Donald Tuohy read and commented on this paper. I also thank Robert Crabtree for providing the ceramic data for several Fremont sites in the BLM Tonopah Resource Area, and Denise Miller for drafting the locational map. Finally, the title for this paper was inspired by an article by White and Thomas (1972).

REFERENCES CITED

(Citations not listed here will be found in the Annotated and Indexed Bibliography of Ceramics at the back of this volume.)

Briuer, Frederick L.
  1976 New Clues to Stone Tool Function: Plant and Animal Residue. *American Antiquity* 41:478-484.

Emslie, Steven D.
  1982 *Archaeological Inventory of Seismic Lines in Newark and Huntington Valleys, Nevada*. Bristlecone Archaeology, Ely. Submitted to USDI Bureau of Land Management, Ely District Office, Ely, Nevada.

Fowler, Don D. (editor)
  1975 *Archeological Reconnaissance of Steptoe Creek Area*. Desert Research Institute, University of Nevada System, Reno. Submitted to Nevada State Highway Department, Carson City.

  1976a *Archeological Survey of Cave Lake State Recreation Area, White Pine County, Nevada*. Desert Research Institute, University of Nevada System, Reno. Submitted to Nevada State Highway Department, Carson City.

  1976b *Preliminary Archeological Investigations of Sites 26WP645 and 26WP649, White Pine County, Nevada*. Desert Research Institute, University of Nevada System, Reno. Submitted to Nevada State Highway Department, Carson City.

Fowler, Don D., and Floyd W. Sharrock
  1973 Survey and Test Excavations. In *Prehistory of Southeastern Nevada*, by Don D. Fowler, David B. Madsen, and Eugene M. Hattori, pp. 97-136. Desert Research Institute 6.

Gifford, James C., and Watson Smith
  1978 Gray Corrugated Pottery from Awatovi and Other Jeddito Sites in Northeastern Arizona. *Papers of the Peabody Museum of Archaeology and Ethnology* 69. Harvard University, Cambridge.

Gruhn, Ruth
1979   Excavation of Amy's Shelter,
        Eastern Nevada. In *The Archaeology
        of Smith Creek Canyon, Eastern
        Nevada*, edited by Donald R. Tuohy
        and Doris L. Rendall, pp. 90-160.
        Nevada State Museum Anthropological
        Society Quarterly 17.

Harrington, Mark R.
1932a   The Kachina Rockshelter in Nevada.
        Masterkey 6(5):148-151.

Hill, James N.
1970   Broken K Pueblo: Prehistoric
        Social Organization in the American
        Southwest. *Anthropological Papers
        of the University of Arizona* 18.

James, Steven R.
1977a   *Archaeological Clearance of Two*
        Seismic Lines for Dome Petroleum
        in Spring Valley, White Pine
        County, Nevada. Cultural Resources
        Report 4-157(P). USDI Bureau of
        Land Management, Ely District
        Office, Ely, Nevada.

1977b   *Clearance of Gulf Oil Seismic Lines
        Near Jakes Wash, White Pine County,
        Nevada*. Cultural Resource Report
        4-155(P). USDI Bureau of Land
        Management, Ely District Office,
        Ely, Nevada.

1978   Archaeological Investigations in
        Lincoln, Nye, and White Pine
        Counties. Paper presented at the
        1978 Great Basin Anthropological
        Conference, Reno.

1979   *Cultural Resources of Eight Springs
        in Northeastern Lincoln County,
        Nevada*. Cultural Resources Report
        4-321(P). USDI Bureau of Land
        Management, Ely District Office,
        Ely, Nevada.

Loy, Thomas H.
1983   Prehistoric Blood Residues:
        Detection on Tool Surfaces and
        Identification of Species of
        Origin. *Science* 200:1269-1271.

Madsen, David B.
1979   The Fremont and the Sevier:
        Defining Prehistoric Agricultur-
        alists North of the Anasazi.
        American Antiquity 44:711-722.

1982   Get It Where the Getting's Good:
        A Variable Model of Great Basin
        Subsistence and Settlement Based
        on Data from the Eastern Great
        Basin. In *Man and Environment in
        the Great Basin*, edited by David
        Madsen and James F. O'Connell,
        207-226. Society for American
        Archaeology Papers 2.

Malouf, Carling I., Charles E. Dibble, and
Elmer R. Smith
1940   *The Archaeology of the Deep Creek
        Region, Utah*. Museum of Anthro-
        pology, University of Utah,
        Archaeology and Ethnology Papers
        5. Reprinted 1950, Paper No. 5,
        University of Utah Anthropological
        Papers 1-9.

McGregor, John C.
1965   *Southwestern Archaeology*. 2nd
        edition. University of Illinois
        Press, Urbana.

Tuohy, Donald R.
1979   *Kachina Cave. In The Archaeology
        of Smith Creek Canyon, Eastern
        Nevada*, edited by Donald R. Tuohy
        and Doris L. Rendall, 1-88.
        Nevada State Museum Anthropological
        Quarterly 17.

Wheeler, S. M.
1938   A Fremont Moccasin from Nevada.
        Masterkey 12:34-35.

White, J. Peter, and David H. Thomas
1972   *What Mean These Stones?: Ethno-
        taxonomic Models and Archaeological
        Interpretations in the New Guinea
        Highlands. In Models in Archae-
        ology*, edited by David L. Clarke,
        275-308. Methuen, London.

York, Robert
1977   *Studies at Adams-McGill Reservoir:
        Exercises in Applying Small Project
        Data to Archaeological Research*.
        USDI Bureau of Land Management,
        Technical Report 1. Reno.

NOTES ON CERAMIC ANALYSIS

SUZANNE GRISET

All participants of the Great Basin/California Pottery Workshop would agree, I believe, that prehistoric ceramics found in the Great Basin and adjacent areas exhibit variations and similarities from region to region, either morphologically or technologically. At the very least, regional geologies affected the paste composition. And while the majority of vessels were constructed by the coiling technique, then thinned and shaped either by scraping or paddling the vessel wall, some were modeled from patches of clay pressed together with the fingers.

Overlying these differences, however, is a perceived areal similarity in overall vessel shape, in uncontrolled firing that produced various shades of gray/brown exteriors, and by the fact that much of the area in which these ceramics are found was inhabited in the protohistoric period by Numic speakers. This impression of commonality is further reinforced by the contrast presented by the ceramic traditions of surrounding areas such as the slipped and painted wares of the Southwestern Pueblo cultures and the buff wares of the southern California desert. Basin wares/types, or whatever they may be called, were brown. Granted that these are subjective impressions, they are difficult nonetheless, to resist, particularly after viewing the roomful of pottery from across the Basin that was assembled at the Workshop.

Interpretations of what these similarities and differences may mean is another matter. Three positions were expressed by Workshop participants when discussing Basin ceramic typology: (1) there is a common Basin ceramic tradition which encompasses the three "wares" described in the literature (Shoshoni Brown Ware, Owens Valley Brown Ware, Southern Paiute Utility Ware); (2) there is much regional variation which needs to be examined in detail prior to constructing an all-encompassing Basin

typology; and (3) all-encompassing typologies do not work and should be avoided in the Basin.

Arguments for the first position are eloquently expressed in three papers in this volume (Prince, Pippin, and Butler). The second position is presented in Bettinger's paper. The third position was expressed at the Workshop by Swarthout and Drover who maintained that ceramic typologies of the type/variety system are unworkable and inappropriate. They cited "The Great Southwestern Type Experiment" (Swarthout and Delaney 1982) in which a group of long-time Southwestern archaeologists was asked to classify a collection of provenienced vessels. None of them was able to "correctly" identify all of the vessels and few successfully identified half. Swarthout and Drover questioned the usefulness of attempting to force all pottery into a single typology purely for the sake of conformity and urged Great Basin researchers not to fall into the trap of the Southwestern ceramic typology.

I will argue here that some of this typological and terminological confusion is due to the confusion of the two steps involved in ceramic analysis. Ideally, ceramic analyses consist of: (1) the initial descriptive analysis, and (2) the interpretive analysis. These parts are often blended or each is partially ignored. Perhaps, by consciously separating these two aspects of analysis we can elicit comparable data bases that will enable and encourage analysts to use ceramic data in formulating and examining research problems.

DESCRIPTIVE ANALYSIS

Carefully selected, accurate description is the foundation of all interpretation and one of the first tasks to confront the archaeologist both in the field and in the laboratory (McGimsey 1980:24).

Even in this era of reputed "scientific" archaeology, site reports often present ceramic analyses which consist of: (1) tallies of the number of sherds, (2) typological attributions based on the site's nearness to the core areas of Shoshonean, Southern Paiute, or Owens Valley Brown wares, and (3) use of the sherds to indicate recent site occupation. Without comparable data bases, it is impossible to begin comparing sherds from site to site, much less from region to region, or to proceed to interpret these data.

McGimsey (1980) presents one of the most lucid discussions of the distinctions between description and typology, which may be very germane to this problem:

> Few if any publications describe every artifact recovered individually, and with material like pottery any such attempt generally is impossible. Most publications resort to a technique that might be labeled "typological description," that is, individual units are described only as exemplifications or members of a particular "type." What is "described" is an idealized unit rather than any observable unit itself. In fact this technique is so prevalent that the basic distinctions between the concepts of description, typology, and classification are at times disregarded and the terms used as synonyms (McGimsey 1980:25).

He goes on to define these terms as follows:

> Description involves the presentation of some or "all" of the characteristics and relations of a single unit or, via typological descriptions, groups of units. Typology refers to the conceptual amalgamation of individual units into groups or types based on their relative identity with respect to one or more characteristics. These diagnostic characteristics normally are selected for and determined by their relevance to a particular problem or group of problems. Classification is the arrangement or ordering of the units or the types that constitute the data according to a definite scheme or hypothesis (McGimsey 1980: 25; emphasis added).

The Southwestern ware/type/variety classification system is actually a time/place typology. A variety of pottery characteristics or attributes has been selected to construct pottery types thought to have time (chronological) and place (cultural) significance (Hargrave 1974). Problems encountered in using this typology are due to the mixed nature of the criteria used in ordering it hierarchically and consequent lack of replicability.

Although attributes of manufacturing technique are used to distinguish ceramics at the ware level, a wide range of manufacturing, surface treatment, design element, and compositional attributes are used to distinguish types. According to Hargrave:

> Type determinants are not predicted, but accrue as a result of decisions made by many individual researchers as the need arises (Hargrave 1974:80).

He rejects the concept of further division of ceramics beyond the level of type: any grouping of attribute variations (varieties or subtypes) is grounds for creation of an additional type.

The problem arises as each researcher adds new types, according to the requirements of the current research problem. The attributes are not necessarily comparable and the rationale for greater and finer splitting of types varies from instance to instance. Thus we have "The Great Southwestern Type Experiment" results.

As contorted as the Southwestern typology may be, it has the weight of tradition and widespread usage behind it, and it still serves as a standard typology. McGimsey uses this "time/place" typology in his own analysis, but uses it as one of the ancillary problem-oriented typologies that amplify and interpret the basic data contained in a "descriptive typology." Each "descriptive type" consists of a specific set of attributes. A sherd either matches all of the attributes described for a specific "descriptive type" or it must belong to another "descriptive type." For convenience sake and to avoid a replication of the proliferation of type names, McGimsey uses numerical labels for these "descriptive types" (Figure 34).

By first sorting sherds into these basic physical types and looking at their distributions within a site (Figure 34 c), it becomes possible to depict the range of physical properties present in a ceramic assemblage and the pattern of their distribution. It also enables resorting of the sherds into other combinations or types by choosing specific groupings of the basic physical properties to form different problem-oriented typologies, i.e., McGimsey looks at selected decorative techniques in his "artisan types" to see if there are any distributional patterns indicative of specific artisan patterns or styles.

These problem-oriented typologies crosscut the distributions seen in the descriptive typology, and can highlight patterns that otherwise might be masked by forcing all sherds into a single ideal typology.

Steponaitis (1980) uses a similar multifaceted approach in analyzing Southeastern vessels. Although he does not describe the

McGimsey's Descriptive Type is composed of four major descriptive classes: Material (Row A), Vessel Shape (Row B), Construction and Surface Finish (Row C), and Decorative Effect (Row D). All variations on these classes are called "modes" and are defined in the appendix of his volume. An example of the modes described for Material (Row A) are listed in Fig. 34A.

These general mode descriptions are then combined and recombined to describe the attributes of the pottery found at each site, and are given numerical designations. An example of the Material (Row A) numerical types at site 601 of Mariana Mesa, is shown below in Fig. 34B. To the right, in Fig. 34C is the summary Distribution Table of all white slipped pottery from site 601. The numbers in Row A of this Table refer to the numerical types described in Fig. 34B, which in turn refer to the modes defined in Appendix A as seen in Fig. 34A.

PASTE: ALL POTTERY

Mode Key A*

Color: average: dull white; range: buff to dark gray. Carbon streak: rare in all forms, most often present on the inner half of jar sherds. Clay texture: generally friable but occasionally dense. Fracture: crumbling or shattering (this seems to vary more with the amount of firing than with the amount of inclusions). Appearance in cross section: irregular and dull (occasional sherds were more angular and had a slight lustrous or vitreous appearance). Inclusions: gray, opaque, angular material with rare rounded and angular, generally clear, sand; fine to medium in size with rare coarse fragments; moderate in frequency.

Mode Key B

Color: average: gray; range: light to dark gray. Carbon streak: rare. Clay texture: friable but occasionally dense. Fracture: crumbling or shattering (varying with amount of inclusions). Appearance in cross section: irregular, dull, and powdery, though occasionally almost angular. Inclusions: dark to light gray, angular opaque material and occasionally clear or cloudy rounded quartz grains, fine to medium in size, sparse.

The larger amount of sand proportionally and the general sparseness of the temper helps to distinguish sherds of mode key B from mode key A.

SLIP: WHITE- AND RED-SLIPPED POTTERY

Mode a: No slip.
Mode b: Slip flat-white in color.
Mode c: Slip creamy white in color.
Mode d: Slip orange in color; range: brown to red; slip tends to crackle.
Mode e: Slip brick-red or maroon in color; slip often has a powdery appearance and tends to wear away fairly readily; it never exhibits crackling.
Mode f: Slip of same material as the paste, dull white in color.
Mode g: Slip thickly applied, and visible in cross section with the naked eye.
Mode h: Slip thinly applied, and visible in cross section only with the aid of a magnifying glass (14x used); slip is not translucent and the paste cannot be seen through it.
Mode i: Watery slip, applied so thinly and/or in such a dilute solution that paste can be seen in patches.

A

(from McGimsey 1980:291)

B

White-slipped Pottery

MATERIAL: ROW A

1. Dense gray paste with opaque angular material and rare sand inclusions — mode key (D)
   Slip flat-white, thinly applied — modes (b) and (h)
   Mineral paint — mode (a)
2. Gray friable paste with sand and rare opaque angular inclusions — mode key (E)
   Slip flat-white, thinly applied — modes (b) and (h)
   Mineral paint — mode (a)
3. Gray friable paste with sand and rare opaque angular incusions — mode key (E)
   Slip flat-white, applied thinly with paste visible in patches — modes (b) and (i)
   Mineral paint — mode (a)
4. Dense cream-colored paste with sand inclusions — mode key (J)
   No slip — mode (a)
   Mineral paint — mode (a)

The dense and the friable gray pastes were about equally popular and exhibited a similar range of decorative elements. The vessels of dense gray paste were better finished than those of the friable gray paste. Similarly it was only on the friable gray paste that the poorly or thinly applied slip was used. These two paste types may represent local production, perhaps the output of two artisans or groups of potters. The hypothesis that the vessels of material type 4 (dense cream-colored paste with sand) were imported rests primarily on their scarcity at the site.

(from McGimsey 1980:251)

C

White-slipped Pottery

Provenience			A	1	1	1	1	1	1	1	1	1	1	2	2	2	2	3	3	4	
Descriptive Types			B	1	2	2	3	3	3	3	3	3	4	4	1	3	3	4	1	1	Bases
			C	2	1	4	1	1	1	1	2	4	1	2	1	3	5	1	1	6	
			D	2	2	1	1	2	3	4	1	1	5	2	6	2	2	?	1	?	
	Totals	511		1	2	1	5	35	45	8	60	1	2	6	3	190	8	1	26	5	112
Room 2	Fill	295			2			33	45	8	60			5						26	5	112
	Floor	7						1						5				7		24		110
Room 3	Fill	113										1	2			110*					
	Floor	78		1												77*					
Room 4	Fill	11															3	3				
Room 5	Fill	6					5	1												5		
Room 6	Fill	1																1			

* Nearly all from a single vessel.

(from McGimsey 1980:254)

Figure 34. Sample of descriptive type formulated by McGimsey (McGimsey, Charles R., III, *Mariana Mesa: Seven Prehistoric Settlements in West-Central New Mexico*. Papers of the Peabody Museum, Vol. 72. Copyright 1980 by the President and Fellows of Harvard College. Reprinted here with their kind permission).

physical properties of each vessel in a single typology, he attempts to depict all of the attribute variety by looking at several different groupings or typologies of these attributes. He establishes a hierarchical type/variety typology of pots sorted first by temper (shell or grog), next by surface finish (burnished vs. unburnished) and lastly by kind of tooled decoration (plain, incised scrolls, incised rectangular, etc.). Crosscutting this type/variety typology is another sorting of groups according to the kind of painted decoration on a pot. A third grouping sorts first by overall shape and further by the kinds of secondary shape features such as lip form, appendages, etc.

The point I wish to stress here is not a new one. There are all kinds of types and therefore, all kinds of typologies. Typologies are sorting tools, created from specific artifact attributes which have been selected by the sorter in the belief that they will reveal some kind of patterning in the archaeological materials. And just as there are multiple patterns in the materials, there are potentially several different typologies which can be used to elicit different information from the same data base.

Some may argue that McGimsey and Steponaitis could easily establish multiple typologies given the extensive pottery assemblages in their areas of concern. Great Basin ceramics, however, also exhibit variation. Witness the variations described for each of the three original "wares." Differences in manufacturing technique have been lumped in all three. Overall vessel shape varies, and vessel dimensions have rarely been specified in assemblage descriptions, even when rim sherds and base sherds are noted. Tuohy and Strawn's examination of the nonplastic inclusions in the paste of pots from across the western edge of the Great Basin has shown that nonplastics may not be discriminative at the level of mineral identification, but may be useful when structurally analyzed for shape, size, spacing, and as a percentage of the paste composition (Tuohy and Strawn, this volume).

Most important, we need to concentrate on more extensive description of the physical properties of the sherds or pots recovered archaeologically, to make the data base more readily available for comparisons between sites, within regions, or across the Basin. It would also be helpful to establish a minimum set of descriptive attributes with standards set for descriptive terminology so that these terms and classifications will be comparable from researcher to researcher. For example, in describing exterior, interior, and core color, the Munsell Soil Color charts provide a readily available standard (Munsell 1971). Tuohy and Strawn use Powers (1953) chart for visual estimation of roundness of nonplastic inclusions in

paste, and suggest that Bennett(1974:105) provides a chart for estimation of percentage composition extending from 0 to 80 percent in 20 percent increments.

Bennett also provides examples of rim/neck form descriptive categories (1974:18-23) that would be applicable to Basin pots. Although her analysis is geared specifically toward coding Southwestern pottery attributes for computer analysis, many of her categories will trigger Basin ceramic analysts to look at the individual attributes of a vessel that otherwise might be overlooked.

From such a list, specific attributes could be selected by the analyst in composing various typologies. It might be useful to pretest potential attributes with a small sample from large collections. This pretest might reveal which attributes are represented consistently in an assemblage and which attributes have potential discriminating value. Bettinger (this volume) singled out and tested variations of surface treatment and found statistically significant differences in pottery samples.

In addition to the description of the physical characteristics of a ceramic assemblage, the descriptive analysis should also include data concerning the specific provenience of the pots or sherds. Their horizontal or vertical deposition within a site may be significant. All too often sherds are viewed out of their archaeological context. They are part of the total tool assemblage and should be viewed as such. Co-occurrences of specific forms with other artifact types and in specific areas may lead to inferences as to overall usage of sites (James, this volume).

An additional element of this contextual description of the sherds can be found in the routine collection and examination of the clay deposits from the area in which the sherds or pots were found. Potters may collect their ceramic materials from traditionally used resource locales, or they may experiment with clays found close at hand. Geologic mapping does not provide the kinds of information ceramic analysts need in order to compare clay artifacts with clay sources. Archaeologists need to become aware of this source of information and incorporate clay collection in their field procedures. Site reports often show unit sidewall profiles with clay lenses or basal strata, but infrequently compare the clay from these on-site sources to the clay composition of the sherds. Still less frequently are comparisons made with samples collected from the surrounding area.

Another source of descriptive comparison may be found in the ethnographic and archaeological literature. This is particularly applicable in the Basin since pottery-bearing archaeological and ethnographic complexes are not too distant in time and are probably part

of a cultural continuum. As more pots and
sherds are reconstructed and dimensions
recorded, these can be compared to whole
vessels collected from specific cultural groups
or areas. Similarities in overall shape can be
tested by comparing ranges of dimensions for
particular vessel forms. Attribute analysis of
whole vessels can be compared for similarities
and differences with attributes described from
sherds. As more descriptive data is published
from these two sources (archaeological/ethno-
graphic), their interpretive potential will
dramatically increase.

INTERPRETIVE ANALYSIS

Perhaps meticulous description and elab-
oration of taxonomic systems serve as
tranquilizers, helping us to forget how
much of vital interest is forever lost,
because these procedures are accepted as
indicative of a thorough scientific job.
But the ethnological record is not a
tranquilizer, and, although it is humbling
to us as archaeologists, it is also
stimulating; it phrases questions that we
have not asked, and suggests where hidden
evidence may be sought (Shepard 1963:1).

Shepard reminds us of the ultimate objective of careful description of a body of data:
explanation. We analyze to explain or interpret
how these data related to the cultural whole.
Pots do not exist in a vacuum--they are part of
the total tool complex a culture used for specific tasks. At a minimum they are containers
for storing, collecting, and preparing food and
medicines. They may also be used to transport
trade goods or to collect or help process other
resources such as basketry materials, or to
hold water to mix clay for making additional
pots. They may be status items or ceremonial
apparatus. Once broken, they can be reused in
a variety of manners as new tool forms, gaming
pieces, or ornaments.
Interpretations as to which of these kinds
of functions was served by particular pots or
potsherds is based on "reading" the information
encoded in the physical properties of the
vessels and in their environmental or arti-
factual contexts. As Shepard suggests, ethnographic analogies have long served as sources
of possible explanation or interpretation for
ceramic analysts. Explanation is after all,
guesswork based on experience. Interpretations
cannot prove or explain anything, nor do they
pretend to do so. Instead, they are an attempt
to put the people back into the archaeological
picture and help the present understand the
past. As long as the data are carefully
described, the assumptions clearly detailed,
and analogies carefully applied, the interpre-

tive analysis should be the objective of the
ceramic analysis.
Many approaches have been utilized to this
end. James' paper in this volume illustrates
one example of a functional analysis predicated
on vessel form, which is then used to examine
the kinds of vessels at a site in order to predict the type of site and subsistence-
settlement pattern operative in a given area.
Thomas (1970) used the occurrence of pottery at
sites in the pinyon-juniper zone to infer subsistence activities which utilized pots.
Vessel form has also been used to predict
population size. Reconstructable fragments or
sherd shape, weight, and curvature were used by
Ericson and a series of coauthors to predict
vessel function, volume, and from these, family
size served by these cooking or serving vessel
capacities (Ericson, Read, and Burke 1972;
Ericson and Stickel 1973; Ericson and DeAtley
1976). These in turn were used to predict
population size at a site. Baumhoff and Heizer
(1959) also used the average weight of different vessel forms to calculate the number of
vessels compared to the number of rooms and
estimated duration of occupation of a site, to
estimate population size.
Braun (1980) and Henrickson and McDonald
(1983) also have used the "form reflects
function" argument. Braun used the rim and
neck attributes of ethnographic pottery from
Southwestern groups to predict prehistoric
form/function from rim and neck attributes of
sherds. Henrickson and McDonald (1983) surveyed basic functional classes of vessels
(cooking, storage, and serving forms) from
worldwide ethnographic literature, compiled
dimensional data for these forms, and
constructed shape and size ranges for each,
then examined an archaeological assemblage of
whole or reconstructable pots and interpreted
their possible function based on comparison of
their shape and dimensions with the ethnographic categories.
Several authors have taken the form/
function argument one step further and
attempted to interpret social practices from
these data. Hargrave and Braun (1981) examined
the physical properties of paste composition
and morphological changes in Woodland pottery
from carbon 14-dated trash pits. By seriating
these attributes chronologically, they hoped to
discern functional changes in the pottery that
reflected the change in Woodland diet and
cooking techniques at the onset of maize horticulture.
Linton's classic article on North American
cooking pots (1944) argued that there were two
basic pot forms: pots with pointed bottoms and
pots with round bottoms. These shapes were
thought to be related to the kind of cooking
techniques employed. Pointed bottoms were used
directly in the fire, lying on their side, for
quick boiling and cooking. Round bottoms were

either placed on supports or suspended above the fire for slow, indirect stewing of the contents. Linton thought these two cooking techniques reflected the differences in settlement system of their owners: wandering groups had little time to cook their food slowly; sedentary peoples could leave pots slowly cooking all day over low, constant temperature fires and thus break down the starchy grains into a palatable stew.

Bronitzky (1982), Hargrave and Braun (1981), Steponaitis (1980), and Rye (1976) have looked at the physical properties of different paste compositions for clues to the functional properties that may have been consciously selected by prehistoric potters. The specific kinds of nonplastic or organic additives to paste, affect manipulability of the clay, impose requisite firing techniques, and determine the ultimate success of the product. Size and percentage of nonplastic inclusions also affect a pot's thermal conductivity and resistances to thermal or mechanical shocks.

Alteration of vessel surfaces during use or postdeposition provide other sources of interpretation. Hally (1983a) examined whole or reconstructable vessels for correlations of wear patterns with specific vessel forms (and hence, functions), and for patterns of soot deposition or oxidation discoloration as indications of proximity of vessel to fire (and thus, cooking techniques). Wilke suggested during the pottery workshop (1983) that carbon deposits on vessels may be useable for radiocarbon dating. Ultimately it may be possible to identify the diet constituents from these kinds of deposits.

Reworked sherds are found in a variety of forms. Interpretations of their functions have been based on occasional ethnographic identification or on pure archaeological speculation. Oppelt (1984) reviewed the literature for explanation and distribution of different shapes of reworked sherds found in the Southwest and found differences in the distributions among the Anasazi, Mogollon, and Hohokam. Foster (1960) looked at the life expectancy of different functional classes of pots in a contemporary Mexican village and demonstrated how these variable survival rates affected the depositional pattern within a site. Some forms of pots were discarded upon breakage, others were recycled as new forms of tools. Hally

(1983b) also used ethnographic analogies of vessel recycling patterns, storage and use locations, use life, and discard processes to interpret archaeological ceramic assemblages.

This brief review of recent approaches to ceramic analysis has sought to emphasize the wide diversity of interpretations possible from ceramic data bases. Ethnographic analogy from the Basin proper (Pippin, this volume) and surrounding areas, as well as analytical approaches taken by ceramic analysts in other regions, can be applied in the interpretation of Basin ceramics.

CONCLUSIONS

To summarize the main points expressed in this paper, ceramic analysis is composed of two parts: (1) descriptive analysis and (2) interpretive analysis. The descriptive analysis first describes the data base--the physical properties of the ceramics and their distribution. It places these properties in their archaeological contexts, and outlines the group or groups of attributes thought to be most relevant to specific research problems.

The interpretive analysis examines the data for its implications on one or more research problems. It attempts to use the archaeological data to reconstruct the original ceramic assemblage and its role in the cultural system. Specific aspects of that cultural system may be examined using parts or all of the ceramic data. Interpretation includes the traditional time/place questions of chronology and culture history, and interactions between cultures or regions, but can be expanded to include processual questions as well.

Great Basin archaeologists, hampered by the ephemeral surficial nature of many of the archaeological deposits, have nevertheless been able to use other classes of artifacts to draw many interpretations of the prehistoric record. Ceramics can be of similar value.

REFERENCES CITED

All sources cited in this paper may be found in the Annotated and Indexed Bibliography of Ceramics at the back of this volume.

ANNOTATED BIBLIOGRAPHY
OF THE CERAMICS OF THE GREAT BASIN
AND ADJACENT AREAS

ABBREVIATIONS USED

This bibliography and index is a compilation of the references deemed most important to pottery analysis by the participants in the Great Basin/California Pottery Workshop, 1983. In consideration of saving space we have used abbreviations for many of the pottery wares and publications commonly cited. These are:

LCBW	Lower Colorado Buff Ware
OVBW	Owens Valley Brown Ware
SBW	Shoshoni Brown Ware
SPUW	Southern Paiute Utility Ware
TBW	Tizon Brown Ware

The bibliographic abbreviations are:

AA	*American Antiquity*
AmAn	*American Anthropologist*
AMNHAP	*American Museum of Natural History, Anthropological Papers.* New York.
ASUARP	*Arizona State University Anthropological Research Papers.* Tempe.
BAEB	*Bureau of American Ethnology, Bulletin.* Washington.
DRI	*Desert Research Institute, Social Sciences and Humanities Publications, Western Research Center, Reno and Las Vegas.*
IA	*Idaho Archaeologist*
JCA	*Journal of California Anthropology*
JCGBA	*Journal of California and Great Basin Anthropology*
MAI	*Museum of the American Indian, Heye Foundation, Indian Notes and Monographs.* New York.
Masterkey	*The Masterkey.* Southwest Museum, Los Angeles.
MNA,B	*Museum of Northern Arizona, Bulletin.* Flagstaff.
MNA,CS	*Museum of Northern Arizona, Ceramic Series.* Flagstaff.
MNA,N	*Museum of Northern Arizona, Notes.* Flagstaff.
NASR	*Nevada Archaeological Survey Reporter*
NASRP	*Nevada Archaeological Survey Research Papers*
NSMAP	*Nevada State Museum Anthropological Papers*
PA	*Plains Anthropologist*
PCASQ	*Pacific Coast Archaeological Society Quarterly*
PPM	*Papers of the Peabody Museum of Archaeology and Ethnology, Harvard University.* Cambridge.
SWJA	*Southwestern Journal of Anthropology*

Tebiwa	*Tebiwa, The Journal of the Idaho Museum of Natural History.* Pocatello.
UCAR	*University of California Anthropological Records.* Berkeley.
UCARFC	*Contributions of the University of California Archaeological Research Facility.* Berkeley.
UCASR	*University of California Archaeological Survey Reports.* Berkeley.
UCAS,AR	*University of California Archaeological Survey, Annual Reports.* Los Angeles.
UCPAAE	*University of California Publications in American Archeology and Ethnology.* Berkeley.
UOAP	*University of Oregon Anthropological Papers.* Eugene.
UUAP	*University of Utah Anthropological Papers.* Salt Lake City.
WAR	*Western Anasazi Reports.* Museum of Southern Utah State College, Cedar City.

Aginsky, Burt W.
1943   *Cultural Element Distributions: XXIV Central Sierra.* UCAR 8:4.

P. 458 lists pottery traits present among Chuckchansi Yokuts.

Aikens, C. Melvin
1966a *Fremont-Promontory-Plains Relationships.* UUAP No. 82.

Fremont pottery.

1966b *Virgin-Kayenta Cultural Relationships.* UUAP No. 79.

Fremont and Anasazi pottery.

1967a *Excavations at Snake Rock Village and the Bear River No. 2 Site.* UUAP No. 87.

Fremont pottery from two sites in western Utah.

1967b Plains Relationships of the Fremont Culture: A Hypothesis. *AA* 32:198-209.

Fremont pottery.

1970   *Hogup Cave.* UUAP No. 93.

Fremont and Shoshoni pottery, clay figurines, and basketry impressions.

Alexander, W., and J. W. Ruby
1963   *1962 Excavations at Summit, Utah: A Progress Report.* NSMAP 9:17-32.

Brief mention of Fremont and Virgin Branch Anasazi pottery recovered from the Evans Mound, southwestern Utah. See Berry (1972) and Dodd (1982) for more details on pottery from this site.

Ambro, Richard D.
1972   Preliminary Observations on the Surface Archaeology of Ridge Village North, an Historic Shoshone Village. In *The Grass Valley Archaeological Project: Collected Papers*, edited by C. W. Clewlow, Jr. and M. Rusco, pp. 85-106. NASRP No. 3.

A fired clay horse and owl figurines recovered with historic items from surface of Shoshone village dated A.D. 1880-1910.

1978   A Second Clay Animal Figurine from Grass Valley, Nevada: Implications for the Distribution and Interpretation of Great Basin Figurines. In *History and Prehistory at Grass Valley, Nevada*, edited by C. W. Clewlow, H. F. Wells, and R. D. Ambro, pp. 105-118. Monograph VII, University of California, Los Angeles.

Describes owl figurine fragment from hearth; reviews ethnographic and archaeological data on Great Basin figurines.

Anderson, K. M.
1963   Ceramic Clues to Pueblo-Puebloid Relationships. *AA* 28(3):303-307.

Statistical analysis of modes of pottery-making techniques to show greater similarity between Snake Valley Gray (Sevier) and North Creek Gray (Virgin) than Fremont/Virgin; lists attributes used.

Angel, M. (editor)
1881 *History of Nevada with Illustrations
and Biographical Sketches of its
Prominent Men and Pioneers*. Thompson
and West, Oakland, California.
Reprinted 1958 with an introduction
by D. F. Myrick, Howell-North Books,
Berkeley.

Early reference to Anasazi pottery
north of the Colorado River on p. 20.
"The pottery is of a dull white
ground, with black stripes running up
and down, the Moqui Tribe of Arizona
having in use at the present time and
same kind of earthern jars."

Anonymous
1924 W. H. Dumble Collection. Ms. #476,
on file UCARF, Berkeley.

Description of private collection
containing a photo of a pot from
northern shore of Kern River, and
bowl from Goose Lake district,
Yokuts area, central California.

Asaro, Frank, and Helen V. Michel
1984 Neutron Activation Analysis of Eight
Sherds of California Pottery Sub-
mitted by Basin Research. Appendix
IX. In *Rockhouse Basin Data Recovery
Project*, edited by A. P. Garfinkel,
L. S. Kobori, J. C. Bard, and R. J.
Dezzani. Manuscript on file, Sequoia
National Forest, Porterville,
California.

Compares eight OVBW sherds, four from
top of Sierras and four from Owens
Valley proper; several differences
are observed, but their significance
is unknown since reference clay
samples have not been collected nor
analyzed for these areas; see also
Meike 1984.

Baldwin, Gordon C.
1942 Archaeology in Southern Nevada. *The
Kiva* 7(1):13-16.

Describes Anasazi pottery from
southern Nevada.

1945 Notes on Ceramic Types in Southern
Nevada. *AA* 10(4):389-390.

Discusses temper differences of
indigenous pottery types of the
Boulder Dam National Recreation area
contrasted to those of southern
Utah and northeastern Arizona.

1950a The Pottery of the Southern Paiute.
AA 16(1):50-56.

Names and describes Southern Paiute
Utility Ware.

1950b Archeological Survey of the Lake Mead
Area. In *For the Dean: Essays in
Anthropology in Honor of Byron Cum-
mings*, edited by E. K. Reed and D.S.
King, pp. 41-49. Hohokam Museums
Association, Tucson, and Southwestern
Monuments Association, Santa Fe.

Brief mention of Virgin Branch
Anasazi pottery.

Barber, E. A.
1876 The Ancient Pottery of Colorado,
Utah, Arizona, and New Mexico.
American Naturalist 10:449-464.

Description of Ute pottery making on
452; most of article deals with
Pueblo pottery from the Four Corners
region; several plates with line
drawings of Pueblo pottery.

Barrett, S. A., and E. W. Gifford
1933 Miwok Material Culture. *Bulletin
of the Milwaukee Public Museum*
2(4):211.

Mentions four clay figurines collected from Sierra Miwok in 1901; no
pottery.

Barrows, David Prescott
1900 *The Ethno-Botany of the Coahuilla
Indians of Southern California*.
University of Chicago Press. Re-
printed 1967 by Malki Museum Press,
Banning.

Discusses pottery making and uses
of vessels by Coahuilla.

Baumhoff, Martin A., and Robert F. Heizer
1959 Some Unexploited Possibilities in
Ceramic Analysis, *SWJA* 15(3):308-316.

Uses average weights of vessel
classes to estimate number of whole
vessels represented by sherd weights
at a single site.

Baumhoff, Martin A. and Jerald J. Johnson
1968 Archaeological Investigations at the
Lorenzen Site (CA-Mod-250), Modoc
County, California. Ms. on file,
Department of Anthropology, Cali-
fornia State University, Sacramento.

Describes potsherds and baked clay
pipes and objects.

Beardsley, Richard K.
   1954   *Temporal and Areal Relationships in Central California Archaeology*. UCASR No. 24 and No. 25.

   Clay figurines from California.

Beck, C. M.
   1981   Shoshoni Brownware from Grass Valley, Nevada. *Annals of Carnegie Museum* 50(1):1-29.

   Excellent descriptive account of attributes and distribution of Shoshoni Brown ware from 56 Grass Valley sites.

Bennett, M. Ann
   1974   *Basic Ceramic Analysis*. Eastern New Mexico University Contributions in Anthropology 6(1).

   Lists and defines ceramic attributes used in coding Southwestern sherds for computerized data storage and analysis.

Berry, Michael S.
   1972   The Evans Site. Special Report, University of Utah Department of Anthropology, Salt Lake City.

   Fremont and Virgin Anasazi pottery.

   1976   Remnant Cave. In *Swallow Shelter and Associated Sites*, by G. F. Dalley, pp. 115-127. UUAP No. 96.

   Provides dates of 950 ± 125 B.P. with Great Salt Lake Gray and 405 ± 60 B.P. with Shoshoni pottery.

Bettinger, Robert L.
   1975   *Surface Archaeology of Owens Valley, Eastern California: Prehistoric Man-Land Relationships in the Great Basin*. Ph.D. dissertation, Department of Anthropology, University of California, Riverside.

   Describes ceramics from surface of sites in central Owens Valley; uses ethnographic data to predict incorporation of vessels in prehistoric subsistence-settlement systems.

   1979   Multivariate Statistical Analysis of a Regional Subsistence-Settlement Model for Owens Valley. *AA* 44(3): 455-470.

   Summarizes Bettinger 1975.

   n.d.   *The Archaeology of Pinyon House, Two Eagles, and Crater Middens: Three Residential Sites in Owens Valley, Eastern California*. AMNHAP (In Press).

   Original report from which Bettinger (this volume) was drawn; has additional data on ceramics.

Bettinger, Robert L., and Martin A. Baumhoff
   1982   The Numic Spread: Great Basin Cultures in Competition. *AA* 47(3): 485-503.

   Uses occurrence of Paiute-Shoshone pottery to mark and date Numic expansion.

Braun, David P.
   1980   Experimental Interpretation of Ceramic Vessel Use on the Basis of Rim and Neck Formal Attributes. In *The Navajo Project: Archaeological Investigations, Page to Phoenix 500kv Southern Transmission Line*, by D. C. Fiero, R. W. Munson, M. T. McClain, S. M. Wilson, and A. H. Zier, Appendix I, pp. 171-231. Museum of Northern Arizona Research Paper No. 11. Flagstaff.

   Uses ethnographic Yuman, Piman and Puebloan vessel shape/size/function correlations to propose similar functional shapes in archaeological assemblages.

   1983   Pots as Tools. Chapter 5 in *Archaeological Hammers and Theories*, edited by J. A. Moore and A. S. Keene, pp. 107-134. Academic Press, New York.

   Relates change in vessel morphological attributes to changes in functional requirements and interprets these as evidence of change in Woodland diet and food processing.

Brauner, David, and Clayton G. Lelow
   1983   A Reevaluation of Cultural Resources Within the Proposed Elk Creek Lake Project Area, Jackson County, Oregon. Phase II: Site Evaluation. Department of Anthropology, Oregon State University, Corvallis.

   Reports an extensive testing of several sites in western Cascades of Oregon, including a brief description of potsherds, possibly associated with a house pit dated to 1150 ± 85 B.P. by carbon-14, found at site 35JA100, a possible Upland Takelma village.

Brauner, David, and Lynne MacDonald
    1983   The Reevaluation of Cultural
            Resources Within the Applegate Lake
            Project Area, Jackson County, Oregon.
            Phase II: Archaeological Sampling of
            Sites 35JA47 and 35JA49. Department
            of Anthropology, Oregon State
            University, Corvallis.

            Describes and illustrates baked clay
            objects, probably figurine fragments,
            from the Late Prehistoric component
            of site in southwestern Oregon.

Brooks, R., D. O. Larson, J. King, R. Leavitt,
and K. Olson
    1977   The Archaeology of the Mariah Site
            26Ln618, White River Narrows, Lincoln
            County, Nevada. Report of the Nevada
            Archaeological Survey, Southern
            Division to the Nevada Highway
            Department. Las Vegas.

            Anasazi and Fremont only--no plain
            brown ware sherds.

Bronitsky, Gordon
    1982   Crackpots and Hotpots: Experiments
            in Ceramic Technology. Paper pre-
            sented at the 81st Annual Meeting,
            American Anthropological Association,
            Washington.

            Experiments examine thermal
            resistance of various plastic/non-
            plastic paste compositions.

Brott, Clark W.
    1963   Pottery and Yuman History. *Omniart*
            2:4. American Institute of Archi-
            tects, San Diego Chapter. San Diego,
            California.

            Presents a summary overview written
            for architects and the general public
            on Yuman prehistory and ceramic
            manufacture; discusses ten stages of
            ceramic production based upon Rogers
            1936.

Brunson, Judy L.
    1985   Corrugated Ceramics as Indicators of
            Interaction Spheres. Chapter 5 in
            Decoding Prehistoric Ceramics, edited
            by B. A. Nelson, pp. 102-127.
            Southern Illinois University Press,
            Carbondale.

            Interesting method for analyzing
            corrugated pottery distributions in
            northeastern Arizona for evidence of
            interaction spheres.

Bryan, Bruce
    1964   A Clay Figurine Found in Southern
            California. *Masterkey* 38:66-69.

            Hohokam figurine found near Lake
            Malibu.

Busby, Colin
    1977   *Civa Shelter, Nye County, Nevada--
            Report of Test Excavations.* UCARFC
            No. 35.

            Shoshone ware recovered as well as
            one B/G.

    1979   *The Prehistory and Human Ecology of
            Garden and Coal Valleys: A Con-
            tribution to the Prehistory of South-
            western Nevada.* UCARFC No. 39.

            Shoshonean and Parowan Fremont sherds
            excavated from Civa Shelter II and
            Slivovitz Shelter. Shoshonean
            Tradition pottery is inferred to have
            been made at Civa Shelter II, one of
            the few sites in the Basin with such
            evidence. Survey of Garden and Coal
            Valleys yielded 22 pottery-bearing
            sites with Shoshonean and/or Fremont
            ceramics.

Butler, B. Robert
    1979a   The Native Pottery of the Upper Snake
            and Salmon River Country. *IA* 3(1):1-10.

            An appraisal of the regional pottery,
            in which the incorrect identification
            of Wilson Butte Plain ware as Sho-
            shonean is perpetuated, but in which
            the presence of Fremont plain wares
            is clearly indicated. It is a pre-
            cursor to Butler 1981b.

    1979b   A Fremont Culture Frontier in the
            Upper Snake and Salmon River Country?
            Tebiwa 18.

    1979c   A Promontory Pottery Find at the Foot
            of the Lost River Range in Eastern
            Idaho. *Tebiwa* 20.

    1980a   Towards a Better Understanding of the
            Fremont Problem in Southern Idaho: A
            Reply to Plew's Comments. *IA* 4(1):
            11-14.

    1980b   Additional Notes on the Occurrence of
            Fremont Basketry in Eastern Idaho.
            IA 4(1):6-7.

    1981a   Southern Idaho Plainware: What Are
            the Facts? *PA* 26(92):157-159.

A critical comment on a proposed, probably spurious pottery type, in which problems relating to the considerable variability in the plain wares of the region are mentioned, along with some preliminary data bearing on these problems.

1981b *When Did the Shoshoni Begin to Occupy Southern Idaho?: Essays on Late Prehistoric Cultural Remains from the Upper Snake and Salmon River Country.* Occasional Papers of the Idaho Museum of Natural History No. 32.

Reviews material culture remains, basketry, pottery, and projectile points in particular, from a series of sites in the region that point to a very late prehistoric—early historic Shoshonean occupation, preceded by a Fremont occupation.

1982 Moapa Black-on-Gray Pottery from South-Central Idaho. *Tebiwa* 19(1): 79-80.

1983a Problems in the Classification of Plain Potsherds from Southern Idaho. Paper presented at Great Basin/California Pottery Workshop, April 23, Bishop.

1983b An Introduction to the Prehistoric Pottery of Southern Idaho. Paper presented at Great Basin/California Pottery Workshop, April 23, Bishop.

1983c *The Quest for the Historic Fremont and a Guide to the Prehistoric Pottery of Southern Idaho.* Idaho Museum of Natural History Occasional Papers No. 33.

Provides brief, generalized descriptions of Great Salt Lake Gray, Promontory Gray, and Shoshonean wares from southern Idaho.

Campbell, E. W. C.
1929a A Museum in the Desert. *Masterkey* 3(3):5-10.

Lower Colorado Buff Ware ollas and bowls cached in the Mojave Desert.

1929b The Finding of the Five. *Masterkey* 3(5):13-19.

Ten Lower Colorado Buff Ware ollas from two Mojave Desert caches.

1931a *An Archaeological Survey of the Twenty-Nine Palms Region.* Southwest Museum Papers No. 7.

Photos and general descriptions of pottery found in southern California desert, probably mainly LCBW.

Campbell, (EWC) Mrs. Wm. H.
1931b Cave Magic. *Masterkey* 4(8):236-241.

Ollas from Twenty-Nine Palms, California; LCBW.

Casjens, Laurel Ann
1974 *The Prehistoric Human Ecology of Southern Ruby Valley, Nevada.* Ph.D. dissertation, Department of Anthropology, Harvard University.

Shoshoni pottery and one Snake Valley Gray sherd were recovered from the excavations of Bronco Charlie Cave in the Ruby Mountains, Elko County, Nevada.

Chace, Paul G.
1973 Clay Figurines, Additional Data. *PCASQ* 9(3):41-43.

Summarizes obscure reports of Southern California figurines.

Chamberlin, Ralph V.
1911 The Ethnohistory of the Gosiute Indians. *AmAn*, *Memoirs* 2(5):329-405.

Describes plants used by Gosiute in making pottery.

Cline, Lara L.
1979 *The Kwaaymii: Reflections on a Lost Culture.* IVC Museum Society Occasional Paper No. 5. El Centro.

Discusses pottery making and uses; photos of pots made 1900-1920; eastern San Diego County.

Coale, George L.
1963 A Study of Shoshonean Pottery. *Tebiwa* 6(2):1-11.

Generalized description of Shoshonean brown wares and argument for their origin from Eskimo wares.

Colton, Harold S.
1935 Naming Pottery Types and Rules of Priority. *Science* 82(2133):462-463.

1939a *An Archaeological Survey of Northwestern Arizona Including the Description of Fifteen New Pottery Types.* MNA,B No. 16.

A taxonomic description of Tizon
Brown Ware and its individual types
based upon Hargrave's 1938 surface
collections from northwestern Arizona
(Cerbat, Aquarius, Prescott, Topoc,
Pyramid Gray, Boulder and Sandy
Brown, Needles R/Bf). See Colton
1952, 1955, 1956 and 1958 for
updates.

1939c *Primitive Pottery Firing Methods.*
MNA,N No. 11(1).

Discusses Southwestern firing methods.

1939b The Reducing Atmosphere and Oxidizing
Atmosphere in Prehistoric Southwestern Ceramics. *AA* 4(3):224-231.

1943 The Principles of Analogous Pottery
Types. *AmAn* 45(2):316-320.

1945 Another Unfired Sherd from Black Dog
Cave, Loganville Gray. *Plateau*
17(4):69-70.

Virgin Branch Anasazi unfired sherd
from Black Dog Cave, Clark County,
southern Nevada; see also McGregor
1945.

1952 *Pottery Types of the Arizona Strip
and Adjacent Areas in Utah and
Nevada.* MNA,CS No. 1.

Virgin, Tusayan and Lino Gray; latter
two revised in Colton 1955, 1956,
1958.

1953 *Potsherds: An Introduction to the
Study of Prehistoric Southwestern
Ceramics.* MNA,B No. 25.

Rudimentary primer on how to analyze
potsherds and describe types, as
applied in the Southwest; good for
standard terminology and guidelines.
See Shepard 1956 for greater detail.

1955 *Pottery Types of the Southwest.*
MNA,CS No. 3.

Describes wares from Northern
Arizona; Tusayan Gray and White,
Little Colorado Gray and White.

1956 *Pottery Types of the Southwest.*
MNA,CS No. 3C.

Describes wares from northeastern
Arizona; San Juan Red, Tsegi Orange,
Homolovi Orange, Winslow Orange,
Awatovi Yellow, Jeddito Yellow, and
Sichomovi Red.

1958 *Pottery Types of the Southwest.*
MNA,CS No. 3D.

Describes wares from central and west
central Arizona (Upland Cerbat):
Alameda Brown (Colton), Tizon Brown
(Euler and Dobyns), Lower Colorado
Buff (Schroeder), Prescott Gray
(Colton), San Francisco Mt. Gray
(Colton).

1965 *Check List of Southwestern Pottery
Types.* MNA,CS No. 2 (revised).

Summarizes pottery types as of that
date; see Oppelt 1976 for more recent
list.

Colton, Harold S., and Lyndon L. Hargrave
1937 *Handbook of Northern Arizona Pottery
Wares.* MNA,B No. 11.

Original Northern Arizona wares
descriptions—see later revisions
(Colton 52, 55, 56, 58, 65).
Ch. 5 gives basic information on
description of types.

Cowan, Richard A., and Kurt Wallof
1974 Final Report, Field Work and Artifact
Analysis, Southern California Edison,
No. 2 Control—Casa Diablo 115 kv
Transmission Line. Report submitted
by Archaeological Research Unit,
University of California, Riverside,
to Southern California Edison.

Pp. 39-40 describe OVBW sherds.

Crabtree, Robert H., and D. D. Ferraro
1980 *Artifact Assemblages from the
Pahranagat Lincoln County, Nevada.*
BLM Nevada, Contributions to the
Study of Cultural Resources Technical
Report No. 4. Reno.

Describes sherds from survey as
variety of Paiute Ware.

Cressman, Luther S.
1942 Pottery. In *Archaeological
Researches in the Northern Great
Basin,* p. 91. Carnegie Institution
of Washington Publication No. 538.

Mentions eight plain sherds from
Catlow Cave No. 1, two of which were
analyzed by F. R. Matson, Jr.

Dalley, Gardiner F.
1976 *Swallow Shelter and Associated Sites.*
UUAP No. 96.

Fremont Great Salt Lake Gray Ware and Shoshone Ware recovered from Swallow Shelter and other sites in northwestern Utah and adjacent northeastern Nevada.

Davis, Edward H.
1928　*Modern Pottery Vessels from San Diego County.* MAI 5:93-96.

Describes manufacture of Diegueño vessels; illustrates large storage jar used for mesquite, piñon, and other seeds.

1967　Diegueño Basketry and Pottery. *PCASQ* 3(1):59-66.

Contains the edited papers of E. H. Davis housed at the Federal Records Center in Bell, California; discusses how Diegueño ceramics were produced; notes the use of sand and ground sherd in unfired clay to prevent shrinkage; defines a series of Diegueño terms for the various ceramic vessel forms and the tools for the production of ollas.

Davis, E. L.
1964　*An Archaeological Survey of the Mono Lake Basin and Two Rockshelters, Mono County, California.* UCAS,AR 6:225-353.

P. 277 notes rarity of pottery in Mono Basin and Montgomery Pass areas.

Davis, James T.
1959　*Further Notes on Clay Human Figurines in the Western U.S.* UCASR No. 48.

Describes a number of clay figurines from California and other western states.

1962　*The Rustler Rockshelter Site (SBr-288), a Culturally Stratified Site in the Mojave Desert, California.* UCASR 57:25-56.

Patayan materials; Owens Valley ceramics, Havasu Buff, Tizon Brown; Lower Colorado Buff and others.

Davis, James T., and Adan E. Treganza
1959　*The Patterson Mound: A Comparative Analysis of the Archaeology of Site Ala-328.* UCASR No. 47.

Several baked clay balls were recovered from this San Francisco Bay site which are inferred to be boiling stones (p. 60).

Dean, Patricia W.
1983　Black Rock Cave Ceramics. In *Black Rock Cave Revisited*, by David B. Madsen, pp. 60-66. Bureau of Land Management, Utah Cultural Resource Series No. 14. Salt Lake City.

Describes seven Snake Valley Gray and 23 Northern Shoshoni/Great Salt Lake Gray sherds.

1984　Similarities in Techniques of Manufacture Between Northern "Numic" and Northern Fremont Pottery. Paper presented at 19th Great Basin Anthropological Conference, Boise.

Deatrick, Stephen Lee
1978　Another Earthenware Vessel from Grass Valley, Nevada. In *History and Prehistory at Grass Valley, Nevada,* edited by C. W. Clewlow, H. F. Wells, and R. D. Ambro, pp. 137-140. Monograph VII, Institute of Archaeology. University of California, Los Angeles.

Describes reconstructed portion of Shoshonean pot (no photo).

DeBoer, Warren R.
1985　Pots and Pans Do Not Speak, Nor Do They Lie: The Case for Occasional Reductionism. In *Decoding Prehistoric Ceramics*, edited by Ben A. Nelson, pp. 347-357. Southern Illinois University Press, Carbondale.

Use-life of pots among the Shipibo-Conibo of eastern Peru; examines effect of size and weight on survival, and looks at applicability of ethnoarchaeological analogy.

Dobyns, Henry F.
1956　Prehistoric Indian Occupation Within the Eastern Area of the Yuman Complex: A Study in Applied Archaeology. Ms. submitted to Marlo and Marks, Phoenix, Arizona.

Upland Cerbat.

Dobyns, Henry F., and Robert C. Euler
1956　Ethnographic and Archaeological Identification of Walapai Ceramics. Paper delivered at 32nd Annual Meeting, American Association for the Advancement of Science, Southwest and Rocky Mountain Division, Las Cruces.

Traces production of Tizon Brown from prehistoric Cerbat to ethnographic Walapai, A.D. 700-1800.

1970 *Wauba Yuma's People: The Comparative Sociopolitical Structure of the Pai Indians of Arizona.* Prescott College Studies in Anthropology No. 3.

Upland Cerbat.

Dodd, Walter A., Jr.
1982 *Final Year Excavations at the Evans Mound Site.* UUAP No. 106.

Fremont site located in the Parowan Valley of southwestern Utah. Ceramics consisted mainly of Snake Valley wares--Gray, Black-on-gray, and Corrugated. Other Fremont and Virgin Branch Anasazi pottery types were also represented.

Donnan, Christopher B.
1964 *A Suggested Culture Sequence for the Providence Mountains.* UCAS,AR 1963-64:1-22.

Outlines culture sequence with Yumans (Lowland Patayan Brown Ware) replaced by incoming Shoshoneans who learn pottery-making from Mojave.

Driver, Harold E.
1937 *Culture Element Distributions: VI. Southern Sierra Nevada.* UCAR 1(2): 53-154. Berkeley.

Pottery manufacture, vessel shapes and decoration (p. 80); additional details and general discussion of pottery east of Sierras (p. 122).

Driver, Harold E., and W. C. Massey
1957 *Comparative Studies of North American Indians.* Transactions of the American Philosophical Society 47(2). Philadelphia.

Chapter 6 discusses uses of ceramic vessels for food preparation in Great Basin California; Map 127 shows distribution; pp. 332-333, 339-341 discusses pottery-making.

Drover, Christopher E.
1975 Early Ceramics from Southern California. *JCA* 2(1):101-107.

Describes fired clay objects.

1978 Prehistoric Ceramic Objects from Catalina Island. *JCA* 5(1):78-83.

Used thermoluminescence to date two fired clay objects.

1979a *The Human Paleoecology of the Northern Mohave Sink, San Bernardino County, California.* Ph.D. dissertation, Department of Anthropology, University of California, Riverside.

Discusses TBW, LCBW and puebloid sherds identified by M. Rogers in the Cronese Basin.

1979b A review of "A southern California indigenous ceramic typology: A contribution to Malcolm J. Rogers research" by R. V. May. *JCGBA* 1(1): 205-206.

Drover, Christopher E., R. E. Taylor, Thomas Cairns and Jonathan Ericson
1979a Thermoluminescence Determinations on Early Ceramic Materials from Coastal Southern California. *AA* 44(2): 285-295.

Used thermoluminescence to date same objects (Drover 1975) from Orange County.

Drucker, Philip
1941 *Culture Element Distributions: XVII Yuman-Piman.* UCAR 6(3):91-230.

Discusses pottery making and vessel shapes (pp. 107-109, 176-178), uses (p. 101) for Diegueño, Akwa'ala, Mohave, Pima, Papago, Yaqui, Yavapai, Walapai, and Shivwits Paiute.

DuBois, Constance G.
1907 Diegueño Mortuary Ollas. *AmAn* 9: 484-486.

Illustrates and describes two ollas from southern California.

Dunnell, Robert C.
1970 Seriation Method and Its Evaluation. *AA* 35(3):305-319.

Critiques use of seriation to construct chronologies; stipulates conditions necessary for chronological inferences.

Elsasser, A. B.
1960 *The Archaeology of the Sierra Nevada in California and Nevada.* UCASR No. 51.

Provides map of pottery sites in region and discusses relation to Great Basin.

1963   Two Fired Clay Figurines from Central
        California. *AA* 29(1):118-120.

        Photos and descriptions of figurines
        from Sacramento and Marin Counties.

1978   Two Unusual Artifacts from the Sierra
        Nevada of California. *JCA* 5(1):
        73-88.

        Describes an incised clay tablet/
        figurine? fragment and notes similar
        objects from other sites.

Elston, R. G.
1979   The Archaeology of U.S. 395 Right-of-
        Way between Stead, Nevada, and
        Hallelujah Junction, California.
        Report submitted to California
        Department of Transportation and
        Nevada Department of Transportation
        by the Nevada Archaeological Survey,
        University of Nevada, Reno. Ms. on
        file, Getchell Library, Special
        Collections, University of Nevada,
        Reno.

        Report contains illustrated descrip-
        tions of 222 fired clay objects from
        site 4Las317, a small winter campsite
        with house remains and other features
        in Long Valley near Hallelujah
        Junction, California. Many of these
        objects were found stratigraphically
        above features C14 dated between A.D.
        740 and A.D. 1430. Most of the clay
        objects appear to be shapeless lumps,
        but many are fragments of figurines,
        including two animals and one bird
        head. Nine objects are discs or disc
        fragments; three objects are pot-
        sherds.

Enfield, R., and G. Enfield
1964   *Mammoth Creek Cave, Mono County,
        California.* UCAS,AR 1963-1964:
        393-424.

        Site report includes description of
        recovered OVBW.

Ericson, Jonathan E., and Suzanne P. DeAtley
1976   Reconstructing Ceramic Assemblages:
        An Experiment to Derive the
        Morphology and Capacity of Parent
        Vessels from Sherds. *AA* 41(4):
        484-489.

        Broke 25 modern vessels of various
        shapes to test whether vessel capac-
        ity and morphology could be recon-
        structed from sherds.

Ericson, Jonathan E., D. W. Read, and C. Burke
1972   Research Design: The Relationships
        Between the Primary Functions and the
        Physical Properties of Ceramic
        Vessels and their Implications for
        Distributions on an Archaeological
        Site. *Anthropology UCLA* 3(2):84-95.

        Presents a hypothesis/test implica-
        tions model of "vessel form equals
        function," and implied behavioral
        correlates that could be derived from
        archaeological data.

Ericson, Jonathan E., and E. Gary Stickel
1973   A Proposed Classification System for
        Ceramics. *World Archaeology* 4(3):
        357-367.

        Experimental attempt to correlate
        vessel capacity with vessel weight so
        that archaeological sherd weights can
        be used to predict assemblage capaci-
        ties and to draw behavioral inferences.

Euler, Robert C.
1958   *Walapai Culture-History.* Ph.D.
        dissertation, Department of
        Anthropology, U. New Mexico, Albuquerqi

        Examines Cerbat Branch of Upland
        Patayan in northwestern Arizona (A.D.
        1150-1776) and relates to modern
        Walapai; summarizes Tizon Brown
        Ware.

1959   Comparative Comments on California
        Pottery. In *Archaeological Resources
        of Borrego State Park,* by C. W.
        Meighan, pp. 41-44. UCAS,AR No.
        1959.

        Compares southern California Tizon
        Brown Ware to Arizonan.

1964   Southern Paiute Archaeology. *AA*
        29(3):379-381.

        Amplifies Baldwin's (1950a) descriptio
        of Southern Paiute pottery.

1966   *Southern Paiute Ethnohistory.* UUAP
        No. 78.

        Pp. 114-115, brief mention of
        historical observations of Southern
        Paiute pottery.

1982   Ceramic Patterns of the Hakataya
        Tradition. In *Southwestern Ceramics:
        A Comparative Review,* edited by A. H.
        Schroeder, pp. 52-69. The Arizona
        Archaeologist No. 15. Arizona
        Archaeological Society, Phoenix.

Most of the discussion concentrates on pottery types from western Arizona; brief note on southern California wares.

Euler, Robert C., and Henry Dobyns
1956   Tentative Correlations of Arizona Upland Ceramics. Paper delivered at the 32nd Annual Meeting, American Association for the Advancement of Science, Las Cruces.

Discusses various origin theories for Tizon Brown Ware.

1958   Tizon Brown Ware, a Descriptive Revision. In *Pottery Types of the Southwest*, edited by H. S. Colton, MNA,CS No. 3D.

Revises Colton 1952 based on ethnographic and archaeological fieldwork for the Hualapai Land Claims case.

Evans, William S.
1969   California Indian Pottery: A Native Contribution to the Culture of the Ranchos. *PCASQ* 5(3):71-81.

Proposes a new type of Tizon Brown Ware distinct from Palomar Brown type, thought to have been produced during the historic period for rancho use.

Ewers, J. C.
1945   The Case for Blackfoot Pottery. *AmAn* 47(2):289-299.

Evidence for brown ware pottery among the Blackfoot.

Fenenga, Franklin
1952   The Archaeology of the Slick Rock Village, Tulare County, California. *AA* 17(4):339-347.

Distinguishes Sierran plain ware as separate from OVBW; names it Tulare Plain, see Lathrap and Shutler (1955) for counter argument.

1977   An Early Account of a Fired Clay Anthropomorphic Figurine from Marin County. *JCA* 4(2):308-310.

Illustrates figurine reported in 1924 newspaper article.

Flaim, F., and A. D. Warburton
1961   Additional Figurines from Rasmussen Cave. *Masterkey* 35(1):19-24.

Fremont figurines from Rasmussen Cave, northeastern Utah.

Flannery, R.
1953   *The Gros Ventres of Montana: Part 1, Social Life.* Catholic University of America, Anthropological Series No. 15.

Notes pottery use by Gros Ventres in Montana.

Fontana, Bernard L., William J. Robinson, Charles W. Cormack, Ernest E. Leavitt, Jr.
1962   *Papago Indian Pottery.* The American Ethnological Society. University of Washington Press, Seattle.

Modern ethnographic account of pottery making; good photos.

Forbes, Jack D.
1961   Pueblo Pottery in the San Fernando Valley. *Masterkey* 65(1):36-38.

Walapai, Mohave and Hopi sherds found in the San Fernando Valley, California.

Foster, George M.
1960   Life-Expectancy of Utilitarian Pottery in Tzintzuntzan, Michoacan, Mexico. *AA* 25(4):606-609.

Ethnographic account of vessel use, reuse, and disposal.

Fowler, Catherine S.
1970   *Great Basin Anthropology ... A Bibliography.* DRI No. 5.

Good resource guide with clear categories and many annotations.

Fowler, Catherine S., and Don D. Fowler
1981   The Southern Paiute: A.D. 1400-1776. In *The Protohistoric Period in the North American Southwest, A.D. 1450-1700*, edited by D. R. Wilcox and W. B. Masse, pp. 129-162. ASUARP No. 24.

Reviews archaeological and ethnographic evidence of Southern Paiute pottery making; photo of incised pot collected by E. Palmer.

Fowler, Don D.
1968a   *Archaeological Survey in Eastern Nevada*, 1966. DRI No. 2.

Reports Snake Valley Gray wares and Deep Creek Buff from two sites in Snake Valley; Shoshonean pottery from numerous sites in Elko and White Pine counties; and presents a table and map displaying distribution of Shoshoni and Southern Paiute pottery in Great Basin.

1968b *The Archaeology of Newark Cave, White Pine County, Nevada.* DRI No. 3.

Shoshoni brown ware and one sherd of Snake Valley B/G.

1975 Current Research: Great Basin and California. *AA* 40(4):489.

Reports B. R. Butler's discovery of Shoshonean pottery with radiocarbon dates of 720 ± 70 B.P. and 450 ± 80 B.P. from excavations at Blackfoot Reservoir, Idaho.

Fowler, Don D., David B. Madsen, and Eugene M. Hattori
1973 *Prehistory of Southeastern Nevada.* DRI No. 6.

Virgin Branch Anasazi, Fremont, and Shoshonean pottery are described from several excavated rockshelters and surface sites.

Fowler, Don D., and J. F. Matley
1978 *The Edward Palmer Collection from Southern Utah, 1875.* UUAP No. 99, Miscellaneous Papers No. 20.

Describes 52 Fremont and Virgin vessels collected by Palmer (1875) from Santa Clara, Utah, mound as well as three ethnographic Southern Paiute vessels, and gambling implements.

1979 *Material Culture of the Numa, the John Wesley Powell Collection 1867-1880.* Smithsonian Contributions to Anthropology No. 26. Washington, D.C.

Unfired "figurines" p. 84, Fig. 81, and North Creek Gray olla p. 84, Fig. 45c.

Fremont, John C.
1845 *Report of the Exploring Expedition to the Rocky Mountains in the Year 1842 and to Oregon and Northern California in the Years 1843-1844.* Glaes and Senton, Printers, Washington, D.C.

See below.

1886 *Memoirs of My Life.* 2 vols. Belford, Clarke, and Co., Chicago and New York.

Recalls seeing a small pot containing squirrel, suspended over a fire, near Elko, Nevada.

Frison, George C.
1973 *The Wardell Buffalo Trap 48SU301: Communal Procurement in the Upper Green River Basin, Wyoming.* Anthropological Papers, Museum of Anthropology, University of Michigan 48:68-70, 81-84.

248 sherds found in meat-processing area; differ from descriptions for Shoshoni or Fremont wares, suggest Woodland or Navajo similarity; mention other pottery found in Wyoming.

Gautier, D. L.
1979 A Brief Look at the Clay Minerals from the Glenn's Ferry Formation, Snake River Plain, Idaho. *Tebiwa* 19.

Gayton, A. H.
1929 Yokuts and Western Mono Pottery-Making. *UCPAAE* 24(3):239-255.

Ethnographic account of pottery making vessel forms, clay sources, etc., with photos.

1948 *Yokuts and Western Mono Ethnography,* I and II. UCAR 10 (1 & 2).

Summarizes the data presented in detail in Gayton 1929, but adds much more data about the cultural context in which the pots were used; pp. 17, 51, 79-81, 148 161, 226, 265.

Gebhard, D., G. A. Agogino, and V. Haynes
1964 Horned Owl Cave, Wyoming. *AA* 29(3): 360-368.

Laramie Mountains: Shoshonean sherds.

Giddings, J. L., Jr.
1952 *The Arctic Woodland Culture of the Kobuk River.* University Museum Monograph. University of Pennsylvania, Philadelphia.

Describes Eskimo pottery which Coale (1963) felt was the source of Shoshonean brown ware tradition.

Gifford, E. W., and W. E. Schenck
1926 Archaeology of the Southern San Joaquin Valley, California. *UCPAAE* 23(1):1-122.

Discusses early fired-clay industry; provides photos of objects.

Gifford, James C. (editor)
1953   A Guide to the Description of Pottery
       Types in the Southwest. Ms. prepared
       by the Archaeological Seminar of the
       Department of Anthropology,
       University of Arizona, Spring 1952.

Gladwin, Harold S.
1929   *The Western Range of the Red-on-Buff*.
       Medallion Papers No. 5. Gila Pueblo.

Goerke, Elizabeth B., and Francis A. Davidson
1975   Baked Clay Figurines of Marin County.
       Journal of New World Archaeology
       1(2):9-24.

       Describes 40 anthropomorphic figu-
       rines found in 15 central California
       sites.

Griffen, Dorothy W.
1963   Prehistory of the Southern Sierra
       Nevada: A Preliminary Investigation.
       Part I, *Masterkey* 37(2):49-57. Part
       II, *Masterkey* 37(3):105-113.

       Discusses pottery occurrences in
       Kawaiisu area sites.

Griset, Suzanne
1981   Ceramic Analysis. In *Archaeological
       Investigation in the Southern Sierra
       Nevada: The Kennedy Meadows and
       Rockhouse Basin Segments of the
       Pacific Crest Trail*, edited by K. R.
       McGuire, pp. 186-197. Ms. on file,
       USFS, Sequoia National Forest,
       Porterville.

       Describes OVBW sherds from test exca-
       vations of Sierra Nevada crest sites.

1982   Pottery. In *Excavations Along the
       Pacific Crest Trail in the Southern
       Sierra Nevada: CA-Ker-1286*, edited
       by K. R. McGuire, pp. 83-89. Ms. on
       file, USFS, Sequoia National Forest,
       Porterville.

       Describes OVBW sherds from site on
       Sierra Nevada crest.

1985a Analysis of Pottery Collections from
       Mitchell Caverns and Surrounding
       Area. Appendix in *The Archaeology of
       Mitchell Caverns*. by Diana G. Pinto.
       California Archeological Reports (in
       press), State of California Resources
       Agency, Cultural Resources Management
       Unit, Department of Parks and
       Recreation, Sacramento.

       Describes TBW, LCBW, and puebloid
       sherds and reconstructed vessels from
       caverns and campsites in Providence
       Mountain area of eastern Mohave
       desert.

1985b Ceramics. In *Archaeological Test
       Investigations at CA-Iny-30: A
       Multicomponent Prehistoric Site Near
       Lone Pine, Inyo County, California*,
       by Mark E. Basgall, Kelly R. McGuire,
       and Amy J. Gilreath, pp. 134-153.
       Report prepared for California
       Department of Transportation,
       District 9, Bishop.

       Describes OVBW assemblage from site
       in Owens Valley.

Grosscup, Gordon L.
1962   Plateau Shoshonean Prehistory. *AA*
       28:41-45.

       P. 44 notes that Fremont and
       Shoshonean pottery both have finger-
       nail incising.

Gruhn, Ruth
1961   *The Archaeology of Wilson Butte Cave,
       South-Central Idaho*. Occasional
       Papers of the Idaho State College
       Museum No. 6.

       Pottery recovered from a radiocarbon-
       dated context; 4 rim and 8 body sherds
       from shallow bowls with wide mouths and
       fingernail indentations on the lips,
       comprising a type called Wilson Butte
       Plain Ware. believedto be an uncommong
       type of Shoshoni pottery characteristic
       of the Dietrich phase in south-central
       Idaho (pp. 98-100); restudy of this
       pottery at the University of Utah in
       1980 led to the conclusion that it
       was typical Great Salt Lake Gray Ware
       (Butler 1981b).

Gunnerson, James H.
1956   Fremont Ceramics. In *Papers of the
       Third Great Basin Archaeological
       Conference*, pp. 54-62. UUAP No. 26.

       Describes variety found in temper of
       Fremont Turner Gray wares from south-
       eastern Utah survey; speculates close
       affinity with western Utah plain grays.

1969   *The Fremont Culture: A Study in
       Culture Dynamics on the Northern
       Anasazi Frontier*. PPM No. 59(2).

       Fremont pottery in Utah.

Guthrie, Georgiana
1957   Southern Sierra Nevada Archaeology.
        *Archaeological Survey Association of
        Southern California Newsletter*
        4(1-2):3-5.

        Describes archaeological evidence of
        pottery in Kawaiisu area.

Hall, M. C.
1985   *Test Excavations of 26-Ek-2710, Elko
        County, Nevada: A Protohistoric
        Rockshelter on the South Fork of the
        Humboldt River.* Archaeological
        Research Services Report, Virginia
        City.

        Describes Shoshoni ware found in
        rockshelter.

Hally, David J.
1983a   Use Alteration of Pottery Vessel
        Surfaces: An Important Source of
        Evidence for Identification of Vessel
        Functions. *North American
        Archaeologist* 4(1):3-26.

        Looks at wear patterns and soot
        deposition on whole vessels for indi-
        cations of vessel function and use.

1983b   The Interpretive Potential of Pottery
        from Domestic Contexts. *Mid-
        Continental Journal of Archaeology*
        8(2):163-196.

        Uses ethnographic examples of vessel
        recycling patterns, storage and use
        locations, use life, and discard pro-
        cesses to interpret archaeological
        ceramics.

1986   The Identification of Vessel
        Function: A Case Study from North-
        west Georgia. *AA* 51(2):267-295.

        Further refinement of Hally 1983a
        and b.

Hargrave, Lyndon L.
1974   Type Determinants in Southwestern
        Ceramics and Some of Their
        Implications. *Plateau* 46(3):76-95.

        Argues against use of "types" as
        cultural designations; rather they
        should be restricted to consistently
        distinct criteria such as color,
        form, temper, etc.

Hargrave, Lyndon L., and Harold S. Colton
1935   *What Do Potsherds Tell Us?* MNA,N
        No. 7(12).

Hargrave, Michael L., and David P. Braun
1981   Chronometry of Mechanical Performance
        Characteristics of Woodland Ceramics:
        Methods, Results, Applications.
        Paper presented at 46th Annual
        Meeting, Society for American
        Archaeology, San Diego.

        Argues that vessel form and construc-
        tion are conditioned by their in-
        tended use, hence changes in mor-
        phology or attributes of mechanical
        performance reflect changes in use.
        Examines dated samples of Woodland
        pottery for changes in these attri-
        butes. Interesting techniques, appli
        cable to plain wares.

Harner, Michael J.
1957   *Potsherds and the Tentative Dating of
        the San Gorgonio-Big Maria Trail.*
        UCASR 37:35-37.

        Describes pottery found on trail which
        extends from San Bernardino to Colorado
        River.

1958   *Lowland Patayan Phases in Lower
        Colorado River Valley and Colorado
        Desert.* UCASR 42:93-97.

        Sets up general pottery typology
        based on stratigraphy of Bouse site.

Harrington, Mark R.
1926   Western Extension of Early Pueblo
        Culture. *MAI* 3(2):69-73.

        Brief note regarding Fremont pottery
        found in rockshelters near Baker,
        eastern Nevada.

1927   A Primitive Pueblo City in Nevada.
        AmAn 29(2):262-277.

        Provides brief preliminary reference
        to Pueblo and Paiute pottery from
        Muddy River Valley, Nevada.

1928   Tracing the Pueblo Boundary in
        Nevada. *MAI* 5(2):235-240.

        Brief descriptions of Virgin Branch
        Anasazi and Fremont pottery from
        several sites in eastern and southern
        Nevada along Harrington's "pottery
        boundary."

1930   *Archaeological Explorations in
        Southern Nevada.* Southwest Museum
        Papers No. 4.

Describes Pueblo pottery from Mesa
House, pp. 71-81; from Paiute Cave,
pp. 114-115; and gives brief description of Paiute pottery, p. 24.

1932   Relics of an Abandoned Colony.
        Masterkey 6(4):115-116.

        Describes two Fremont vessels,
        sherds, and other artifacts from
        caves near Garrison, western Utah,
        found by a local resident and given
        to the Southwest Museum.

1955a   Ancient Life Among the Southern
        California Indians. *Masterkey*
        29:79-88, 117-129, 153-167.

        Anecdotal account of Luiseño pottery
        making and use.

1955b   Unique Olla. *Masterkey* 29(6):203.

        Diegueño incised water olla.

Harrison, R. R., and J. Hanson
1980   *Fremont-Shoshoni Relationships in
        Southwestern Idaho: Comments on Use
        and Misuse of Published Data.* IA
        No. 3(3).

        Critiques Plew 1979a.

Hawley, Florence M.
1936   *Field Manual of Prehistoric
        Southwestern Pottery Types.*
        University of New Mexico Bulletin
        291, Anthropology Series 1(4)
        (revised 1950).

        First comprehensive compilation of
        type descriptions, particularly for
        eastern Arizona and New Mexico areas.

Hedges, Ken
1973   Hakataya Figurines from Southern
        California. *PCASQ* 9(3):1-40.

        Discusses figurines and effigy pots
        and relates them to Hakataya, Hohokam
        and Yuman traditions; good photos.

Heizer, Robert F.
1937   Baked Clay Objects of the Lower
        Sacramento Valley, California. *AA*
        3:34-50.

        Discusses and illustrates variety and
        distribution of baked clay objects in
        central California and compares them
        to others in Southwest and Great
        Basin.

1949   *The Archaeology of Central California
        I: The Early Horizon.* UCAR 12(1).

        Brief note on baked clay objects from
        central California.

Heizer, Robert F. (editor)
1954   *Notes on the Utah Utes by Edward
        Palmer, 1866-1877.* UUAP No. 17, pp.
        7-14.

        Brief note, p. 12, on pottery manu-
        facture and description of conical
        cooking pots; describes cooking tech-
        niques, including stone boiling in
        pots, and drilled holes for suspen-
        sion as well as for repairing cracks.

Heizer, Robert F., Martin A. Baumhoff and C. W.
Clewlow, Jr.
1968   *Archaeology of South Fork Shelter
        (NV-EL-11), Elko County, Nevada.*
        UCASR 71:1-58.

        Pp. 18-20 describe 12 sherds of
        Shoshoni ware and speculate on west-
        ward diffusion of Great Basin
        pottery making from the plains

Heizer, Robert F., and Richard K. Beardsley
1943   Fired Clay Human Figurines in Central
        and Northern California. *AA* 9(2):
        199-217.

        Illustrates California figurines and
        compares their distribution to those
        found in the Southwest.

Heizer, Robert F., and D. M. Pendergast
1954   Additional Data on Fired Clay Human
        Figurines from California. *AA*
        21(2):181-185.

        Describes 25 figurines from Marin,
        Sonoma, and Humboldt Counties.

Heizer, Robert F., and Adan E. Treganza
1944   Mines and Quarries of the Indians of
        California. *California Journal of
        Mines and Geology* 40:291-359.

        Lists ethnographic clay resource loca-
        tions in California; provides a general
        map of locations.

Henrickson, Elizabeth F., and Mary M. A.
McDonald
1983   Ceramic Form and Function: An Ethno-
        graphic Search and an Archaeological
        Application. *AmAn* 85:630-643.

Assumes that similar functions require
similar vessel forms, and compiles
average vessel dimensions for different functional classes from
world-wide ethnographic sample; uses
these data to predict the function of
archaeological vessels.

Ceramic materials (p. 16); approximately 1,000 sherds analyzed and
divided into several wares (pp.
193-194, 202-224); petrography of the
pottery by C. B. Hunt (pp. 195-201);
illustrations of vessel shapes, rims
and designs (pp. 211, 216, 218, 221);
baked and unbaked figurines;
miniatures (pp. 224-230).

Hester, Thomas R.
  1973 *Chronological Ordering of Great Basin
        Prehistory.* UCARFC No. 17.

        Brief discussion of Great Basin ceram-
        ics.

Heuett, M. L.
  1974 Boulder Springs: Cerbat-Hualapai
        Rock Shelter in Northwestern Arizona.
        M.S. thesis, Department of
        Anthropology, Northern Arizona
        University, Flagstaff.

        Chapter 4 analyzes Tizon Brown from
        site near Kingman, dated A.D. 900-
        1200; uses Rouse's modal analysis.

Heye, George G.
  1919 Certain Aboriginal Pottery from
        Southern California. *MAI* 7(1):3-48.

        Summarizes shapes, contents, use, and
        deposition of 42 cached, 422 buried
        Diegueno pots, 82 of which had been
        used as cremation urns; gives ranges
        of measurements; many photos.

Hildebrand, Timothy S.
  1974 The Baird Site. In *Excavation of Two
        Sites in the Coso Mountains of Inyo
        County, California.* Maturango Museum
        Monograph No. 1. China Lake.

        Mentions 19 plain sherds.

Hindes, Margaret G.
  1962 *The Archaeology of the Huntington
        Lake Region in the Southern Sierra
        Nevada, California.* UCASR No. 58.

        Compared to Martis-Kings Beach,
        Pinto, etc., Owens Valley Paiute,
        Washo; notes on Owens Valley Brown
        Ware.

Hunt, Alice
  1960 *Archaeology of the Death Valley Salt
        Pan, California.* UUAP No. 47.

Hunt, Charles B.
  1953 Pottery Thin Sections. In *Archaeo-
        logical Survey of Western Utah,* by
        Jack R. Rudy. UUAP No. 12.

        Thin-section analysis of sherds used
        by Rudy (1953) for type descriptions.

  1960 Petrography of the Pottery. In
        *Archaeology of the Death Valley Salt
        Pan, California*, by A. Hunt, pp.
        195-201. UUAP No. 47.

        Petrographic analysis of sherds and
        discussion of probable source areas
        based on the geology of Death Valley.

Huntley, J. L., and M. G. Plew
  1981 A Pottery Vessel from the Mud Springs
        Site. *IA* 5(1):1-3.

        Describes Shoshoni pot from South-
        western Idaho.

Huscher, Betty H., and Harold A. Huscher
  1940 Potsherds from a Pinyon Tree!
        Masterkey 14(4):137-142.

        An Uncompahgre, Colorado Ute pot with
        analysis by A. Shepard and com-
        parisons to Paiute, Yuman, and
        eastern California pots.

Irving, W.
  1868 *The Adventure of Captain Bonneville,
        U.S.A. in the Rocky Mountains and Far
        West.* G. F. Putnam, New York.

        Mentions a Shoshoni cooking salmon in
        vessel near Twin Falls, Idaho.

Irwin, Charles N.
  1980 *The Shoshoni Indians of Inyo County,
        California: The Kerr Manuscript.*
        Ballena Press Publications in
        Archaeology, Ethnology and History
        No. 15.

        Panamint Shoshoni account (1930s) of
        pottery-making and uses, p. 28; photo
        of pot, p. 29.

James, Steven R.
1981   Prehistory of the Elko and Ely
       Districts. In *Prehistory, Ethno-
       history, and History of Eastern
       Nevada: A Cultural Resources Summary
       of the Elko and Ely Districts*, edited
       by S. R. James, pp. 89–147. Nevada
       Bureau of Land Management, Cultural
       Resource Series No. 3.

       Distribution of Fremont and Numic
       pottery in eastern Nevada is
       discussed on pp. 136–147, along with
       other traits of these cultures.

James, Steven R., and Robert G. Elston
1983   *A Class II Archaeological Survey in
       the Mt. Hope Vicinity, Eureka County,
       Nevada.* Report on file, Inter-
       mountain Research, Silver City,
       Nevada.

       One Shoshoni Brown Ware rim sherd
       with fingernail incising was recov-
       ered from site 26EU834.

James, Steven R., and Charles D. Zeier
1981   An Archaeological Reconnaissance of
       Eight Candidate Siting Locations in
       White Pine County, Nevada. In *The
       White Pine Power Project: Cultural
       Resource Considerations*, vol. 2.
       Report on file, Intermountain
       Research, Silver City, Nevada.

       A Snake Valley Black-on-gray bowl rim
       sherd and six gray sherds were recov-
       ered from site 26WP1244 in Spring
       Valley. Shoshoni Ware was recovered
       from 26WP1247 in Spring Valley and
       26WP1203 in northern Steptoe Valley,
       eastern Nevada.

Janetski, Joel C.
1981   Ethnohistory/Ethnography of the Elko
       and Ely Districts. In *Prehistory,
       Ethnohistory, and History of Eastern
       Nevada: A Cultural Resources Summary
       of the Elko and Ely Districts*, edited
       by S. R. James, pp. 149–210. Nevada
       Bureau of Land Management, Cultural
       Resource Series No. 3.

       Brief mention of Shoshoni and
       Southern Paiute pottery and vessel
       forms on pp. 190–191.

Jenkins, Dennis L.
1981   *Cliffs Edge: A Pueblo I Site on the
       Lower Virgin River.* M.A. thesis,
       Department of Anthropology,
       University of Nevada, Las Vegas.

       Describes ceramics from excavated
       site contrasted to surface collec-
       tions of 18 Virgin Anasazi sites in
       northwestern Arizona.

1983   Denning Springs Ceramics. Appendix
       in *Excavations at the Denning Springs
       Rockshelter, Avawatz Mountains,
       California,* by Mark Sutton. Ms. on
       file, University of California,
       Riverside, Archaeological Research
       Unit.

       Describes five sherds excavated from
       rockshelter: two brown (SPUW?),
       three false corrugated from single
       vessel; south of Death Valley
       National Monument.

1984   Ceramic Compositions and Cultural
       Influences at Three Sites in Southern
       Nevada and California. Paper pre-
       sented at Southern Nevada Regional
       Ceramic Workshop, University of
       Nevada, Las Vegas, October 27.

       Describes distributions of SPUW/TBW/
       OVBW/LCBW and puebloid wares at three
       sites in southern Nevada/Mohave
       Desert, California, and their impli-
       cations of occupations of these areas
       by different cultures through time.

1985a Spatial and Temporal Distributions of
       Ceramics at Ft. Irwin. Paper pre-
       sented at Annual Meeting of the
       Society for California Archaeology,
       San Diego, March.

       Discusses distribution and chronology
       of brown, buff, and gray wares at Ft.
       Irwin, in the Mojave Desert.

1985b Ceramics of Southcott Cave. Manu-
       script prepared for inclusion in
       archaeological report by Mark Sutton,
       on file at University of California,
       Riverside, Archaeological Research
       Unit.

       Describes six reconstructed vessels
       and three ground sherd disks; TBW
       (possibly some Paiute?), LCBW
       (including a stucco cooking pot and
       fugitive red jar); discusses possible
       vessel functions and cultural affil-
       iations.

1985c Ceramics of Afton Canyon (4-SBr-85).
       Manuscript prepared for inclusion in
       archaeological report by Joan
       Schneider, on file at University of
       California, Riverside, Archaeological
       Research Unit.

Reports 24 buff, gray, and brown
sherds from surface and excavated
samples in central Mojave Desert.

Jennings, Jesse D.
1957   *Danger Cave*. Society for American
Archaeology, Memoirs, No. 14.

Lists quantity and types of Fremont
and Shoshoni sherds found at Danger
and Juke Box Caves, Utah.

1978   *Prehistory of Utah and the Eastern
Great Basin*. UUAP No. 98.

Photos of reconstructed Southern
Paiute and Shoshoni vessels, pp.
237-238.

Johnson, Jerald J. (editor)
1966   *The Archaeology of Site 4-Ama-56*.
Ms. on file, Department of
Anthropology, University of
California, Davis.

Several baked clay objects recovered
(pp. 55-56).

1976   *Archaeological Investigations at the
Blodgett Site (CA-Sac-267) Sloughouse
Locality, California*. Ms. submitted
to National Park Service, Western
Region, Contract No. CX8880-6-0002.

Describes potsherds from site on
Consumnes River, Sacramento County,
which he calls Consumnes Brown Ware.

Judd, Neil M.
1926   *Archaeological Observations North of
the Rio Colorado*. BAEB No. 82.

Includes Fremont pottery from western
Utah.

Kehoe, Alice B.
1959   Ceramic Affiliations in the Northwestern Plains. *AA* 25(2):237-246.

Outlines the wares and ethnic affiliations of three ceramic traditions
in Northwestern Plains: Shoshone,
Pisamiks, and Mandan; describes Great
Falls ware--a Shoshoni tradition
pottery closely affiliated with Snake
River ware.

Kelly, Isabel T.
1964   *Southern Paiute Ethnography*. UUAP
No. 69.

Describes Panguitch unfired pots (p.
186), and Kaibab man's pottery-making
effort after visiting the Hopi (pp.
77-78).

Kelly, William H.
1977   *Cocopa Ethnography*. Anthropological
Papers of the University of Arizona
No. 29.

1940s ethnographic observations of
Cocopa woman making pots.

Kielusiak, Carol M.
1982   *Variability and Distribution of Baked
Clay Artifacts from the Lower
Sacramento-Northern San Joaquin
Valleys of California*. M.A. thesis,
Department of Anthropology,
California State University,
Sacramento.

Surveys baked clay tradition in
central California.

King, Chester, and Dennis G. Casebier
1976   *Background to Historic and Pre-
historic Resources of the East Mojave
Desert Region*. Report prepared for
USDI, BLM California Desert Planning
Program, Riverside, California, by
Archaeological Research Unit,
University of California, Riverside.

Appendix 4 contains discussion of the
numerous pottery types found in the
east Mojave Desert (Anasazi, Tizon
Brown, Colorado Buff, Parker Buff,
and others).

King, Thomas F.
1967   Three Clay Figurines from Marin
County. *Masterkey* 41:138-141.

Describes three anthropomorphic
figurines from central California.

1976   A Cache of Vessels from Cottonwood
Spring (Riv-937). *JCA* 3(1):136-142.

Describes Lower Colorado Buff Ware
olla cached with burden basket, iron
pan, spirit sticks in southeastern
California.

King, W. M.
1875   Account of the Burial of an Indian
Squaw, San Bernardino County,
California, May, 1874. Annual Report
of the Board of Regents of the
Smithsonian Institution, 1874, p.
350. Government Printing Office,
Washington.

Describes burial ceremony (ethnicity
not specified) in which a water olla
is broken over the grave after the
fire has burned out.

Knight, Lavinia
1973   A Figurine from China Ranch
        (4-Iny-962). *PCASQ* 9(3):48-51.

        Fragment from rockshelter in eastern
        California.

Koerper, Henry C., and Arthur E. Flint
1978   Some Comments on "Cerritos Brown"
        Pottery. *PCASQ* 14(2):19-25.

        Critiques creation of this new type
        (Evans 1969) as not distinct from
        Palomar Brown type of southern
        California TBW.

Koerper, Henry C., Christopher E. Drover,
Arthur E. Flint and Gary Hurd
1978   Gabrieleño Tizon Brown Pottery.
        PCASQ 14(3):43-58.

        Uses neutron-activation analysis to
        test local manufacture of Tizon
        Brown.

Kowta, Makoto
1954   Preliminary Report on Excavation in
        Kern County. Ms. #210 on file,
        UCARF, Berkeley.

        Discusses pottery and baked clay
        objects recovered from Ker-62.

Kramer, Carol
1985   Ceramic Ethnoarchaeology. *Annual
        Review of Anthropology* 14:77-102.

        Reviews ethnoarchaeological litera-
        ture concerning ceramic production,
        stylistics, use, disposal, and
        changes in ceramic traditions.

Kroeber, Alfred L.
1925   *Handbook of the Indians of
        California.* BAEB No. 78.

        Ethnographic accounts for W. Mono
        (p. 537); Yokuts (p. 537, Pl. 51);
        Kawaiisu (p. 605); Tubatulabal (pp.
        537, 608); Gabrielino (pp. 628, 822);
        Luiseno (pp. 653, 702, 822); Cahuilla
        (pp. 702-703, 822, Pl. 62); Serrano
        (pp. 702, 822); Diegueño (pp. 702,
        722, 822); Mohave (pp. 702-703,
        737-739, 822, Pl. 68); Yuma (p. 702);
        other Colorado River groups (p. 803);
        general discussion (pp. 822-823).

1935   *Walapai Ethnography.* AmAn, Memoir,
        No. 42.

        Upland Cerbat.

Kroeber, Alfred L., and Michael J. Harner
1955   *Mohave Pottery.* UCAR No. 16(1).

        Describes pots collected by Kroeber
        in 1902-08; gives native terms for
        designs and forms; dimensions;
        photos; clay sources and petrography;
        Harner describes Parker Red-on-buff,
        Fort Mohave variant.

Lanning, Edward P.
1963   Archaeology of the Rose Springs Site,
        Iny 372. *UCPAAE* 49(3):237-336.

        Describes OVBW recovered from strat-
        ified site south of Owens Lake.

Larson, Daniel O.
1981   *A Study of the Settlement Pattern of
        Southern Nevada as Reflected by the
        Archaeological Record.* WAR No. 3(1).

        Uses ceramics as cultural and chrono-
        logical indicators.

Larson, Daniel O., and Katharyne Olson
1984   A Refined Ceramic Chronology for the
        Southern Great Basin. Paper pre-
        sented at 19th Great Basin
        Anthropological Conference, Boise.

        Compares traditional Virgin ceramic
        chronologies with carbon 14-dated
        sites and statistically examines
        ceramic attributes.

Lathrap, Donald W., and C. W. Meighan
1951   *An Archaeological Reconnaissance in
        the Panamint Mountains.* UCASR
        11:11-32.

        Potsherds from four sites in the
        Panamint Mountains analyzed and
        described (pp. 21-23); illustration
        of reconstructed vessel (Plate 3A).

Lathrap, Donald W., and D. Shutler, Jr.
1955   An Archaeological Site in the High
        Sierra of California. *AA* 20(3):
        226-240.

        Excavation of site in Vermillion
        Valley, Fresno County; describes 22
        sherds as OVBW and discounts
        Fenenga's (1952) distinction of
        Sierran sherds as separate Tulare
        Plain ware.

Layton, Thomas N.
1970   *High Rock Archaeology: An Inter-
        pretation of the Northwestern Great
        Basin.* Ph.D. dissertation,
        Department of Anthropology, Harvard
        University, Cambridge.

Describes small sample of sherds and posits it is Shoshoni.

1973   Evidence for Pottery Manufacture on the Northwestern Periphery of the Great Basin. *Masterkey* 47(1):23-27.

Describes two potsherds, four coils, four shaped fragments from Hanging Rock Cave, northwestern Nevada.

Leonard, Zenas
1839   *Narrative of the Adventures of Zenas Leonard, a Native of Clearfield County, PA Who Spent Five Years in Trapping for Furs, Trading with the Indians &c., &c., of the Rocky Mountains.* D. W. Moore, Clearfield, Pennsylvania.

Describes use of pottery near Humboldt Sink (or Mono Lake?).

1934   *The Narrative of the Adventures of Zenas Leonard, Written by Himself,* edited by M. M. Quaife. The Lakeside Press, R. R. Donnelly and Sons, Co., Chicago.

Same as above.

Lerch, Michael K.
1985   *Archaeological Studies at the Colosseum Mine: Surface Collections and Test Excavations at CA-SBr-4889, 5300, and 5303, Clark Mountain Range, San Bernardino County.* Report prepared for Amselco Minerals, on file at University of California, Riverside, Archaeological Research Unit.

Describes ceramics from three sites, identified by D. Jenkins as SPUW, LCBW, and puebloid sherds.

Lillard, J. B., R. F. Heizer and F. Fenenga
1939   *An Introduction to the Archaeology of Central California.* Sacramento Junior College Department of Anthropology Bulletin No. 2. Sacramento.

Reports extensive baked clay (non-pottery) tradition.

Lindsay, A. T., and K. Gratz
1974   Ceramic Repository. Ms. on file, Nevada State Museum. Produced by the Department of Anthropology, Museum of Northern Arizona.

Describes services and data available at Museum of Northern Arizona.

Lindsay, La Mar W., and Kay Sargent
1979   *Prehistory of the Deep Creek Mountain Area, Western Utah.* Utah Division of State History, Antiquities Section Selected Papers 6(14). Salt Lake City.

Fremont and Shoshonean pottery recovered from several sites in western Utah.

Linton, Ralph
1944   North American Cooking Pots. *AA* 9(4):369-380.

Attributes two main traditions of cooking pot shape to the kind of lifestyle (nomadic vs. sedentary) and the cooking method favored by each (pot in the flame vs. suspended over it). This would place Great Basin cooking pots in the Northern tradition with ultimate origins in Northern Asia.

Lister, R. H., and H. W. Dick
1952   Archaeology of the Glade Park Area: A Progress Report. *Southwestern Lore* 17(4):69-72.

Non-Pueblo ceramics; Colorado-Utah border, near Grand Junction.

Longacre, William
1985   Pottery Use-Life Among the Kalinga, Northern Luzon, the Philippines. Chapter 13 in *Decoding Prehistoric Ceramics*, edited by Ben A. Nelson, pp. 334-346. Southern Illinois University Press, Carbondale.

Ethnoarchaeological study of use-life and changing composition of household pottery assemblages.

Lowie, Robert H.
1909   The Northern Shoshone. *AMNHAP* 2(2): 165-306.

Earthen pots referred to by several informants, but not described, p. 177.

1924   Notes on Shoshonean Ethnography. *AMNHAP* 20(3).

Describes pottery making and usage, and notes location of museum specimens.

Lyneis, Margaret M.
1980   *Residual Archeology of the Main Ridge
       Locality, Pueblo Grande de Nevada.*
       Report prepared for the USDI Water
       and Power Resources Service by the
       Department of Anthropology,
       University of Nevada, Las Vegas.

       Summarizes Olson 1980 ceramic analy-
       sis.

McCown, B. E.
1955   *Temeku: A Page from the History of
       Luiseno Indians.* The Archaeological
       Survey Association of Southern
       California Paper No. 3.

       Reports potsherds and data on clay
       figurines from California.

McGimsey, Charles R., III
1980   *Marina Mesa: Seven Prehistoric
       Settlements in West-Central New
       Mexico.* PPM No. 72.

       Includes interesting discussion of
       ceramic typology.

McGregor, J. C.
1945   An Unfired Sherd from Black Dog Cave.
       Plateau 17(4):68-69.

       Black Dog Cave, Clark County, Nevada;
       see also Colton 1945.

Mack, Joanne M.
1983   *Archaeological Investigations in the
       Salt Cave Locality: Subsistence
       Uniformity and Cultural Diversity
       Along the Klamath River, Oregon.*
       UOAP No. 29.

       Describes Siskiyou Utility Ware,
       related to Shoshone Brown Ware.

McKinney, Aileen
1972   Two Mortuary Urns from San Diego
       County. *PCASQ* 8(3):38-46.

       Describes two cremations, one in a
       single narrow mouthed olla with asso-
       ciated grave goods, the other in a
       wide-mouthed olla covered with a
       cooking bowl and surrounded by three
       small bowls; both associated with
       milling feature near Descanso, San
       Diego; TBW.

McKinney, Aileen, and Lavinia Knight
1973   Baked Clay Figurines from Mason
       Valley, San Diego: Bowers Museum,
       Strandt Collection. *PCASQ* 9:44-47.

       Describes 15 fragments from southern
       San Diego County.

McNutt, C. H.
1973   On the Methodological Validity of
       Frequency Seriation. *AA* 38(1):45-60.

       Criticizes frequency seriations as
       methodologically unsound; uses ce-
       ramic examples.

Madsen, David B.
1970   Ceramics. In *Median Village and
       Fremont Culture Regional Variation,*
       by J. P. Marwitt, pp. 54-75. UUAP
       No. 95.

       Describes ceramics recovered and
       types assigned--99 percent Snake
       Valley; unfired paint pot, pipes,
       ground sherds and reconstructed
       vessel forms.

1975   Dating Paiute-Shoshoni Expansion in
       the Great Basin. *AA* 40(1):82-85.

       Uses dated sites containing
       Paiute-Shoshoni pottery to argue a
       time plan and direction of Numic
       expansion.

1983   Great Basin Ceramics. Ms. in prep-
       aration for *Handbook of North
       American Indians*, vol. 11, Great
       Basin. Smithsonian Institution,
       Washington, D.C.

       Reviews all ceramics found in Great
       Basin.

Madsen, David B., and La Mar W. Lindsay
1977   *Backhoe Village.* Utah Division of
       State History, Antiquities Section
       Selected Papers No. 4(12).

       Fremont ceramics, clay pipes, and
       figurines from this Fremont site in
       southwestern Utah on the edge of the
       eastern Great Basin.

Madsen, Rex E.
1972   Evans Mound Ceramics. In *The Evans
       Site*, by M. S. Berry, pp. 45-96.
       A Special Report, Department of
       Anthropology, University of Utah.

       Fremont ceramics.

1977   *Prehistoric Ceramics of the Fremont.*
       MNA,CS No. 6.

The only collective guide to Fremont
pottery types; includes added technical details, synonyms, references,
etc.

Magee, Molly
1964   A Flat-Bottomed Earthenware Vessel
        from Central Nevada. *AA* 30(1):96-98.

        Compared to other Great Basin finds;
        probably historic Shoshoni; illustra-
        tions.

1966   The Grass Valley Horse: A Baked Clay
        Head of a Horse Figurine from Central
        Nevada. *PA* 11(33):204-207.

        Describes horse figurine fragment and
        suggests it is recent, possibly
        Plateau Shoshoni.

1967   A Report on Perforated Sherds from
        Central Nevada with a Tentative
        Suggestion for Their Use. *AA* 32(2):
        226-227.

        Shoshoni ware.

Malouf, Carling
1940   The Archeology of Sites Along
        Fifteen-Mile Creek. In *The
        Archeology of the Deep Creek Region,
        Utah*, by Carling Malouf, Charles E.
        Dibble and Elmer R. Smith. UUAP
        No. 5:50-64.

        Describes attributes of Knolls ware,
        Sevier Gray, Great Salt Lake ware,
        Plain Gray, Shoshone ware, Corrugated
        and Black-on-gray found at temporary
        habitations; does not provide distri-
        bution data.

1944   Thoughts on Utah Archaeology. *AA*
        9(3):319-328.

        Mentions pottery traits associated
        with each of the "cultures" of the
        Great Salt Lake area: Shoshoni,
        Promontory, Puebloid, Black Rock, and
        Bonneville.

1946   The Deep Creek Region, the North-
        western Frontier of the Pueblo
        Culture. *AA* 12(2):117-121.

        Notes difficulty in distinguishing
        Shoshoni pottery from Great Salt Lake
        Buff.

Marwitt, J. P.
1968   *Pharo Village*. UUAP No. 91.

        Fremont pottery recovered from this
        site in western Utah.

1970   *Median Village and Fremont Culture
        Regional Variation*. UUAP No. 95.

        See Madsen 1970 for detailed ceramic
        description; Marwitt summarizes ce-
        ramic traits for Fremont regional
        variations.

Matson, Frederick (editor)
1965   *Ceramics and Man*. Viking Fund
        Publications in Anthropology 41.
        Wenner-Gren Foundation for
        Anthropological Research, New York.

        Papers from 1961 symposium which
        attempted to interpret ceramic analy-
        ses from a cultural context; many
        interesting papers.

Matson, R. G.
1972   *Adaptation and Environment in the
        Cerbat Mountains, Arizona*. Ph.D.
        dissertation, Department of Anthro-
        pology, University of California,
        Davis.

        Upland Cerbat.

May, Ronald V.
1976   An Early Ceramic Date Threshold in
        Southern California. *Masterkey*
        50:103-107.

        A carbon-14 date from San Diego
        County falls between Amargosan and
        Hakatayan cultures.

1978   A Southern California Indigenous
        Ceramic Typology. *Archaeological
        Survey Association Journal* 2(2).
        LaVerne.

        Proposes types for Californian Tizon
        Brown Ware. See Drover 1979b.

1980   Ceramic Artifacts. In *An Investi-
        gation in the Southern Sierra: The
        Lamont Meadow and Morris Peak
        Segments of the Pacific Crest Trail*,
        edited by A. P. Garfinkel, R. A.
        Schiffman, and K. R. McGuire. BLM
        Bakersfield District, Cultural
        Resources Publications, Archaeology.

        Proposes Sierra Brown type of OVBW
        identified from sherds recovered atop
        the southern Sierras.

1981 An Analysis of Ceramics from the
     Scodie Mountains Segment of the
     Pacific Crest Trail, Sequoia National
     Forest. In *Archaeological Investi-
     gation for the Scodie Mountains
     Segment of the Pacific Crest Trail,
     Kern County, California,* by R. D.
     Ambro, M. K. Crist, B. J. Peck and
     D. M. Varner. Ms. submitted to
     Sequoia National Forest, Porterville,
     USFS Contract #R5-04-80-02.

     Identifies additional specimens of
     his proposed Sierra Brown type of
     OVBW; notes two varieties within this
     type.

1982 When Did Pottery Making Technology
     Enter California and What Impact Did
     It Have on Native Culture? *Society
     for California Archaeology Newsletter*
     16(4):7.

     Reviews existing carbon-14 dates for
     earliest Tizon Brown Ware in San
     Diego region.

Meighan, Clement W.
1953a *Ancient Pottery Figurines and their
     Significance in the Study of Pre-
     history.* Ph.D. dissertation,
     Department of Anthropology,
     University of California, Berkeley.

     Clay figurines.

1953b *The Coville Rock Shelter, Inyo
     County, California.* UCAR No. 12(5).

     Describes two pottery sherds, p. 180,
     which more closely resemble Southern
     Paiute Ware than OVBW.

1954 A Late Complex in Southern California
     Prehistory. *SWJA* 10(2):215-227.

     Clay figurines from California.

1955 *Notes on the Archaeology of Mono
     County.* UCASR 28:6-28.

     Reports conical OVBW vessels from two
     sites in Chidago Canyon and proposes
     that firing atmosphere may be used to
     distinguish OVBW from Southern Paiute
     Utility Ware.

1959a A New Method for the Seriation of
     Archaeological Collections. *AA*
     25(2):203-211.

     Demonstrates a quick method of
     graphically seriating pottery
     assemblages.

1959b *Archaeological Resources of Borrego
     State Park.* UCAS,AR 1958-59:25-44.

     Names and describes Palomar Brown
     type (Tizon Brown Ware) and contrasts
     it with OVBW and Parker Buff; also
     describes pottery found in surveys of
     Borrego Desert; photos of several
     reconstructed pots.

Meighan, Clement W., et al.
1956 *Archaeological Excavations in Iron
     County, Utah.* UUAP No. 25.

     Fremont ceramics.

Meike, Annemarie
1984 X-Ray Diffraction and Fluorescence
     Analyses. Chapter 9, Ceramics, in
     *Rockhouse Basin Data Recovery
     Project*, by Alan P. Garfinkel, Larry
     S. Kobori, James C. Bard, and Raymond
     J. Dezzani. Ms. on file, Sequoia
     National Forest, Porterville, and
     California.

     XRD and XRF analysis of some eight
     OVBW sherds (four from a southern
     Sierra site, and four from an Owens
     Valley site) that were analyzed by NA
     by Perlman and Asaro 1984.

Meister, C. W., E. N. Tomihama, and T. Kaboy
1966 *Pottery from the New York and
     Providence Mountains Survey Sites.*
     UCAS,AR 8:275-278.

     Describes sherds recovered from areal
     survey in southeastern California--
     TBW, LCBW, SPUW.

Minto, J.
1901 Reminiscences of Experiences on the
     Oregon Trail in 1844. *Oregon
     Historical Quarterly* 2(3):209-259.

     Notes earthenware pot in a Shoshoni
     village near Salmon Falls, Idaho.

Mook, M.
1935 *Pottery. Walapai Ethnography.* AmAn,
     Memoir No. 42.

     Two Walapai women with only oral tra-
     dition to guide them attempted to
     make pots for Kroeber's students; the
     value of the article lies in the
     discussion of the experiment and
     information gained from informants.

Moratto, Michael J.
   1984   The Sierra Nevada. Chapter 7 in
          California Archaeology, edited by M.
          J. Moratto, pp. 285-338. Academic
          Press, Orlando.

          Reviews excavations and proposed
          archaeological sequences for the
          area; discusses OVBW on west side of
          Sierras among Yokuts and Western Mono
          groups.

Morss, N.
   1931   *The Ancient Culture of the Fremont
          River in Utah.* PPM No. 12(3).

          First major work on the Fremont;
          includes descriptions of Fremont pot-
          tery and figurines.

   1954   *Clay Figurines of the American
          Southwest.* PPM No. 49(1).

          Major reference on Fremont figurines.

Mulloy, William
   1942   *The Hagen Site, a Prehistoric Village
          on the Lower Yellowstone.* University
          of Montana Publications in Social
          Science No. 1.

          Describes flat-bottomed "Shoshonean"
          pots found in association with
          Woodland pottery at site near
          Billings.

   1958   *A Preliminary Historical Outline for
          the Northwestern Plains.* University
          of Wyoming Publication in Science
          22:1.

          Contains the original definition of
          Intermountain ware, the flat-bottomed
          pottery attributed to the Shoshoni
          and sometimes called Shoshonean ware,
          but which Mulloy emphasized was a
          regional style made by several dif-
          ferent tribes, including Shoshoneans
          (see also Simon 1979).

Munsell
   1971   *Munsell Soil Color Chart.* Munsell
          Color Division, Kollmorgen Corpo-
          ration, Baltimore.

Nelson, Ben A. (editor)
   1985   *Decoding Prehistoric Ceramics.*
          Southern Illinois University Press,
          Carbondale.

          Compendium of various pottery analy-
          sis articles organized under five
          headings: stylistic variation and
          social organization; organization of
          ceramic production; assignments of
          form, function and context; lessons
          from ethnoarchaeology; and commentary
          on theoretical approaches to sty-
          listic analysis. Though the examples
          may be from other areas, the methods
          and cautionary tales are applicable
          to Basin ceramics.

Olsen, William H.
   1963   *The Comparative Archaeology of the
          King Brown Site (CA-Sac-29)
          Sacramento County, California.*
          M.A. thesis, Department of Anthro-
          pology, California State University,
          Sacramento.

          Describes baked clay objects.

Olson, Kathryne
   1978   *Attribute Analysis of Muddy River
          Ceramics.* M.A. thesis, Department of.
          Anthropology, University of Nevada,
          Las Vegas.

          Tests various attributes of Virgin
          Anasazi ceramics to see which have
          discriminating value.

   1979   An Attribute Analysis of Muddy River
          Ceramics. *WAR* 2(4):303-361.

          Seriation study of 18 attribute
          classes on Virgin Branch Anasazi
          pottery from seven sites near
          Overton.

   1980a Ceramic Analysis. Appendix 1 in *Test
          Excavations at Bird Springs, Clark
          County, Nevada (26CK1),* by C. William
          Clewlow, Jr. and Helen Fairman Wells.
          Report prepared by Ancient
          Enterprises for Bureau of Land
          Management, Las Vegas District, Las
          Vegas.

          Reports BM-PIII Puebloid sherds from
          southern Nevada and northern Arizona,
          as well as SPUW and SBW.

   1980b Ceramic Analysis. In *Residual
          Archaeology of the Main Ridge
          Locality, Pueblo Grande de Nevada,* by
          M. Lyneis. Report prepared for USDI
          Water and Power Resources Service by
          Department of Anthropology,
          University of Nevada, Las Vegas.

          Virgin Branch Anasazi pottery.

Opler, M. K.
   1939   Southern Ute Pottery Types.
           Masterkey 13(5):161-163.

           Pottery-making techniques described
           for southern Colorado as well as
           shapes and uses.

Oppelt, Norman T.
   1976   *Southwestern Pottery: An Annotated
           List of Types and Wares.* University
           of Northern Colorado, Occasional
           Publications in Anthropology,
           Archaeology Series No. 7 (2 vols.).

           Excellent reference; one volume lists
           pottery types alphabetically and
           cites references, the other volume is
           the bibliography.

   1984   Worked Potsherds of the Prehistoric
           Southwest: Their Forms and
           Distribution. *Pottery Southwest*
           11(1):1-6.

           Reviews literature and compares
           distributions of various forms of
           reworked sherds.

Osborne, Douglas
   1941   Archeological Reconnaissance in
           Western Utah and Nevada. *Masterkey*
           15(5):189-195.

           Brief mention of Fremont pottery in a
           private collection in Ely, Nevada.

   1957   Pottery in the Northwest. *AA* 23(1):
           28-34.

           Summarizes known distribution of
           fired clay objects and pottery.

Palmer, Edward
   1878   Plants Used by the Indians of the
           United States. *American Naturalist*
           12:593-606, 646-655.

           Notes the Pah-ute use of earthen pots
           to parch seeds of *Pinus monophylla*,
           p. 595.

Panlaqui, Carol
   1974   The Ray Cave Site. In *Excavation of
           Two Sites in the Coso Mountains of
           Inyo County, California.* Maturango
           Museum Monograph No. 1. China Lake.

           P. 17 mentions OVBW bowl cached in
           canyon near site.

Peck, Stuart L.
   1953   *Some Pottery from the Sand Hills,
           Imperial County, California.* The
           Archaeological Survey Association of
           Southern California Publication No. 1.

           Describes Sand Hills Red, Gray, Black
           in Red, and Cream in Black (Lower
           Colorado Buff Wares?).

Pendergast, D. M.
   1957   Further Data on Pacific Coast Fired
           Clay Figurines. *AA* 23:178-180.

           Argues for independent development of
           figurine complex in central
           California.

Pilles, P. J., Jr.
   1981   A Review of Yavapai Archaeology. In
           *The Protohistoric Period in the North
           American Southwest, A.D. 1450-1700,*
           edited by D. R. Wilcox and W. B.
           Masse, pp. 163-182. ASUARP No. 24.

           Discussion of ethnographic and
           archaeological finds of Yavapai
           pottery, i.e. Tizon Brown Ware, Orme
           Ranch Plain, and Wingfield Plain,
           from Arizona.

Pilling, Arnold R.
   1952   The British Museum Collection from
           Near Avila, California. *AA* 18(2):
           169-172.

           Describes three sherds, presumed from
           a single vessel, found in a grave in
           San Luis Obispo County in 1894-95 by
           Freer and Summers. Pilling thinks
           the sherds are distinct from OVBW and
           Mission period pottery, and similar
           to Southern Paiute Utility Ware.

Pippin, Lonnie C.
   1984   *Limited Test Excavations at Selected
           Archaeological Sites in the NNWSI
           Yucca Mountain Project Area, Southern
           Nye County, Nevada.* DRI, Social
           Sciences Technical Report No. 40.

           Reports potsherds found at sites in
           area.

Plew, Mark G.
   1979a   Southern Idaho Plain: Implications
           for Fremont-Shoshoni Relationships in
           Southwestern Idaho. *PA* 24(86):
           329-335.

           Proposes a new pottery type different
           from Shoshoni ware based on sherds
           from a variety of sites across Idaho.

1979b   A Tentative Re-Classification of
        Idaho Shoshoni Ware. Ms. on file,
        Nevada State Museum, Carson City.

1980a   The Use and Misuse of Published Data:
        A Reply to Harrison and Hanson.
        IA 4(1):4-6.

1980b   Comment on Butler's "Native Pottery
        of the Upper Snake and Salmon River
        Country." *IA* 3(3):4-6.

1980c   *Archaeological Investigations in the
        Southcentral Owyhee Uplands, Idaho.*
        Archaeological Reports No. 7, Boise
        State University.

1981   *Archaeological Test Excavations at
        Four Prehistoric Sites in the Western
        Snake River Canyon near Bliss, Idaho.*
        Project Reports No. 5, Idaho Archaeo-
        logical Consultants. Boise.

1982   Thin Section Analysis of Pottery from
        Site 10GG1, Southcentral Idaho.
        IA 5(2):9-15.

Plew, Mark G., and J. Woods
    1980   Fired Clay Cylinders from Nahas Cave,
            Southwestern Idaho. *IA* 4(1):8-11.

Powell, John Wesley
    1893   Are There Evidences of Man in the
            Glacial Gravels? *Popular Science
            Monthly* 43:316-326 (July).

            Questions the antiquity of the Nampa,
            Idaho, figurine; see Wright 1890, 1891.

Powers, M. C.
    1953   A New Roundness Scale for Sedimentary
            Particles. *Journal of Sedimentary
            Petrology* 23:117-119.

            Useful for describing shape of non-
            plastics in thin-sections.

Prince, Eugene R.
    1959   Shoshonean Pottery of the Western
            Great Basin. Paper presented at 24th
            Annual SAA Meeting, Salt Lake City.
            Ms. on file, University of California
            Archaeological Research Facility,
            Berkeley. (Published in this
            volume.)

            Describes sherds from Elko, Lander,
            Lincoln, Mineral, Nye, and White Pine
            Counties, Nevada and proposes
            collapsing OVBW, SPUW, and Shoshoni
            Ware into an overall Great Basin
            Plain Ware.

Rice, Prudence M.
    1976   Rethinking the Ware Concept. *AA*
            41(4):538-542.

            Argues for separating paste com-
            position attributes from ware
            descriptions and using them as a
            separate unit of analysis which
            crosscuts types.

Riddell, Francis A.
    1950   An Archaeological Survey in Lassen
            County, California. Ms. in
            possession of the author, Sacramento,
            California.

            Reports potsherds discussed in this
            volume.

    1956   *Summary Report of the Excavation of
            the Karlo Site.* UUAP No. 26:63-73.

            See below.

    1960   *The Archaeology of the Karlo Site
            (CA-Las-7), California.* UCASR No.
            53.

            Fired and unfired figurines from a
            site located in Great Basin portion
            of northeastern California.

    1978   *Honey Lake Paiute Ethnography*
            (revised edition; originally
            published 1960). Nevada State Museum
            Occasional Papers No. 3.

            Notes use of mud by children to make
            toys.

Riddell, Harry S., Jr.
    1951   *The Archaeology of a Paiute Village
            Site in Owens Valley.* UCASR
            12:14-28.

            Defines OVBW.

Riddell, Harry S., Jr., and Francis A. Riddell
    1956   *The Current Status of Archaeological
            Investigations in Owens Valley,
            California.* UCASR 33:28-33.

            Discusses possible origins of OVBW
            and relation to Southern Paiute
            Utility Ware.

Rogers, Malcolm J.
    1928   A Question of Scumming. *Arizona Old
            and New* 1(2):5, 18, 20-21.

            Compares southern Arizona and
            Colorado Desert wares.

1936   *Yuman Pottery Making.*   San Diego
Museum of Man Papers No. 2.

Archaeological and ethnographic data
for Diegueño, Luiseño, Cupeño, Kamia,
Yuma, Mohave, Chemehuevi; vessel
shapes.

1945a   Letter to E. W. Gifford Dated March
2, 1945. Filed at San Diego Museum
of Man, Malcolm Rogers Notes.

Discusses southern California pottery
types as he envisioned them at that
date.

1945b   An Outline of Yuman Prehistory. *SWJA*
1(2):157-198.

Discusses changes in ceramics produced during Yuman I, II, and III
periods along the Colorado River and
into Baja California.

n.d.a   Yuman and Intrusive Pottery Types.
Ms. on file, Curatorial Department,
San Diego Museum of Man.

The type descriptions Rogers was
revising at the time of his death;
based upon his field work in the
California coast, desert, and
Colorado River areas.

n.d.b   File Folders 1-14 on Yuman Ceramics.
Filed at San Diego Museum of Man.

The folders contain drawings,
photographs, notes, tables, ceramic
descriptions, lists of ceramic
vessels in the Museum collection,
preliminary ceramic typology, and
correspondence.

Ruby, J.
1966   Southwestern Pottery in Los Angeles
County, California. *AA* 31(3):440.

Correction to Ruby and Blackburn 1964
article.

Ruby, J., and T. Blackburn
1964   Occurrence of Southwestern Pottery in
Los Angeles County, California. *AA*
30(2):209-210.

Southwestern types found in Los
Angeles County include Cibola White
ware (see Ruby 1966), Sacaton Red-on-
buff, Lower Colorado River Buff ware,
and possibly Jeddito.

Rudy, Jack R.
1953   *Archeological Survey of Western Utah.*
UUAP No. 12.

A basic reference work on artifact
types and distributions in western
Utah; contains definitions of pottery
types that are still in current use.

Rudy, Jack R., and R. D. Stirland
1950   *An Archeological Reconnaissance in
Washington County, Utah, 1949.*
UUAP No. 9.

Describes attributes of Plain Gray,
Corrugated, North Creek Grays,
Tusayan and Dogoszhi Black-on-whites,
Tusayan Red wares, Patayan and Paiute
sherds; whole vessels and 18 reworked
sherds from Virgin River area.

Rusco, Mary
1978   A Partially Restored Pottery Vessel
from Elko County, Nevada. *NASR*
11(1-2):21-26.

Describes small flanged-base pot,
thought to be Shoshoni ware.

Rusco, M. K., J. D. Davis, and A. Jensen
1979   *Archaeological Investigations near
Carlin, Elko County, Nevada.* Nevada
State Museum Archaeological Services
Report, Carson City.

Describes Shoshoni Brown Ware;
illustrates partially reconstructed
pointed bottom vessel.

Rusco, M. K., and C. S. Kuffner
1984   *Further Archaeological Evaluation of
Seven Sites on Public Land, South
Fork Recreational Area, Elko County,
Nevada.* Archaeological Research
Services, Virginia City.

Describes sherds from surface collection on site near rockshelter
described by Hall 1985; these sherds
have been identified as a Fremont
gray ware pot drop.

Rye, O. S.
1976   Keeping Your Temper Under Control:
Materials and the Manufacture of
Papuan Pottery. *Archaeology and
Physical Anthropology in Oceania*
11(2):106-137.

Shows that particular pottery production techniques may be related to the
nature of the available resources,
not simply cultural proscriptions.

Schellbach, L.
   1930   Mr. Schellbach's Researches in Idaho.
          Museum of the American Indian, Heye
          Foundation, Museum Notes 7:123-125.

          Shoshonean pottery.

Schenck, W. E., and E. J. Dawson
   1929   Archaeology of the Northern San
          Joaquin Valley. *UCPAAE* 25(4):289-413.

          Describes baked clay industry,
          central California.

Schroeder, Albert H.
   1952   *A Brief Survey of the Lower Colorado*
          River from Davis Dam to the Inter-
          national Border. Ms. prepared for
          National Park Service, Santa Fe, on
          file Bureau of Reclamation, Boulder
          City, Nevada.

          Describes pottery types of LCBW found
          in surface collections along Colorado
          River.

   1953   A Few Sites in Moapa Valley, Nevada,
          I, II. *Masterkey* 27:18-24, 62-68.

          Virgin Branch Anasazi ceramics.

   1955   *Archeology of Zion Park.* UUAP No. 22.

          Virgin Branch Anasazi ceramics;
          intrusives include Lower Colorado
          Buff Wares, Fremont, and Southern
          Paiute Brown Ware.

   1958   Lower Colorado Buff Ware: A
          Descriptive Revision. In *Pottery*
          Types of the Southwest, edited by H.
          S. Colton, Ware 16. MNA,CS No. 3D.

          Based on his (1952) and M. Rogers'
          (n.d.) data.

   1961   *The Archaeological Excavations at*
          Willow Beach, Arizona, 1950. UUAP
          No. 50.

          Describes stratigraphic deposition of
          eight wares and suggested cross-
          dating; experiments with clay from
          site to replicate observed variety in
          sherds.

   1963   Comment on Gunnerson's "Plateau
          Shoshonean Prehistory." *AA* 28(4):
          559-560.

          Argues that Virgin branch peoples of
          southern Nevada were replaced by
          Shoshonean speakers; cites ceramic
          evidence of cultural discontinuity.

   1975   *The Hohokam, Sinagua and the*
          Hakataya. Imperial Valley College
          Museum Occasional Paper No. 3. El
          Centro. Printed from 1960 microcard,
          Archives of Archaeology No. 5,
          published by Society for American
          Archaeology and University of
          Wisconsin Press.

          Describes cultural traits and ceramic
          types associated with Sinagua and
          Hohokam in the Verde Valley, and
          defines a new cultural root, the
          Hakataya.

   1979   The Hakataya. In *Southwest*, edited
          by A. Ortiz, pp. 100-107. *Handbook*
          of North American Indians, vol. 9,
          W. G. Sturtevant, general editor.
          Smithsonian Institution, Washington.

          Discusses introduction of paddle-
          anvil pottery and its spread north
          and west from Gila Valley area.

Schroeder, Albert H. (editor)
   1982   *Southwestern Ceramics: A Comparative*
          Review. The Arizona Archaeologist
          No. 15. Arizona Archaeological
          Society, Phoenix.

          Papers on Hakataya (Euler 82),
          Apache, Navajo, Mogollon, Anasazi,
          and Rio Grande ceramics, and
          Schroeder's theory of origin of
          southwestern pottery making.

Schumacher, Paul
   1880   *The Method of Manufacturing Pottery*
          and Baskets Among the Indians of
          Southern California. 12th Report of
          the Peabody Museum, Harvard
          University, pp. 521-525. Cambridge.

          Describes Cahuilla pottery making.

Schwartz, Douglas W.
   1955   *Havasupai Prehistory: Thirteen*
          Centuries of Cultural Development.
          Ph.D. dissertation, Department of
          Anthropology, Yale University, New
          Haven.

          Uses San Francisco Gray and Tizon
          Brown wares to support contention
          that Cohonina developed into Pai
          culture.

Shapiro, Gary
   1984   Ceramic Vessels, Site Permanence and
          Group Size: A Mississippian Example.
          AA 49(4):696-712.

Uses diameters and volumes of different vessel shapes, estimated from rim sherds, to examine differential site population and permanence.

Shepard, Anna O.
1956 *Ceramics for the Archaeologist.* Carnegie Institution of Washington, Publication No. 609.

The analyst's bible. Discusses clay minerology, manufacturing techniques, as well as analytical approaches.

1963 Beginnings of Ceramic Industrialization: An Example from the Oaxaca Valley. In *Notes from a Ceramic Laboratory*, by A. O. Shepard, pp. 1-26. Carnegie Institution of Washington.

Looks at contemporary household production of pottery and local distribution in Oaxaca, for clues to explanations of archaeological ceramics.

Shipek, Florence
1951 *Diegueño Pots.* El Museo, New Series 1:2. San Diego Museum Association, San Diego, California.

A nontechnical overview of Diegueño ceramic production with a discussion on clay types (mountain and desert), vessel shapes, use, firing techniques, fuel, clay additives, and the surface treatment of the ceramic vessels.

Shutler, Richard, Jr.
1961 *Lost City: Pueblo Grande de Nevada.* NSMAP No. 5.

A major reference on Virgin Branch Anasazi pottery from southern Nevada, though most of discussion on the pottery is limited to tables on distributional data from the site. Southern Paiute Brown Ware is also mentioned. Photos of various vessels and sherds are provided.

Shutler, Mary E., and Richard J. Shutler, Jr.
1962 *Archaeological Survey in Southern Nevada.* NSMAP No. 7.

Notes the occurrences of Virgin Branch Anasazi types, Lower Colorado River Buff Ware, and Southern Paiute Brown Ware from sites in the Valley of Fire and Red Rock Canyon, southern Nevada.

1963 *Deer Creek Cave, Elko County, Nevada.* NSMAP No. 11.

Two rims and 16 body sherds of Shoshoni Ware were recovered from the excavations.

Shutler, R., Jr., M. E. Shutler, and J. S. Griffith
1960 *Stuart Rockshelter: A Stratified Site in Southern Nevada.* NSMAP No. 3.

Virgin Branch Anasazi pottery recovered.

Simon, Arleyn
1979 Pottery Manufacture Analysis: Experimental Assessment of Technological Continuity in the Altamont Region. *Archaeology in Montana* 20(2):1-78.

A study concerned with reconstruction of pottery manufacture which involves analysis of flat-bottomed pottery found on the High Plains; has application elsewhere.

Simpson, Ruth Dee
1962 Report of Archaeological Investigation Conducted in the Greater Owens Valley-Mono Region. Ms. on file, Inyo National Forest, Bishop, California.

Mentions OVBW in Big Pine/Independence and Casa Diablo areas; describes one reconstructed flat-bottom vessel.

Smith, Gerald A.
1963 *Archaeological Survey of the Mojave River Area and Adjacent Regions.* San Bernardino County Museum Association, Redlands.

Site survey records describe distribution of pottery and illustrate unique examples.

Smith-Emery Company
1945 A Report on the Chemical Composition of Some California Clays. In Rogers (n.d.a: Folder No. 2).

Rogers submitted a sample of rock used to temper ceramics; Smith identified plagioclase feldspar, probably oligoclase and suggested further chemical analysis or petrographic examination.

Smith, Marion F., Jr.
    1985   Economic Interpretation of Ceramics.
            Chapter 11 in *Decoding Prehistoric
            Ceramics*, edited by Ben A. Nelson,
            pp. 250-309.   Southern Illinois
            University Press, Carbondale.

            Attempts to predict vessel morphol-
            ogy, and ultimately use, from sherd
            measurements.

Soule, E. C.
    1976   Lost City II. *Masterkey* 50(1):10-18.

            Photos of Virgin Branch Anasazi
            vessels from sites near Overton,
            southern Nevada.

    1978   Pottery Wares of the Moapa Valley.
            Masterkey 52(3):101-104.

            Brief description of Logandale Gray
            Ware and Logandale Black-on-gray,
            Virgin Branch Anasazi pottery from
            southern Nevada.

    1979   Pottery Types of the Moapa Valley:
            Moapa Gray Ware. *Masterkey*
            53(1):27-33.

            Brief discussion of Moapa Gray Ware,
            a Virgin Branch Anasazi pottery found
            in southern Nevada, northwestern
            Arizona, and southwestern Utah.

Spaulding, A. C.
    1953   Statistical Techniques for the
            Discovery of Artifact Types. *AA*
            18(4):305-313.

            Uses Chi square to test significance
            of the degree of association between
            attribute modes.

Spencer, J. E.
    1934   Pueblo Sites of Southwest Utah.
            AmAn 36(1):70-80.

            Describes 13 pottery types found
            along Virgin River in southern Utah:
            North Creek grays, Shinarump browns,
            Middleton reds, Virgin Black-on-
            whites, and Washington Black-on-
            cream.

Stansbury, H.
    1852   *Exploration and Survey of the Valley
            of Great Salt Lake of Utah, Including
            a Reconnaissance of a New Route
            through the Rocky Mountains*. 32nd
            Congress, Special Session, Senate
            Executive Document No. 3(2).
            Lippincott, Grambo, and Co.,
            Philadelphia.

            An early reference to pottery found
            on the northwestern shore of Great
            Salt Lake.

Stephenson, R. L., and K. Wilkinson
    1969   *Archaeological Reconnaissance of the
            Winnemucca-Battle Mountain Area of
            Nevada*. NASRP No. 1.

            17 sherds from single vessel, similar
            to Snake Valley Gray or Shoshoni
            wares.

Steponaitis, Vincas Petra
    1980   *Ceramics, Chronology, and Community
            Patterns at Moundville, a Late Pre-
            historic Site in Alabama*, vols. I and
            II. Ph.D. dissertation, Department
            of Anthropology, University of
            Michigan. Available from University
            Microfilms.

            Presents a multi-level sorting system
            for whole vessel assemblages.

Steward, Julian H.
    1928   Pottery from Deep Springs Valley,
            Inyo County, California. *AmAn*
            30:348.

            Early description of sherds, probably
            OVBW.

    1933a   *Ethnography of the Owens Valley
            Paiute*. UCPAAE No. 33(3).

            Describes pot making by Owens Valley
            informants; lists known specimens
            from Owens and Death Valleys, relates
            story of commercial revival of ceram-
            ic art by Death Valley man and his
            methods (pp. 266-269; Fig. 1; Plate
            5).

    1933b   *Archaeological Problems of the
            Northern Periphery of the Southwest*.
            MNA,B No. 5.

            Fremont pottery.

    1933c   *Early Inhabitants of Western Utah.
            Part 1, Mounds and House Types*.
            University of Utah Bulletin No.
            23(7).

            Fremont pottery.

    1937   *Ancient Caves of the Great Salt Lake
            Region*. BAEB No. 116.

            Describes plain ware sherds found in
            Promontory caves; notes differences
            between these and Shoshonean plain
            wares; adduces Puebloan association.

1938   *Basin-Plateau Aboriginal Socio-political Groups*. BAEB 120. Reprinted 1970, University of Utah Press, Salt Lake City.

    Brief note about Promontory and Shoshoni pottery (p. 5).

1941a   *Archaeological Reconnaissance of Southern Utah*. BAEB 128:277-365.

    Describes unbaked pots, ground sherds and vessel profiles of various south-western types found in Johnson Canyon, Paria River and Glen Canyon areas.

1941b   *Culture Element Distributions: XIII, Nevada Shoshoni*. UCAR No. 4(2).

    General description of western Shoshoni pottery and its relation to that of the Owens Valley Paiute and of the Southern Paiute people (pp. 242-243); details of pottery manufacture (pp. 294-295); additional notes (p. 339).

1943   *Culture Element Distributions: XXIII, Northern and Goshute Shoshone*. UCAR 8(3):263-392.

    Lists pottery-making traits (p. 319); comments on pp. 273-274.

Stewart, Omer C.
1941   *Culture Element Distributions: XIV, Northern Paiute*. UCAR 4(3):361-446.

    No data on pottery; p. 435 disputes Leonard's (1839) account of pottery use in Humboldt Sink.

1942   *Culture Element Distributions: XVIII, Ute-Southern Paiute*. UCAR 6(4):231-360.

    P. 330 discusses pottery making reported for Pahvant Ute and Shivwits Southern Paiute.

Sutton, Mark
1979   Three Baked Clay Figurines from Antelope Valley, California. *JCGBA* 1(2):367-369.

    Describes three figurines from south-western Mohave Desert.

Swanson, E. H., R. Powers, and A. L. Bryan
1964   The Material Culture of the 1959 Southwestern Idaho Survey. *Tebiwa* 7(2):1-27.

    Estimates date of A.D. 1700 for earliest presence of Shoshonean pottery.

Swarthout, Jeanne K.
1979   A Discriminant Analysis of Cerbat Ceramics. Ms. on file, Arizona State University, and Museum of Northern Arizona.

    Upland Cerbat.

1981   *Final Report for an Archaeological Overview for the Lower Colorado River Valley, Arizona, Nevada and California*, 4 vols. Submitted by Museum of Northern Arizona to Bureau of Reclamation, Boulder City, Contract 9-07-30-X0035.

    Provides descriptions of previous investigations and pottery types found in area; good bibliography.

Swarthout, Jeanne, and A. Delaney
1982   A Description of the Ceramic Collections from the Railroad and Transmission Line Corridors. In *The Coronado Project*, edited by R. Simms. MNA, Research Papers No. 26.

Taylor, Dee C.
1954   *The Garrison Site: A Report of Archaeological Excavations in Snake Valley, Nevada-Utah*. UUAP No. 16.

    Fremont pottery.

Terry, R. D., and G. V. Chilingar
1955   Chart for Estimating Percentage Composition of Rocks and Sediments. *Journal of Sedimentary Petrology* 25:229-234. Also reprinted as Data Sheet 6 of *Geotimes*, American Geological Institute, 2101 Constitution Ave. N.W., Washington, D.C.

    Useful in describing thin sections.

Thomas, David H.
1970   Review of "Archaeological Survey in Eastern Nevada, 1966," and, "The Archaeology of Newark Cave, White Pine County, Nevada," by D. D. Fowler. *AmAn* 72(3):695-697.

    Proposes positive correlation between Shoshoni Brown Ware and the pinyon-juniper lifezone in the central Great Basin.

1982   An Overview of Central Great Basin Prehistory. In *Man and Environment in the Great Basin*, edited by D. B. Madsen and J. F. O'Connell, pp. 156–171. Society for American Archaeology Papers No. 2. Washington, D.C.

Overview mentions Shoshoni ceramics and calls for more investigation of ethnographic vs. archaeological patterns (pp. 163, 166).

Thomas, D. H., A. Leventhal, and L. Williams
1976   Additional Piñon Ecotone Settlements of the Reese River Valley. In *Prehistoric Piñon Ecotone Settlements of the Upper Reese River Valley, Central Nevada*, edited by D. H. Thomas and R. L. Bettinger, pp. 328–346. AMNHAP 53(3):265–365.

Describes Shoshoni pottery and possible figurine fragment from two sites.

Thomas, Scott, John Loring, and Andrew Goheen
1983   An Aboriginal Pottery Site in South-eastern Oregon: A Preliminary Report. In *Contributions to the Archaeology of Oregon, 1981–1982*, edited by D. E. Dumond, pp. 82–98. Association of Oregon Archaeologists Occasional Papers No. 2.

Describes surface-collected pottery similar to Shoshoni ware from Snake River Plateau from late prehistoric Lost Dune site (35HA792).

Tomten, David
1983   Ceramic Thin Sections. In *Black Rock Cave Revisited*, by D. Madsen, Bureau of Land Management, Utah Cultural Resource Series 14:117–121. Salt Lake City.

Mineralogical description of four sherds from Black Rock Cave and one from Deadman's Cave.

Townsend, G., and R. G. Elston
1975   *Evaluation of Impacts on Archaeological Resources from Proposed Realignment of U.S. 395 from Washoe Valley North to Panther Siding*. Report to Environmental Impact Planning Corporation, submitted by Nevada Archaeological Survey, University of Nevada, Reno. Ms. on file, Nevada Department of Transportation, Carson City, Nevada.

Includes a description of site 26WA2028, an isolated find of a single body sherd "... similar to Shoshone Plain Ware" located near Brown's Creek at 5460 feet near the foot of Slide Mountain, southwest of Reno, Nevada.

Treganza, Adan E.
1942   An Archaeological Reconnaissance of Northeastern Baja California and Southeastern California. *AA* 8: 152–163.

Describes Diegueño brown and buff surface wares collected from this area; provides pot profiles, but no locational data.

1946   *California Clay Artifacts*. R. E. Schenck Archives of California Archaeology Papers No. 22. San Francisco State University.

Describes baked clay objects from central California.

1947   Possibilities of an Aboriginal Practice of Agriculture among the Southern Diegueño. *AA* 12(3):169–172.

Suggests Colorado River Yumans as source of pottery-making techniques and horticulture, westward to Diegueño Yumans.

1955   *The Examination of Indian Shellmounds within San Francisco Bay with Reference to the Possible 1579 Landfall of Sir Francis Drake*. Project No. 1, Nova Albion Explorations, Inc. Reporter Publishing Co., Vacaville, California.

Several clay figurines from Marin County, California.

1958   *Salvage Archaeology in the Trinity Reservoir Area, Northern California*. UCASR 43:1–38.

Clay pipe recovered from one site.

True, D. L.
1957   Fired Clay Figurines from San Diego County, California. *AA* 22:291–296.

Clay figurines from southern California.

1965 *Archaeological Differentiation of
     Shoshonian and Yuman Speaking Groups
     in Southern California.* Ph.D.
     dissertation, Department of Anthro-
     pology, University of California, Los
     Angeles.

     Compares archaeological ceramics of
     Diegueño/Luiseño Tizon Brown Ware.

1970 *Investigation of a Late Prehistoric
     Complex in Cuyamaca Rancho State
     Park, San Diego County, California.*
     Archaeological Survey Monograph,
     Department of Anthropology, Uni-
     versity of California, Los Angeles.

     Describes TB and LCBW ceramic arti-
     facts excavated from upland southern
     California (Diegueño) area.

True, D. L., and Claude N. Warren
1961 A Clay Figurine from Santa Monica,
     California. *Masterkey* 35:152-155.

     Describes a figurine recovered from
     Los Angeles basin which they attrib-
     ute to Colorado Desert influences,
     possibly historic.

Tuohy, Donald R.
1956 Shoshoni Ware from Idaho. *Davidson
     Journal of Anthropology* 2(1):55-72.
     Seattle.

     A detailed, pioneering study of a
     series of four flat-bottomed,
     earthenware vessels and 154 sherds,
     in which the writer concludes that
     "the predominant vessel form from the
     state of Idaho is the flat-bottomed,
     basal-flanged, undecorated cooking
     pot [;] only ten sherds indicate the
     possibility of other forms within the
     state" (p. 67).

1963 *Archaeological Survey in Southwestern
     Idaho and Northern Nevada.* NSMAP No.
     8.

     Shoshoni ware sherds recovered from
     six sites in Elmore and Owyhee
     Counties, southwestern Idaho, are
     described on pp. 62-64. A possible
     Deep Creek Buff sherd was also found
     at one site in Elmore County.

1965 Stone Age Missiles from a Modern Test
     Site. *Masterkey* 39(2):44-59.

     Mentions that pottery from the Nevada
     Test Site in southern Nevada includes
     Southern Paiute Brown Ware, North
     Creek Black-on-gray, and Washington
     Corrugated.

1973 Nevada's Non-Ceramic Culture Sphere.
     Tebiwa 16(1):54-68.

     Discusses areas where pottery occurs
     vs. those it does not; reviews excep-
     tions and pottery/baked clay tradi-
     tions in surrounding areas.

1974 *In the Path of Electrical Energy: A
     Preliminary Report of Archaeological
     Work along Sierra Pacific Power
     Company's Power Corridors in Central
     Nevada.* Nevada Archaeologist No. 2(1).

     Illustrations of Snake Valley Gray
     and Black-on-gray pottery from an
     excavated but unidentified rock-
     shelter in eastern Nevada.

1980 Nevada Shoshoni Ceramics. Paper pre-
     sented at 17th Great Basin Anthro-
     pological Conference, Salt Lake City,
     Utah, September 4-6.

1981 Cultigens, Pit Vipers, Camel Hair,
     and Shoshoni Pots. *Docent Council
     Newsletter, Nevada State Museum*
     11(1):4-5.

1983 Problems and Recent Work with Nevada
     Shoshoni Pottery. Paper presented at
     Great Basin/California Pottery Work-
     shop, April 23, Bishop.

     Report on preliminary findings of
     thin-section analysis of sample of
     sherds from across Nevada.

1984 Thin Section Analysis of Mission
     Pottery from Baja California. Paper
     presented at 19th Great Basin
     Anthropological Conference, Boise.

     Continuing thin-section sample into
     Baja California.

Tuohy, Donald R., and William Jerrems
1972 *A Pottery Jar from Lake Tahoe, Placer
     County, California.* NASR 6(2):3-5.

     Describes and presents photo of
     Shoshoni pot.

Tuohy, Donald R. and Barbara Palombi
  1972   A Basketry Impressed Shoshoni Pottery
         Vessel from Central Nevada. *Tebiwa*
         15(1):46-48.

         Describes and presents photo of
         Shoshoni ware pot.

Van Camp, Gena R.
  1979   *Kumeyaay Pottery: Paddle and Anvil*
         Techniques of Southern California.
         Ballena Press Anthropological Papers
         No. 15, edited by L. J. Bean and T.
         C. Blackburn.   Socorro.

         Van Camp concentrates on Tizon Brown
         Ware from prehistoric and proto-
         historic San Diego and Imperial
         Counties, and Baja California;
         reviews Kumeyaay subsistence patterns
         and social organizations as they
         relate to variations in ceramic
         style, shape, physical composition
         and distribution; examines manufac-
         turing techniques, forms, decoration,
         clay, ware styles, types and
         aesthetics; utilizes Rogers un-
         published material and collections at
         San Diego Museum of Man, collections
         and research data from Bower's
         Museum, the Malki Museum, and Santa
         Ysabel Reservation.

Voegelin, Erminie W.
  1938   *Tubatulabal Ethnography.*   UCAR 2(1).

         Describes pottery making (pp. 34-35).

Wallace, William J.
  1955   *An Archaeological Survey of the*
         Southern California Edison Company
         Electric Distribution Line in Death
         Valley National Monument.   Contri-
         bution to California Archaeology No.
         6. Archaeological Research Associates.

         P. 12 notes presence of pottery, spec-
         ulates on relationships.

  1957a A Rock-Shelter Excavation in Death
         Valley National Monument. *Masterkey*
         31(5):144-154.

         Hole-in-the-Rock Shelter; Shoshoni
         ware, OVBW, compared to Promontory
         ware.

  1957b A Clay Figurine from Death Valley
         National Monument, California.
         Masterkey 31(4):131-134.

         Describes unfired female figurine
         from rockshelter.

  1958   *Archaeological Investigations in*
         Death Valley National Monument,
         1952-57.   UCASR 42:7-22.

         Summarizes the results of surveys;
         cites presence of brown ware similar
         to Owens Valley Brown, as well as
         occasional puebloan sherds, and
         unbaked figurines; cites pottery as a
         trait of Period IV, late prehistoric
         and historic occupations of Death
         Valley.

  1965   A Cache of Unfired Clay Objects from
         Death Valley, California. *AA* 30(4):
         434-441.

         From Stovepipe Wells; persistence
         of Anasazi trait into 19th century;
         Shoshonean.

  1970   Seasonal Indian Campsites in the Lake
         Isabella area, California. *Masterkey*
         44(3):84-95.

         Notes presence of potsherds at Yokuts
         sites.

Wallace, William J., and Donald W. Lathrap
  1975   *West Berkeley (CA-Ala-307):   A*
         Culturally Stratified Shellmound on
         the East Shore of San Francisco Bay.
         UCARFC No. 29.

         Baked clay (p. 43).

Wallace, William J., and Edith S. Taylor
  1952   *Excavations of Sis-13, a Rockshelter*
         in Siskiyou County, California.
         UCASR 15:13-39.

         Clay figurine from northern
         California border.

  1955   Archaeology of Wildrose Canyon, Death
         Valley National Monument. *AA* 20:
         355-367.

         Southern Paiute/Owens Valley Brown
         wares recovered from several sites.

  1960a The Surface Archeology of Indian
         Hill, Anza-Borrego Desert State Park,
         California. *Masterkey* 34(1):4-18.

         TBW and LCBW.

  1960b The Indian Hill Rockshelter: Pre-
         liminary Excavations. *Masterkey*
         34(2):66-82.

         One pipe fragment and sherds of TBW
         and LCBW; from stratigraphic deposit
         in southern California.

Wallace, William J., and Edith Wallace
  1978 *Ancient Peoples and Cultures of Death
        Valley National Monument.* Acoma
        Books, Ramona.

        Brief description of pottery (p. 23);
        illustrations of vessel shapes (p.
        24).

  1979 *Desert Foragers and Hunters, Indians
        of the Death Valley Region.* Acoma
        Books, Ramona.

        General account of pottery making
        (pp. 19, 22); illustrations of vessel
        forms (p. 21).

Warren, Claude N.
  1984 The Desert Region. Chapter 8 in
        California Archaeology, edited by M.
        J. Moratto, pp. 339-430. Academic
        Press, Orlando.

        Reviews major excavations and pre-
        historic sequences proposed for
        southern California desert area;
        LCBW, TBW and Puebloan sherds found
        in the area.

Washburn, Dorothy K.
  1982 Academically Speaking: Earthquake
        Sherds. *Pacific Discovery* 35(5):
        28-31.

        Photographs and descriptions of
        modern Mohave pots collected by
        Kroeber which were thought to have
        been destroyed in the 1906 earth-
        quake, but were recently rediscovered
        and repaired.

Waters, Michael R.
  1982a The Lowland Patayan Ceramic
         Tradition. Chapter 7 in *Hohokam and
         Patayan: Prehistory of Southwestern
         Arizona*, edited by R. H. McGuire and
         M. B. Schiffer, pp. 275-297.
         Academic Press, New York.

         Proposes new typology for Lower
         Colorado Buff wares.

  1982b The Lowland Patayan Ceramic Typology.
         In *Hohokam and Patayan: Prehistory
         of Southwestern Arizona*, edited by R.
         H. McGuire and M. B. Schiffer,
         Appendix G, pp. 537-580. Academic
         Press, New York.

         Presents descriptions and illustra-
         tions of LCBW types.

Waterworth, Robert M. R., and Eric Blinman
  1986 Modified Sherds, Unidirectional
        Abrasion, and Pottery Scrapers.
        Pottery Southwest 13(2):4-7.

        Analyzes 900+ modified Southwestern
        sherds for shape, size, types of
        abrasion, direction of beveling, and
        types and orientation of striations,
        in an attempt to interpret function.

Weaver, Richard A.
  1983 Pottery Distribution Concordance for
        Inyo County, California, Mono County,
        California and Inyo National Forest
        Lands Located in Portions of Fresno,
        Madera, Tulare Counties, California,
        and Esmeralda and Mineral Counties,
        Nevada. Ms. presented at Great
        Basin/California Pottery Workshop,
        Bishop.

        OVBW; see paper, this volume.

Wedel, Waldo R.
  1941 *Archaeological Investigations at
        Buena Vista Lake, Kern County,
        California.* BAEB No. 130.

        Sherds and baked clay objects.

  1954 Earthenware and Steatite Vessels from
        Northwestern Wyoming. *AA* 19(4):
        403-409.

        Shoshonean affiliation noted.

  1957 *Observations on Some Nineteenth-
        Century Pottery Vessels from the
        Upper Missouri.* BAEB 164:87-114.

        Discusses Arikara, Mandan, Hidatsa.

Weide, D.
  1978 *Temper Analysis of Southern Nevada
        Prehistoric Ceramics: A Test Case of
        X-Ray Diffusion.* WAR No. 1(3).

        Identifies source of olivine found in
        Moapa Gray Ware of southern Nevada.

Wells, H. F.
  1980 An Overview of Cultural Resources in
        Grass Valley, Eureka and Lander
        Counties, Nevada. In *A Program of
        Cultural Resource Preservation,
        Protection and Research on the Gund
        Ranch, Grass Valley, Nevada*, edited
        by R. G. Elston. Submitted to The
        Division of Historic Preservation and
        Archaeology, Nevada State Department
        of Conservation and Natural
        Resources, Carson City.

Lists number of sites containing
Shoshoni Brown Ware; no analysis.

Werlhof, J. C.
1960   Notes on Various Tulare and Kern
        Counties Sites. Ms. #292 on file,
        University of California Archae-
        ological Research Facility, Berkeley.

        Notes presence of pottery at various
        sites in central California; OVBW.

Werlhof, J., and J. Vierhus
1956   Survey Report and Supplementary
        Report on the Tachi Indians. Ms.
        #235a, b, on file, University of
        California Archaeological Research
        Facility, Berkeley.

        Describes pot and sherds found at
        various Yokuts sites including
        village of Oudjiu, central Cali-
        fornia.

Wheeler, S. M.
1936   A Pueblo II Site in the Great Basin
        Area of Nevada. *Masterkey*
        10(6):207-211.

        Various Fremont types recovered from
        the Baker site in Snake Valley,
        eastern Nevada.

1937   An Archaeological Expedition to
        Nevada. *Masterkey* 11(6):194-197.

        Pueblo II site with "plain grey
        sherds."

1942   *Archaeology of Etna Cave, Lincoln
        County, Nevada*. Reprinted 1973 as
        *The Archaeology of Etna Cave, Lincoln
        County, Nevada*, edited by D. D.
        Fowler. DRI No. 7.

        Virgin Branch Anasazi and probably
        Fremont ceramics and clay figurines
        from this southeastern Nevada site.

Wiens, Carol
1982   *The Meaning of Variability in
        Ceramics of the Fremont Area*. M.A.
        thesis, Department of Anthropology,
        University of Utah, Salt Lake City.

Williams, P. A., and Robert I. Orlins
1963   *The Corn Creek Dunes Site*. NSMAP No.
        10.

        Brief distribution data on Virgin
        Branch Anasazi and Southern Paiute
        Brown Ware from three sites in Clark
        County, southern Nevada.

Wilson, A. L.
1978   Elemental Analysis of Pottery in the
        Study of Its Provenance: A Review.
        Journal of Archaeological Science
        5(3):219-236.

        Discusses problems and limitations,
        especially in problem design and data
        interpretation.

Wilson, K. L.
1976   Baked Clay. In *Archaeological
        Investigations at the Blodgett Site
        (CA-Sac-267), Sloughhouse Locality,
        California*, edited by J. Johnson, pp.
        301-328. Ms. on file at National
        Park Service, Western Region, San
        Francisco.

Windes, Thomas C.
1977   Typology and Technology of Anasazi
        Ceramics. In *Settlement and
        Subsistence Along the Lower Chaco
        River*, edited by C. A. Reher, pp.
        279-370. The University of New
        Mexico Press, Albuquerque.

        Interesting use of oxidation studies
        to differentiate clays and ceramic
        traditions.

Witt, D.
1962   Remarks on Paiute Pottery, Inyo and
        Tulare Counties. *The Digger's Digest*
        5(5):2-3. Northwestern California
        Archaeological Society.

        Discusses sherds found on both sides
        of the Sierra Nevada; OVBW.

Worman, F. C. V.
1963   *Anatomy of the Nevada Test Site*.
        U.S. Los Alamos Scientific
        Laboratory.

        Southern Paiute Utility Ware sherds
        found.

1969   *Archaeological Investigations at the
        U.S. Atomic Energy Commission's
        Nevada Test Site and Nuclear Rocket
        Development Station*. Los Alamos
        Scientific Laboratory Report LA-4125.
        Springfield, Virginia.

        Reports Lino Gray, Logandale Gray,
        Boulder Gray, Moapa Creek B/G, North
        Creek Corrugated, Tsegi Orange, and
        Southern Paiute Utility Ware.

Wormington, H. M.
    1955   *A Reappraisal of the Fremont Cultures
           with a Summary of the Archaeology of
           the Northern Periphery*. Denver
           Museum of Natural History Proceedings
           No. 1.

           Fremont pottery from Utah.

Wright, G. A.
    1978   The Shoshonean Migration Problem. *PA*
           23(80):113-137.

           Uses Intermountain ware to argue
           timing of Shoshoni move to north-
           western Wyoming.

Wright, G. F.
    1890   *Nampa Image*. Boston Society of
           Natural History Proceedings No.
           24:424-450.

           See below.

    1891   *Additional Notes Concerning the Nampa
           Image*. Boston Society of Natural
           History Proceedings 25:242-246.

           Fired clay human figurine recovered
           near Nampa, Idaho.

INDEX TO THE CERAMIC BIBLIOGRAPHY

Special Ceramic Forms

Baked clay; Basket Impressions; Figurines; Miniatures; Pipes; Worked Sherds.

Methodology

Analytical Methods; Clay Analysis; Ethnographic Data; Neutron Activation; Petrography; Pottery-Making Techniques; Seriation; Statistical Comparison of Attributes; Thermoluminescence; Thin Sections; Vessel Function; XRD: XRF.

The index lists topics alphabetically and cites the author's last name and the year of publication (e.g. "Smith 66" refers to "Smith 1966" in the bibliography).

King 67; Kowta 54; Kroeber 25; Lathrap and
Shutler 55; Lilliard et al. 39; Moratto 84;
Olsen 63; Pendergast 57; Pilling 52; Schenck
and Dawson 29; Treganza 55, 58; Wallace 70;
Wallace and Lathrap 75; Wedel 41; Werlhof
60; Werlhof and Vierhus 56; Wilson, K. 76;
Witt 62.

California--Eastern:
Asaro and Michel 84; Bettinger 75, 79, n.d.;
Campbell 29a, b; Cowan and Wallof 74; Davis
62; Davis, E. L. 64; Donnan 64; Drover 79a;
Elsasser 60, 63; Enfield and Enfield 64;
Griset 81, 82, 85a, b; Guthrie 57; Harner
57, 58; Hildebrand 74; Hunt, A. 60; Hunt, C.
60; Irwin 60; Jenkins 83, 84, 85a, b, c; King
76; King and Casebier 76; Knight 73; Kroeber
25; Lanning 63; Lathrap and Meighan 51;
Lerch 85; May 80, 81; Meighan 53b, 55; Meike
84; Meister et al. 66; Panlaqui 74; Riddell
51; Riddell and Riddell 56; Simpson 62;
Smith 63; Steward 28, 33a; Sutton 79;
Swarthout 81; Tuohy and Jerrems 72; Wallace
55, 57a, b, 58, 65; Wallace and Taylor 55;
Wallace and Wallace 78, 79; Washburn 82;
Voegelin 38; Warren 84; Waters 82; Weaver
83; Witt 62.

California--Northern:
Baumhoff and Johnson 68; Elsasser 78; Elston
79; Heizer and Beardsley 43; Heizer and
Pendergast 54; Kroeber 25; Mack 83; Riddell
50, 56, 60, 78; Treganza 58; Wallace and
Taylor 52.

California--Southern:
Barrows 1900; Brott 63; Bryan 64; Cameron
82; Campbell 31a, b; Chace 73; Cline 79;
Davis 67; Drover 75, 78, 79a, b; Drover et
al. 79; Drucker 41; DuBois 07; Elsasser 60;
Euler 59, 82; Euler and Dobyns 58; Evans 69;
Forbes 61; Harrington 55a, b; Hedges 73;
Heye 19; Irwin 80; King 1875; Koerper and
Flint 78; Koerper et al. 78; Kroeber 25;
Kroeber and Harner 55; McCown 55; McKinney
72; McKinney and Knight 73; May 76, 78, 82;
Meighan 54, 59b; Peck 53; Rogers 28, 36,
45a, b, n.d. a, b; Ruby 66; Ruby and
Blackburn 64; Schroeder 52, 81, 82; Treganza
42, 46, 47; True 57, 65, 70; True and Warren
61; Van Camp 79; Wallace and Taylor 60a, b.

Cerbat:
Baldwin 50b; Dobyns 56; Euler 58, 59, 82;
Euler and Dobyns 58; Heuett 74; Matson, R.
72; Schroeder 52, 61; Swarthout 79, 81.

Cerritos Brown Ware:
Koerper and Flint 78.

Clay Analysis (see also *Neutron Activation,
Petrogaphy, XRD, XRF*):
Braun 83; Bronitsky 82; Gautier 79; Griset
81; Heizer and Treganza 44; Hunt, C. 60;
Huscher and Huscher 40; Kroeber and Harmer
55; Meike 84; Munsell 71; Rogers 36; Rye 76;
Schroeder 61; Shepard 56; Smith-Emery 45;
Windes 77.

Cocopa:
Kelly 77; Rogers 36.

Cohonina:
Schwartz 55.

Colorado:
Barber 1876; Huscher and Huscher 40; Lister
and Dick 52; Lowie 24; Opler 39; Oppelt 76,
84; Stewart 42.

Cosumnes Brown Ware:
Johnson 76; Kielusiak 82; Wilson, K. 76.

Cupeño:
Rogers 36, n.d. b.

Death Valley Brown Ware (see also *Owens Valley
Brown Ware*):
Hunt, A. 60; Hunt, C. 60; Wallace and
Wallace 78, 79.

Deep Creek Buff (see also *Fremont Ceramics*):
Fowler, D. 68; Malouf et al. 40.

Desert Ware:
Rudy 53.

Diegueño:
Chace 73; Cline 79; Davis 67; DuBois 07;
Harrington 55b; Heye 19; Kroeber 25;
McKinney 72; May 76, 78, 82; Rogers 36, n.d.
b; Shipek 51; Treganza 42, 47; True 65, 70;
Van Camp 79.

Ethnographic Data:
Barber 1876; Barrows 1900; Braun 80; Cline
79; Driver 37; Fontana et al. 62; Foster 60;
Fowler and Fowler 81; Fremont 1887; Gayton
29, 48; Heizer 54; Henrickson and McDonald
83; Huscher and Huscher 40; Irwin 80; Kelly,
I. 64; Kelly, W. 77; Kroeber 25; Kroeber
and Harner 55; Leonard 1839, 1934; Mook 35;
Rogers 36; Steward 33a, 41b, 43; Stewart 41,
42; Voegelin 38.

Figurines:
Aikens 70; Ambro 72, 78; Barrett and Gifford
33; Beardsley 54; Brauner and MacDonald 83;
Bryan 64; Chace 73; Davis 59; Drover 75;
Elsasser 63, 78; Elston 79; Fenenga 77;
Flaim and Warburton 61; Fowler and Matley
79; Goerke and Davidson 75; Hedges 73;
Heizer and Beardsley 43; Heizer and
Pendergast 54; Hunt, A. 60; Kielusiak 82;

Petrography:
Butler 83a; Coale 63; Dean 84; Hunt, C. 53, 60; Olson 78, 79; Plew 82; Powers 53; Prince 59; Shepard 56; Terry and Chilingar 55; Tomten 83; Tuohy 83, 84.

Pipes:
Baumhoff and Johnson 68; Gayton 29; Griset 85b; Heye 19; Lanning 63; Madsen 70; Madsen and Lindsay 77; Opler 39; Rogers 36; Steward 33a; Treganza 58; True 70; Wallace and Taylor 60b.

Pismakis:
Kehoe 59.

Plains:
Aikens 66a, 67b; Ewers 45; Flannery 53; Kehoe 59; Mulloy 42, 58; Simon 79; Wedel 54, 57.

Plateau:
Cressman 42; Grosscup 62; Magee 66; Osborne 57; Schroeder 63; Steward 38; Stewart 41; Thomas, S. et al. 83.

Pottery-Making Techniques (see also *Ethnographic Accounts*):
Barber 1876; Barrows 1900; Brott 63; Busby 79; Chamberlin 11; Cline 79; Driver 37; Driver and Massey 57; Drucker 41; Fontana et al. 62; Fowler and Fowler 81; Gayton 29; Harrington 55b; Heizer 54; Huscher and Huscher 40; Irwin 80; Kelly, I. 64; Kelly, W. 77; Kramer 85; Kroeber and Harner 55; Lowie 24; Mook 35; Opler 39; Rogers 36; Schroeder 79; Schumacher 1880; Shepard 56, 63; Shipek 51; Steward 33a, 41b, 43; Voegelin 38; Wallace and Wallace 79.

Prescott Gray Ware:
Colton 58; Colton and Hargrave 37; Crabtree and Ferraro 80.

Promontory:
Aikens 66a; Butler 79b, 81a, b, 83a, b, c; Jennings 57, 78; Madsen 83; Malouf 40, 44, 46; Rudy 53; Steward 37; Wallace 57a.

Pueblo:
Aikens 66b; Anderson 63; Angel 1881; Barber 1876; Bennett 74; Brunson 85; Drover 79a; Forbes 61; Harrington 28; Hawley 36; Jenkins 81; Lerch 85; McGimsey 80; Madsen 83; Malouf 44, 46; Oppelt 84; Rogers 45b; Ruby and Blackburn 64; Spencer 34; Tuohy 65; Wallace 58; Warren 84; Waterworth and Blinman 86.

Pyramid Gray:
Rogers n.d. a; Schroeder 52, 61.

San Francisco Mountain Gray Ware:
Colton 58; Colton and Hargrave 37; Euler 58; Schwartz 55.

San Juan Wares:
Colton 56; Colton and Hargrave 37.

Sand Hills Wares (see also *Lower Colorado Buff Wares*):
Peck 53.

Seri:
Rogers 36, n.d. b.

Seriation:
McNutt 73; Meighan 59a.

Serrano:
Campbell 29a, b, 31a, b; Chace 73.

Shoshoni Brown Ware:
Beck 81; Berry 76; Bettinger and Baumhoff 82; Busby 77, 79; Butler 79a, b, 81a, b, 83a, b, c; Casjens 74; Coale 63; Crabtree and Ferraro 80; Cressman 42; Dean 83; Deatrick 78; Desart 70; Elston 79; Fowler, D. 68a, b, 75; Frison 73; Gebhard et al. 64; Giddings 52; Grosscup 62; Hall 85; Harrison and Hanson 80; Heizer et al. 68; Hunt, A. 60; Hunt, C. 60; Huntley and Plew 81; Irving 1868; James 81; James and Elston 83; James and Zeier 81; Janetski 81; Jennings 57, 78; Kehoe 59; Layton 70, 73; Leonard 1839, 1934; Lindsay and Sargent 79; Lister and Dick 52; Lowie 09, 24; Mack 83; Madsen 75, 83; Magee 64, 66, 67; Malouf 40, 44, 46; Minto 01; Mulloy 42, 58; Plew 79a, b, 80b, 82; Prince 59; Rudy 53; Rusco 78; Rusco et al. 79; Rusco and Kuffner 84; Schellbach 30; Schroeder 63; Shutler and Shutler 63; Stephenson and Wilkinson 69; Steward 28, 33a, 37, 38, 41b, 43; Swanson et al. 64; Thomas 70, 82; Thomas, D. et al. 76; Thomas, S. et al. 83; Townsend and Elston 75; Tuohy 56, 63, 73, 80, 81, 83; Tuohy and Jerrems 72; Tuohy and Palombi 76; Wallace 55, 57a, 65; Wedel 54; Wells 80.

Shoshoni Culture:
Aikens 70; Ambro 72, 78; Baldwin 45; Beck 81; Butler 81b; Clewlow and Rusco 72; Clewlow et al. 78; Dalley 76; Desart 70; Donnan 64; Fowler et al. 73; Gruhn 61; Harrison and Hanson 80; Irwin 80; Lowie 24; Madsen 75; Steward 41b, 43; Wright 78.

Sichomovi Red Ware:
Colton 56.

Sierra Brown:
May 80, 81.

Siskiyou Utility Ware:
Brauner and Lelow 83; Mack 83; Thomas, S. et al. 83.